STUDENT MINISTRY

# ESSENTIALS

REACHING. LEADING. NURTURING.

STUDENT MINISTRY

# ESSENTIALS

REACHING. LEADING. NURTURING.

## STEVE VANDEGRIFF
## & RICHARD BROWN

MOODY PUBLISHERS
CHICAGO

All Scripture quotations, unless otherwise indicated, are taken from The Holy Bible, English Standard Version® (ESV®), copyright © 2001 by Crossway, a publishing ministry of Good News Publishers. Used by permission. All rights reserved.

Scripture quotations marked AMP are taken from *The Amplified Bible*. Copyright © 1965, 1987 by The Zondervan Corporation. *The Amplified New Testament* copyright © 1958, 1987 by The Lockman Foundation. Used by permission.

Scripture quotations marked KJV are from the King James Version.

Scripture quotations marked NASB are taken from the *New American Standard Bible*®, Copyright © 1960, 1962, 1963, 1968, 1971, 1972, 1973, 1975, 1977, 1995 by The Lockman Foundation. Used by permission. (www.Lockman.org)

Scripture quotations marked THE MESSAGE are from *The Message*, copyright © by Eugene H. Peterson 1993, 1994, 1995. Used by permission of NavPress Publishing Group.

Scripture quotations marked NIV are taken from the Holy Bible, New International Version®, NIV®. Copyright © 1973, 1978, 1984, 2011 by Biblica, Inc.™ Used by permission of Zondervan. All rights reserved worldwide. www.zondervan.com. The "NIV" and "New International Version" are trademarks registered in the United States Patent and Trademark Office by Biblica, Inc.™

Scripture quotations marked NLT are taken from The Holy Bible, New Living Translation, copyright © 1996, 2004, 2007, 2013 by Tyndale House Foundation. Used by permission of Tyndale House Publishers, Inc., Wheaton, Illinois 60188. All rights reserved.

Scripture quotations marked TLB are taken from *The Living Bible* copyright © 1971. Used by permission of Tyndale House Publishers, Inc., Wheaton, Illinois 60188. All rights reserved.

Edited by Jim Vincent
Interior design: Design Corps
Cover design: Faceout Studio
Cover images of silhouettes copyright © by Vertyr/Thinkstock 460475865.
    skateboarder silhouettes copyright © by ChrisGorgio/Thinkstock 450592817.
    crowds of people silhouettes copyright © by grynold/Thinkstock 188030824.
    silhouettes copyright © by fogaas/Thinkstock 185447315.
    little crowds silhouettes copyright © grynold/Thinkstock 482354451.
    All rights reserved on all of these images.

Library of Congress Cataloging-in-Publication Data

Vandegriff, Steve
  Student ministry essentials : reaching. leading. nurturing / Steve Vandegriff and Richard Brown.
      pages cm
  Includes bibliographical references.
  ISBN 978-0-8024-1265-2
  1.  Church work with young adults.  I. Title.
  BV4446.V85 2015
  259'.24--dc23

                              2014035348

    We hope you enjoy this book from Moody Publishers. Our goal is to provide high-quality, thought-provoking books and products that connect truth to your real needs and challenges. For more information on other books and products written and produced from a biblical perspective, go to www.moodypublishers.com or write to:

Moody Publishers
820 N. LaSalle Boulevard
Chicago, IL 60610


3 5 7 9 10 8 6 4 2

*Printed in the United States of America*

# CONTENTS

## PART 1: LEADING

## PART 2: NURTURING

## PART 3: REACHING

# ACKNOWLEDGMENTS

Rich and I are grateful to the many people who have helped contribute to the writing of this book, both directly and indirectly.

A big thank-you to those who have helped contribute to this book with encouragement and wisdom: Dr. Frank Schmitt, who has been a mentor and advisor for all my professional ministry life; Dr. Elmer Towns, who ignited the desire to write; and Doug Madill, who has been a best buddy and has walked many miles with me in student ministry. I am also grateful for the help of Craig Robinson, Patrick Gillen, Deana Dickerson, Derik Idol, and Jonathan Geukgeuzian.

I also want to acknowledge those who are the most important part of my life: my wife, Pam, my mom (who is still a church pianist), my three kids, Josh, Jonathan, and Vanessa; their spouses, Jamie, Amanda, and Matt, and their little ones who always make me smile: Ryah Leanne, Lorelai Reagan, Norah Peyton, Cadence Luanne, Judah Rose, Ezra Kennedy, Waverly Victoria, and Harrison Joshua.

*Steve Vandegriff*

As I think of what this project represents, I have so many to thank. I realize all my blessings come from the Lord; therefore, I must start with the One who first reached out to me. Where would I be without Him?

I want to thank my King for placing me in the family He did. To my dear father and mother, you were the ones who loved me, prayed for me, and led me from the very onset of my life. Dad, thank you for being my pastor, my mentor, my coach, and my example. Most men would give anything to hear their father say just one time, "Well done, son" and yet you have showered me with words of affirmation and kindness my entire life. Thank you for your steadfast faithfulness. Mom, although I know you are enjoying your time now with Jesus, I wish you could have read this book. You were my greatest prayer warrior, encourager, fan, and godly example. Finally, I want to say to my brother, Dathan, and sisters Dalene and Daneal, it is so fun that we can still be close and have such love for one another. If you weren't my siblings, I would still want to be your friend and hang out with you.

Lord, I want to thank You for my bride. Janet, for a man who gets paid to talk, I feel inadequate in attempting to communicate the depth of how much you mean to me. You light up every room you enter and grace everyone you meet. Your love for Jesus, me, our children, and others is so evident to all. Ever since I first met you, you have been about serving Jesus.

Lord, thank You for my children. Rich, Jenna, and Ryan, each of you is unique in personality and gifts, and I am so thankful for what love and joy you each bring to me. I am blessed to call you my children.

Father, thank you for each lead pastor who brought me on the team and believed in me. I want to thank the numerous volunteer leaders who served alongside Janet and me, and especially each student who participated in our student ministries. You were the ones who kept me going in student ministry.

*Rich Brown*

Moody Publishers and the authors of *Student Ministry Essentials* would like to acknowledge the significant efforts of Dr. Lee Vukich who was the initiator and co-author of *Timeless Youth Ministry: A Handbook for Successfully Reaching Today's Youth.* For over a decade, *Timeless Youth Ministry* has served the body of Christ, in equipping a generation of youth ministry workers. As the needs of youth workers have expanded, it became evident that further concentration should be given. It was this book which provided the incentive for *Student Ministry Essentials. Timeless Youth Ministry* has had a far reaching impact on those who take student ministry seriously and the authors of *Student Ministry Essentials,* along with Moody Publishers, would like to express our gratitude for Dr. Vukich's efforts.

# PREFACE

We have had the privilege of being in some level of student ministry all of our adult lives. Someone has claimed that if you love what you do on your job, you'll never work a day in your life. Well, frankly, that's how we feel when it comes to vocational student ministry. Sure, there have been disappointing times along this journey, sometimes self-inflected, but most of the time beyond our control. But that has not deterred us from this important task of student ministry. We have a bigger perspective of student ministry as well for Whom we serve in this adolescent context. In fact, after years of frontline ministry, we still have that freshman enthusiasm for student ministry.

We started as volunteers in youth ministry and quickly moved into vocational student ministry once we graduated from college and seminary. We both served in local churches both big and small, in the south, the west, the Ohio Valley, and in Canada. We've also been involved in Christian youth organizations (Youth for Christ), and are currently in our most important role, professors of student ministry. A lot of discussion about student or youth ministry today is in the context of validity and relevancy questions. With that kind of discussion going on, it has brought youth ministry back to the forefront. In spite of the questions and criticisms, it has forced student ministry to refine its role as well as how student ministry fulfills that role.

Even in the midst of all this enthusiasm for student ministry, an undercurrent of misunderstanding has been directed toward this important ministry. This has been fostered by a number of factors. Wrong perceptions of student pastors and leaders have been sketchy at best: baby sitter; recreation director; rock star; stepping-stone to the pastorate. There's no doubt that some have brought this upon themselves. We would argue that those in the role of student pastor are truly pastors (as discussed in chapter 2).

There has also been massaged incriminating research when it comes to student attrition rate of church attendance and involvement. There has been much debate on this attrition rate of students leaving church for college and never returning. There are obviously enough stats to raise an alarm regardless of what survey you believe but to put the blame solely on student ministry is biased and skewed. Let's weigh in on this ecclesiastical issue with a probable solution. It involves an element of student ministry. The way to lower the attrition rate among college students is to have a vibrant and active college student ministry (discussed in chapter 7). This is the link that is missing in many churches between high school and adulthood.

In her book *The Adolescent Journey: An Interdisciplinary Approach to Practical Youth Ministry*, Amy Jacober does a thorough job in suggesting that to do effective ministry among students, one most know two things: the students themselves and the culture in which they live. There's no doubt those two subjects must be addressed and we will take a look at both. Yet anyone in student ministry also knows that there is definitely a third axis point to what we will suggest, forming a triangular approach to student ministry: a knowledge of students, a knowledge of culture, *and* a knowledge of ministry. The practice of practical theology in student ministry can be a bit of a moving target. It can be like the study of popular culture . . . it changes by the hour. So what we have attempted to do in this book is present what we feel, are the critical elements or the essentials that will enable you to influence students for the kingdom.

# DO TEENAGERS HAVE A PRAYER?

A number of evangelistic tools and methods have been effective among teenagers over the years, including 3 Story Evangelism (Youth for Christ), Dare2Share, and The Way of the Master. Campus Crusade (CRU) popularized an evangelistic tool years ago (The Four Spiritual Laws) by stating that God loves you and has a wonderful plan for your life. It was and still is great news. But we also need to be alert to another truth: Satan hates you and has a terrible plan for your life.

## THE ENEMY'S PLANS

The apostle Paul said of the Corinthian believers that they were not ignorant of Satan's devices (2 Corinthians 2:11). They knew his tactics. They understood his methods of attack. Bible scholar Merrill Unger explained it this way:

> This foe is dedicated to alienate man from God and to keep him from Christ's saving grace. When men do believe the Gospel, Satan exerts every effort to turn them away from God's will. He knows that once they are saved they are beyond his power insofar as their position before God and their eternal destiny are concerned. So he determines to do them as much damage as he can in ruining their Christian life and testimony for God.

> Satan is relentless and pitiless in his hatred for God and the people of God. What makes the devil a fearful foe is the fact of his great power. This is augmented by the assistance of innumerable fallen angels or demons.
>
> Satan . . . is . . . dedicated to doing as much damage as possible to mankind, especially the redeemed . . . The saints represent his ultimate destruction . . . because they are united to Christ and share His triumph over him and his hosts (I Cor. 12:12; Eph. 1:20–23; Rev. 20:1–3, 10).
>
> The saints must realize that they are the bull's-eye . . . against which Satan and his demon helpers aim their most fiery darts . . . This is the reason why saints dare not be oblivious of Satan's malignity or "ignorant of his devices" (II Cor. 2:11).[1]

As a result of Satan's evil toward God, it is reasonable to assume that anyone or anything that aligns himself with God immediately becomes the object of Satan's agenda. There have been religious movements, projects, churches, and leaders who have "suddenly" disappeared off the landscape. Now his focus is on the young, vulnerable, and impressionable.

John 10:10 happens to be my life verse. It was the verse of Scripture that finally made faith in Christ real for me as a junior in high school. Life abundant and being full and meaningful was what I was all about. I was not interested in dying. I was interested in living. But it's that first part of the verse that is most disturbing. As Jesus speaks in His own words (the red letters), He lists Satan's three-part strategy. He says, "The thief comes only to steal, and to kill, and to destroy." There it is in a succinct statement. The enemy's agenda is a simplistic yet catastrophic three-pronged plan. To steal. To kill. To destroy. That is his only agenda for young people. This is his only agenda for you and me. Frightening, isn't it? This truly is a worst-case scenario, if Satan has his way.

Christian teenagers are enjoying the abundant life that Christ promised to every believer. Unbelieving teenagers are clearly looking for that abundant life. The enemy, Satan, is not happy about it. We need to understand that a battle is underway for the hearts, minds, and even lives of young people. Unlike the good news of God's love, Satan's plan for your teenager(s) is to steal, to kill, and to destroy them. We need to examine Satan's three-fold strategy for our students.

# TO STEAL

First, Jesus says that Satan's plan is to steal. When our family was living in Alberta, Canada, we returned home one afternoon to discover that someone had pushed in our door lock, leaving the door ajar. As we went into the house, we realized that it would probably be a good idea to call the police.

During my phone call, the officer asked us an unusual question. "Where are you calling from?"

"From our house," I answered.

He immediately ordered us to get out of the house. I guess we hadn't thought about the unnerving fact that the thieves may still be in the house! So we quietly hurried our kids outside and waited out in the cool Canadian air. The police came and did a sweep through our house. Thankfully, no one was found.

I am not sure as to the intelligence of the thieves since we didn't have a whole lot worth stealing. Our furniture was mostly Early American Garage Sale. Regardless, the thieves had one purpose in mind: to get as many significant items of value as quickly as they could and to make their getaway without being caught.

If a thief broke into your home, what would he take? What would he be interested in? He certainly wouldn't be interested in going through your dirty laundry. He would only want to take those items of significant value.

Satan's purpose is to steal, and he only wants to steal those things in adolescent lives that are of significant value. He wants to rob them, first of all, of their earthly potential. God has a plan and purpose for each one of those teenagers' lives. It is greater than we can even begin to imagine. The Scripture declares, "What no eye has seen, what no ear has heard, and what no human mind has conceived—the things God has prepared for those who love him" (1 Corinthians 2:9 NIV). This is not just referring to eternity, but to the abundant life and to the wonderful plan—a purpose that God has designed for each one. Romans 12:1 brings on new significance when putting it in the context of adolescents. "In view of God's mercy, to offer your bodies as a living sacrifice, holy and pleasing to God—this is your true and proper worship" (NIV). Worship has become a meaningful and participatory element in our churches and young people have largely redefined it. And what better age group to be challenged with an incredible act of worship than offering their physical bodies, not as a lifeless sacrifice, but a living sacrifice, with plenty of potential years of service to present to God.

Psalms 40:6 (TLB) says, "It isn't sacrifices and offerings that you really want from your people. Burnt animals bring no special joy to your heart. But you have accepted the offer of my lifelong service." Not to minimize the evangelism of adults, but without exception, adults who have found faith in Christ have one common and consuming regret: that they did not make this all-important decision earlier in their lives!

Walking in the path of God's purpose maximizes the lives of adolescents for fruitfulness and eternal potential. And that is exactly what Satan wants to steal from young people. He wants them to be so concerned about earthly things that they have little or no time for eternal things. He wants them to become so wrapped up and absorbed in this world's way of thinking that their lives make no significant impact upon eternity.

Secondly, the enemy wants to rob teenagers of those things that are their birthright as Christians. He wants to rob them of their joy and peace. Jesus said "Peace I leave with you; my peace I give to you. Not as the world gives do I give to you. Let not your hearts be troubled, neither let them be afraid. . . . These things I have spoken to you, that my joy may be in you, and that your joy may be full" (John 14:27; 15:11). The apostle Paul wrote regarding joy and peace. "Rejoice in the Lord always; again I will say, rejoice. . . do not be anxious about anything, but in everything by prayer and supplication with thanksgiving let your requests be made known to God. And the peace of God, which surpasses all understanding, will guard your hearts and your minds in Christ Jesus" (Philippians 4:4–7).

Joy and peace are the birthright of every child of God, yet so many young Christians today are being robbed of what is rightfully theirs. Satan is the one who robs us of our joy and peace. We lose our peace because our focus is on circumstances, and we have believed Satan's lies. We lose our joy because we view our circumstances, from a temporal rather than eternal perspective.

Thirdly, Satan wants to steal the innocence of adolescents. Any kind of sexual moorings are ridiculed and trivialized. Never has this battle been so blatant. Gone are the days of even the slightest social and moral restraints. The leader's guide of *Good Sex, A Whole-Person Approach to Teenage Sexuality & God*, puts it this way.

> Something has gone wrong with our appetite for sex. By virtually any objective measure, our cultural preoccupation with sex has grown out of proportion to its actual significance. That may be hard to see since—other than more convenient access to pornography—not much has changed in the last decade.
>
> Nothing has changed for the kids we serve. They've grown up largely unprotected from what grownups cynically refer to as adult content. Our younger brothers and sisters never knew a world without home video and cable sex, descriptive sexual language on pop radio, one-click access to Internet material . . .

They also never knew a world without HIV/AIDS and rampant outbreaks of sexually transmitted infections—a world where careless sex can sterilize or even kill.[2]

Culture seems to dictate to young people that since their physical beings are screaming for sexual involvement, then why all the fuss with sexual boundaries and traditions. There is a dichotomy of beliefs and behavior, even for the Christian teenager. Christians continue to look prudish, as if we are against sex. Yet many times our message, at least perceived message, is NO, NEVER, NOT IN YOUR LIFETIME, when our message should be one that is clearly biblical: WAIT. And not only should you wait but if you wait, the benefits of waiting outweigh the consequences of not waiting.

Culture definitely has two messages that are against waiting. First, a couple should see if they are physically compatible. This classic human rationalization is fatally flawed. Compatibility cannot be measured, for there is nothing else to compare it to! By virtue of waiting and remaining faithful, they will become physically compatible. The second message that culture propagates to support premature sexual involvement is that a couple should gain sexual experience so they will know what they are doing. It certainly sounds good, from a baser level. Even public education continues to push sex education with an emphasis on the mechanics of sex (at the exclusion of sexual responsibility and commitment). My argument is that even though a person does not know the mechanics of sex, what better person to "figure it out" than with the person he or she has waited for and committed oneself to for a lifetime. If you don't get it right on your honeymoon, you'll have a lifetime to work on it!

# TO KILL

Satan's second purpose is to kill. This is not always figurative. It is a clear and present danger. Our spiritual enemy's agenda is to physically kill young people. This is so clearly obvious to the destructive behavior of teenagers, as if they have some kind of death wish. It goes beyond the nature of adolescence that permeates with white-knuckle adventure and constant urge for adrenaline. He wants to take them out! Satan desires to kill Christian young people, but since he can't do that without God's permission, he'll tell young people to do it for him. There are only two instances when Satan can harm us. One is when we step outside of God's protective hedge. If there is rebellion in our life, then we give Satan opportunity. That is why 1 Samuel 15:23 says, "For rebellion is as the sin of divination." A person who is involved in witchcraft (divination) has given himself over to Satan and his power. Exactly the same thing happens when you have a stubborn, rebellious attitude; you expose yourself to the destructive forces of Satan.

The only other instance when Satan is able to attack us is when he has God's full permission to do so. These are the circumstances surrounding the first few chapters of the book of Job. An increasing number of young people are convinced that taking their own life is the only way out. Satan cannot harm us without God's permission or unless we are outside of God's protection. But many Christian young people who have opened themselves up to spiritual oppression struggle daily with thoughts of self-destruction. So the battle is not exclusive to non-Christian teenagers. Suicide is made to look more attractive as an alternative of peaceful nonexistence than continuing in a warlike battleground in the mind. Sadly, young people not only attempt suicide, young people are "successful" in taking their lives.

Some Christian teenagers have revealed that they have heard voices in their head, like there was a subconscious voice talking to them. Others have said they frequently entertain thoughts of suicide. Every one of these young people had been involved in some activity that could easily have opened them up to dark supernatural powers. Many had been involved in a "harmless" party or video games where they had actually called for evil spirits to manifest themselves. Even though this kind of activity may appear to be harmless fun, the spirits on the other side of the "seen" world take a different view. To them it truly becomes an "opportunity."

Never has the fact of Satan's killing agenda been more evident to me than in my own family while growing up. I come from a blended family. When it came to our total of seven kids, it was yours, mine, and ours. My natural father had left my mom, my sister, and me. In God's perfect timing, my mother remarried. She fell in love with a man who had gained custody of his own three children. (It was the exception and not the rule, back in the late 1950s, for a father to gain custody of all the children in a divorce. The circumstances were exceptional that my soon-to-be father was able to keep his kids.) Life moved quickly as my mother remarried and I suddenly had a new older "brother." My stepbrother and I simply didn't get along. His name was Joe. He'd wear my clothes without permission, steal my girlfriends without my permission, and pretty much make my life miserable. He was stronger and better looking than I was, and he reminded me of those facts. For reasons I may never know, my older "brother" constantly rebelled against my parents, especially his own father. One issue that my stepbrother fought more about was smoking. My parents argued with him over this issue all the time, yet to no avail. Joe would refuse to obey.

I remember at one point he would try to disguise the smell of smoking by going into the bathroom and spraying aerosol deodorant directly into his mouth to cover up the smell. This simply didn't make sense to me. But his downhill spiral continued with several more incidents that would embarrass our family and especially my father. I had moved on to Liberty University to study youth ministry. During my first few years at LU, Joe would call from wherever he was and just talk. The subject would always turn to decisions, decisions he was beginning to regret. But in all our conversations, I would try to offer Joe some hope, especially with the fact that he could change with the help of Christ in his life. He would assure me that Christ was in his life but he wasn't living like it. He would always tell that there was no way he could change. It was as if he truly couldn't—this "grip" on his life would never loosen.

During my junior year in college, my stepfather called me, and all I could make out of what he was saying was, "Steve, Joe is dead." As I stood there somewhat numb, I heard our pastor get on the phone and began to tell me that Joe had been smoking in bed and he apparently fell asleep. When the firemen got there, they found my stepbrother stretched out on the floor, with his arm just short of the door. He had died of smoke inhalation. The spiral was over.

I would never want to excuse my stepbrother's behavior due to Satan's agenda. He made some choices that eventually killed him. He had made some choices that would eventually lead him to his premature death. But somehow, I cannot overlook the evil influences that came across the path of my stepbrother's life. Was it the evil group of kids he hung around at school with who were hell-bent on doing wrong? Was it the evil guys in our high school who introduced him to pornography, which led to his own quest for gratification with as many girls as possible? Was it the hypocritical kids in the youth group who sent the wrong message by drinking on Saturday night and "testifying" on Sunday morning? Frankly, no one held a gun to my stepbrother's head and told him to do wrong or choose evil. It was by his own volition.

Yet I cannot overlook the fact that Satan is the originator of all that is wrong, evil, and sinful. And even though we must all learn how to gingerly navigate through life's moral minefield, someone has placed those "mines" there for one purpose . . . to kill us. I hold this spiritual enemy responsible for everything that facilitated the death of my stepbrother.

Many TV programs, movies, online content, and music give Satan opportunity to work in the lives of our teens. As parents and youth leaders, we need to be alert to the activities our youth are exposed to. We need to earnestly pray that God would bind all supernatural powers that may be influencing our young people, while providing them with the critical media skills they will need to make their own right choices.

# ANOTHER KILLING FIELD

Another killing field that Satan has is in the gender arena. Pop culture has leveled the playing field in favor of gender blending and the acceptance of a perceived normalcy in homosexual tendencies and behavior. If one chooses to stand against this type of thinking, you are immediately branded as intolerant at the very minimum. Christians and non-Christians alike have been ridiculed into silence. So our enemy is getting away with it again. In *Four Pillars of a Man's Heart*, Stu Weber has some strong words with relation to this issue:

> Satan loves dark tunnels. And he knows that this one, this gender-destroying detour from God's intentions, has the potential to do more damage than we can begin to dream. Our ancient adversary knows very well what most of us have forgotten: Gender is one of the most far-reaching expressions of the image of God. And the enemy loves nothing better than to distort the image of God he hates ...
>
> The Book of Revelation calls him "the great dragon . . . that serpent called the devil, or Satan, who leads the whole world astray." When he acts, it is according to an established pattern, old as Eden, old as the earth itself:
>
> *Distort the Word of God. Mar the image of God. And never stop attacking man, the creation of God formed in His very image.*
>
> God created mankind "in His image . . . male and female He created them." The image and glory of God on this planet is tied to our human masculinity and femininity. *Anything* Satan can do to bend, blur, or deface that image is a big-time coup for him. So he is at it with a vengeance today, in your lifetime and mine ...
>
> Hear me, please, when I say that these issues represent a rock-bottom, down-in-the-trenches, gut-tearing attack on our society's vital organs.
>
> To tinker with the image of God, represented in male and female, is to slap God in the face. This is something more than politics, economics, social studies, or some bleeding-heart, feel-good crusade for "equality." This is a culture killing disease. It also represents an ancient, long-simmering attack on the very person of God and His loving intentions for His children.[3]

Young people are caught in the crossfire of this moral dilemma. There is definitely some confusion. There is going to be a need for clear teaching of the

Scriptures in order to make the proper stand on this issue, a stand that demonstrates grace, while being clear about the Scripture's expectations on sexuality.

# TO DESTROY RELATIONSHIPS

The third purpose of Satan is to destroy. A primary target is relationships—the most significant aspect of any teenager's life. Teens value and need relationships with their peers, including the opposite sex. They need relationships with their siblings; relationships with their parents. And they need a relationship with a loving and personal God.

Satan's purpose is to destroy relationships, especially among family members and among church members. This is the reason so many Christian marriages are ending in divorce. This is the reason so many Christian young people are living in rebellion against their parents, school, church, and society in general. It is the reason so many churches are dividing and members of the same congregation harbor bitterness and refuse to talk to one another. And it is the teenager who is caught in the wake of such relational disasters.

Most young people who are bitter don't realize it. Rather than admitting they are bitter, they simply say they that have been hurt or disappointed or offended by another person. But bitterness is like a cancer, and unless it's checked it will quickly spread and produce devastating consequences. Paul wrote, "Be angry and do not sin; do not let the sun go down on your anger, and give no opportunity to the devil" (Ephesians 4:26–27). If the young believer cultivates in his life any known sin, he is giving Satan an opportunity to get a foothold, a beachhead in his life. Satan will use this opportunity to invade and take over other areas. The word translated "opportunity" simply means a place, such as a city or building. But it carries the idea of a foothold or opportunity, a chance to operate.

In 2 Corinthians 2, Paul exhorted the Corinthian believers to forgive a repentant Christian brother who had been involved in immorality. "Anyone whom you forgive, I also forgive. Indeed, what I have forgiven, if I have forgiven anything, has been for your sake in the presence of Christ, so that we would not be outwitted by Satan; for we are not ignorant of his designs" (vv. 10–11).

If young people hold resentment and unforgiveness in their hearts against anyone, the same thing will happen to them. They will give the enemy ground to torment them. Most Christians would never think of becoming involved in the occult and giving ground in their lives for the enemy to operate; but bitterness is one of the major inroads that Satan has to gain ground in a Christian's life. Adolescent Christians who have a bitter, unforgiving spirit open themselves up to spiritual attack.

# TO DESTROY INTEGRITY

The destruction of your teen's own personal integrity and effectiveness is certainly on the to-do list of Satan. It is a type of neutralizing. It is a strategy that does whatever it takes to make the Christian young person ineffective. It could be subtle intrusions into the adolescent's life like being overwhelmed by loneliness, certain private and personal disorders or addictions, or unbridled preoccupations like the Internet and social media. It could be disguised as more recognizable factors like financial success or athletic prowess or popular personae. These recognized factors do not necessarily mean spiritual bankruptcy in a teenager's life. But unless the young person keeps them in their proper perspective, they could become an end in themselves. These factors could become the god that replaces God.

# CONCLUSION

We cannot and should not prevent young people from learning about the dangers of this world. But like the young of any species, our teens require the care, protection, and guidance of parents and adults. When we make the mistaken conclusion that teenagers are fully capable to deal with some of these morally complex issues, we discourage them from seeking the support and counsel that can only come from adults. And we adults have something going for us that teenagers can learn and benefit from . . . experience.

No one is saying that this conflict is going to be an easy one to resolve. In the biblical sense of things, this conflict will always be with us. We do know the outcome. We win. The enemy loses. But until that divinely appointed time, we will have to be diligent and responsible with what God has entrusted to us . . . namely our teenagers.

The second part of John 10:10 says, "I have come that they may have life, and have it to the full" (NIV). I would suggest that our message is simple . . . life both now and forever. It's not about dying. It's about living. It's essential.

*Steve Vandegriff*

# NOTES

1.  Merrill F. Unger, *What Demons Can Do to Saints* (Chicago: Moody, 1977), 10, 11, 12.

2.  Jim Hancock & Kara Eckmann Powell, *Good Sex, A Whole-Person Approach to Teenage Sexuality & God, Leader's Guide* (Grand Rapids: Zondervan Publishing House, 2001), 17.

3.  Stu Weber, *Four Pillars of a Man's Heart* (Sisters, Oreg.: Multnomah, 1997), 34–35.

STUDENT MINISTRY

# ESSENTIALS

## PART 1: LEADING

# 1

# THE ESSENTIAL OF

# LEADERSHIP IN STUDENT MINISTRY

The average churchgoer may not completely understand what it means to be a leader in the church. In fact, many assume that the student ministry leader only works two days a week, and when he is around he is just playing ultimate Frisbee and playing music just a little too loud. Unless someone needs to unload some old couches or is looking for some cheap movers, the churchgoer is satisfied in letting the students live in their world as long as it doesn't mess with their own. The student ministry leader can have the unique task of helping students pursue God, shepherding them and being examples, while navigating the waters of conflicting church culture around them.

For the purpose of this chapter, I have decided to define this position as the "student ministry leader." There are many reasons for this, but the primary one is this: it is simply difficult to paint this position with a broad brush. As we will discuss, many different variations can appear among leaders who work with students. So when you see "student ministry leader" mentioned, feel free to apply that term to your own context, understanding that we are doing our best to come to an agreement that this is anyone who desires to lead and shepherd the minds and souls of students toward a greater love and devotion to Jesus Christ.

For those already in student ministry, the following story of student ministry resistance and hesitation may not be of any surprise. For those who are looking forward to, or are beginning student ministry, this might surprise you.

> When I was in a seminary course for youth ministry, our Professor brought in our Greek Professor who was relatively well known—in the kind of strange circles that seminary professors have name recognition, that is. He shared with our class that youth ministry was a failed experiment. It was unbiblical, he said, and we should all quit. While I think it is a good thing to bring in different perspectives in an educational environment, this decision lacked direction and conviction. Our visiting Professor's arguments were many, but primarily he argued that intergenerational churches create better disciples than those with segmented groups. His argument wasn't completely invalid, but it did ignore a fundamental understanding in the exercise of contextualization.
>
> Being that we were in a youth ministry class, many of us were youth pastors already or we were training to be one in the future. One of the students raised his hand and said, "Sir, you have successfully talked me out of a job!" My heart sank. While nothing compares to my love for my Savior, my love for seeing students embrace Him as well was a close second. I asked our guest lecturer if he planned to retire. He indicated that he did indeed plan to retire one day. I reminded him that retirement was not a Biblical concept, yet it was something that existed within our culture. To ignore retirees and tell them that they don't exist because of their unseen recognition within Scripture is to truly misunderstand what it means to reach out to our culture. Contextualization takes culture into consideration. It helps us bridge the gap between the message of the Gospel and the world that we live in. I hope that in that classroom I was able to encourage a few students who had otherwise felt as if they were being led down the wrong path in pursuing student ministry.[1]

Student ministry is consistently on the frontlines and is challenged repeatedly. There are those who say that youth ministry is a "50-year failed experiment."[2] These are well-meaning people who misunderstand the purpose of student ministry. Youth pastors used to be the third hire, after the senior pastor and a worship pastor, but this is changing. We are seeing a de-emphasis on student ministry in many churches across denominations. While this chapter doesn't aim to accomplish the task of affirming student ministry itself, it does intend to validate our role as leaders and disciplemakers of students. Student pastors are making a difference and do play an important role in ministry.

## THE CHANGING FACE OF STUDENT MINISTRY

It is worth noting that the face of student ministry is changing. And while it is important to understand that student ministry is still a prevailing and important part of our church culture—there is not one way to *do* student ministry just as there is not just one way to *be* a student ministry leader. It should come as no surprise that the face of leadership within student ministry is changing, since the culture in which students live is itself moving at a rapid pace. Years ago ministry to students would change or evolve slowly, with the biggest threat being a TV station. (MTV anyone?) Today, trends can wear out in mere weeks or even days, not years. Student ministries chasing relevancy are chasing a moving target.

So, what does the state of leadership look like in student ministry and what can we do to be the best at it we can be?

## KINDS OF LEADERS IN STUDENT MINISTRY

Of course, many of the differences found in student ministry leadership are on the surface. Different faith expressions or denominations handle the position of the student leader in a variety of ways. While this is in no way an exhaustive list, here are a few examples of these differences:

*The Student Pastor.* This may be a position that we are most aware of and usually involves a specific calling to ministry. The student pastor is often seen as a staff position of the pastoral team, though there are occasions where a student pastor may sit at the table as a plural elder, but often the student pastor is seen as an associate pastor who may carry duties outside of student ministry. Depending on the size of the church, the student pastor may also oversee worship or children as a part of his expectations. In larger churches this position may have the opposite effect, where the role is more specific and more specialized.

*The Student Director.* The student director typically may hold less authority than a pastor might. While there is similarity in job description, often churches will use the term *director* when they expect the leader's role to be more confined within the student ministry itself. While the director is still a part of the overall leadership team, this term can often signify that the leader may be bivocational or lacks certain scholastic or other ritualistic expectations, such as a seminary degree or an ordination.

*The Volunteer Student Leader.* The volunteer leader is almost certainly bi-vocational. The leader usually has a desire to help students grow, or maybe has a child of their own in the student ministry. The volunteer leader is not to be overlooked, as this person is an extremely common part of leadership and can be very well suited for the position. This position is typical in a smaller church that may have only a few students and does not require a very dedicated person to excel.

*Student Ministry Advisory Board.* Many of the more traditional settings will have something similar to an advisory board. This group could work in conjunction with either of the previously mentioned positions as well and generally includes people from all walks of life from the church. The group typically oversees the direction and activities of the student ministry. Members of the board monitor budget, concerns from parents, and can act as a go-between to the senior pastor.

Many factors are leading to nontraditional understandings of the above definitions. Such modifications in titles for the student ministry leader can be interpreted as a change in theological understanding and/or an overall pragmatic change in the role itself. Many treat the role as a stepping-stone to a senior pastor position, or as an entry-level position. What we need to understand is that God can call someone specifically to student ministry with no expectations of moving to be a "real pastor" (a phrase the student pastor becomes all too familiar with). In one church that I am aware of, a student pastor served the church twenty-nine years and retired at age sixty-seven.[3] There are those men and women out there who are doing a great job and not looking to use the ministry as a tool to build their resume and experience. It is a joy to see someone who understands and embraces the calling to lead students—finding their satisfaction in blossoming where they're planted and not looking for what's next.

# MEET DEANA

Deana Dickerson is a student leader who has navigated this path of leadership in student ministry.[4] She represents an often-overlooked segment of women who struggle to find a place serving in student ministry. While there are differing opinions on the roles of women in ministry, she has walked through this and her story is compelling. She is one of the most gifted middle school student leaders I (Steve) know, and she certainly has much to offer to the discussion. Here is her view of her place in youth ministry within the church:

I realize that the central issue for me in leadership was not so much about gender or acceptance, but about gifting and, even more, about calling. Saying yes to this was saying yes to Jesus and the way He gifted me. In the church, spiritual gifts of women and men should be recognized, developed, and used in serving and teaching ministries like small groups, counseling, administration, pastoral care, and worship. In doing so, the church honors God as the source of our gifts.

Dallas Willard says it well, "It is not the rights of women to occupy 'official' ministerial roles, nor their equality to men in those roles that set the terms of their service to God and their neighbors. It is their obligations that do so: obligations which derive from their human abilities empowered by divine gifting. It is the good they can do, and the duty to serve that comes from that, which impels them to serve in all ways possible. Women and men are indeed very different, and those differences are essential to how God empowers each to induce the Kingdom of God into their specific life setting and ministry."[5]

She realizes her role as a woman in ministry is an area "that has never been free from controversy. I know that my gender can be an issue for some and because of this I have sometimes felt alone." She cites her monthly meetings with other youth workers in the area: "I am usually one of three ladies in a room full of guys."

Deana has found true support in her church's male leaders who regularly encourage her. She calls the experience of leading the middle school group "fun and exciting."

I have realized over the years that my role as a woman in leadership is vital and important to the overall church. Furthermore, I do a disservice to God and His purposes if I do not embrace the gifts He has given me, step faithfully into the opportunities He has put before me, and trust that He is with me wherever I go.

So instead of marrying a youth pastor, I became one. This was not how I saw my life playing out. Choosing to trust Jesus with my life and step into the calling of full-time youth ministry has stretched and challenged me in many ways, but it has also been the most rewarding thing I have ever done.

Deana understands her context and is doing her best to excel in the role God has placed her in.

# EXPECTATIONS ABOUT STUDENTS AND STUDENT MINISTRY

While each and every expression can have its merits and disappointments, we must keep in mind that ultimately it is important to gain an adequate understanding of how the particular church you serve understands and utilizes each leader it brings to this role. Not fully understanding what may be expected of you, or even to what authority you may have, can be a death sentence—especially if you're finding those things out as you move through the position. Regardless of which position you walk into, make sure you have a crystal clear understanding of the expectations of you and what the system of leadership is.

Lifeway Research states that roughly 70 percent of young adults drop out of church.[6] This number is lower than the often-touted "86 percent" of students who don't stick around; however, it is still a cause for concern. One implication of young adults not sticking around could be that while they connect with the student ministry, they aren't connecting with the church as a whole. When they make the transition to adult worship, it looks nothing like the silly games and loud music they are most accustomed to. Another factor influencing this outcome is that the students don't adequately own their own faith before reaching adulthood. When a student is at their most impressionable, we are missing opportunities to invest the gospel into their lives.

Misplaced priorities have held us back and riddled our ministries with great losses of effectiveness. Many leaders have experienced hurt and shouldered the pain of others so much that it has misdirected our own intentions and passions. Pastors have found themselves leading from a negative place, and can even lead from a place of low self-esteem—seeking the approval of others rather than the approval of God.[7]

# BETWEEN PRIDE AND GENUINENESS

One of the largest pitfalls of a leader is pride, which applies to both effective and ineffective leaders. The perceived *cool* leader can lean too much on his own confidence and completely lose sight of his dependence on God, while the perceived *uncool* leader can be so focused on trying to impress others to make up for his shortcomings that he has the same result. Whatever the case, we need to grasp that when we fall into one of these pitfalls as a leader that we aren't just handling a business or an organization, but we are handling the very truth of God.

We all may need to embrace that to be called and follow God into the unknown world of working with students often draws those of us who may be a little different. I want to encourage you to embrace who God has made you and equipped you to be. Don't try to be someone you aren't. Don't shop at stores geared for teenagers and be that forty-year-old wearing V-necks and slim jeans. Be yourself and let your walk with God be the most obvious thing about you—people will remember your character over your style. (And if they remember your style, it's probably not a good thing.)

Success defined in student ministry can almost always lead to what one pastor labeled as the Three B's: Butts, Budgets, and Buildings. We focus on how many butts are in the seats. (Yes, I know there is some artistic license with this "B.") In fact, one of the first questions one student ministry leader will ask another is, "How many students do you run?" It's the instant size-up. Our concerns play more into our comparisons and self-worth defined by attendance rather than the number of students who are embracing Jesus. Effective leadership in student ministry is not just numbers. You can find a gimmick (that will work for a short period of time, most likely) that can get feet in the door, but it's what you do with them at that point that matters. Focus on the message. Focus on the gospel, the only thing that can change their lives for eternity and give them a greater purpose in life today. Redefine success as a leader and wear it proudly on your sleeve. Our collective strive toward effectiveness is not to see more seats filled, but more hearts filled with the love of Christ.

# ATTRIBUTES OF STUDENT MINISTRY LEADERS

There are many things we can do to improve as leaders to help students grow in their transition into adulthood. Here is another nonexhaustive list of many current attributes of the ever-shaping student ministry leader.

## TEACHABLE

Effective student ministry leaders are teachable. While this statement may seem simple, it's extremely accurate. Leaders are learners, and student ministry doesn't have the latitude to offer any exceptions to this rule. The student ministry leaders who are really making an impact are the ones who are seeking to learn from other effective leaders, as well as from the culture itself. These leaders understand that networking is important not just to help your career in ministry, but also to catch a glimpse of something that is catching the attention of the culture. They are finding ways to leverage their influence with today's student culture, and not just going through the motions.

## MORE SPECIALIZED

Student ministry leaders are becoming more specialized. There seem to be fewer broad positions found in churches today. This could be in part to the fact that smaller churches are shutting down in droves as people navigate to larger churches.[8] These larger churches tend to have a more contemporary worship style and are less likely to have a position for a student leader that is a catchall for many youth ages. Many churches are also realizing that keeping a sixth-grade student and a twelfth-grade student in the same room for worship and instruction can be beyond challenging. With the split of middle school and high school ministries often comes the more specialized hiring of leaders to head up each of those specific ministries. So while the older model may have found student pastors who also have a passion for speaking to the XYZ Senior Group, this new breed of leader is much more specialized and laser focused to their specific group.

## OFTEN BI-VOCATIONAL

Many student leaders are still bi-vocational. Student ministry leaders aren't always the third hire on staff any longer. As churches grow, they are looking for roles that may fit their growth needs and they may not have an immediate need for a specialized position for student ministry. Many leaders found in this role are found through their volunteer status or came on at the church in a part-time role that expanded as the church continues to grow. As mentioned before, as the church abandons the "catch all" position that student pastors once held, they are quicker to hire several part-time positions before hiring one full time.

## KINGDOM-MINDED AND MISSIONAL

Student ministry leaders are becoming more kingdom-minded and missional in their approaches. When the medium becomes the message, eventually you lose a generation's attention when that medium changes. For many years we have experienced this in our churches in the music medium. Music is not headed toward extinction, although its forms (records, tapes, CDs, downloads) continually change, as do its styles. A generation worships a certain style of music instead of the reason that music had a huge impact in the first place—its message. In other words, we make a decision on whether we like the music (our preference), not on what it does or does not accomplish (its message). Student leaders should focus more on the message and less on style. Wise student ministry leaders are careful to understand that the goal isn't to entertain a student (and to keep up with the current music trend), but to disciple a student. Discipleship supersedes cultural styles. The students today are looking for raw, real truth.[9] They thrive when they are challenged and are not looking for anything that would even appear fake or insincere. They aren't concerned with petty arguments or silly disagreements.

While styles in which we convey our messages can change, the message never changes. Focus on the most important part of the great need and teach students to love Jesus more—not their style of worship.

## EQUIP PARENTS

Student ministry leaders excel when they equip parents. One survey found that 61 percent of students value family in their lives.[10] There is a certain expectation that they have when they see their student ministry leader share the gospel—but when students witness their parents telling others about Jesus it shapes them considerably more than the impact that the leaders may have. Effective student ministry leaders are learning that to have a greater impact in the lives of students, they need to have a greater influence in the lives of parents.

While student ministry in the past may have been a situation where a parent dropped his or her child off in hopes that the leader will "fix" them and lead them spiritually, the best thing we can do for that parent is help the mother or father embrace and understand that a parent has the biggest impact on the life of the son and daughter.

Student ministry leaders are spending large amounts of time and resources in more effectively reaching parents through training, equipping, and sometimes simply informing parents as to cultural trends they may be unaware of. This has quickly become an irreplaceable part of effective ministry. There is no substitute for a healthy ministry to parents.

# A WIDENING GAP AMONG MINISTRY LEADERS

The final attribute of student ministry leaders deserves special mention. It is this: The gap of differences between student ministries is getting wider. Although many churches are facing declining attendance or actually closing their doors, many new churches are starting, seemingly taking their places. Fewer traditional churches are embracing change and new churches are opening with a new dynamic that isn't restricted by tradition. As such, the gap between these churches is getting wider, not narrower.

The role of student ministry leaders in each of these churches is looking just as dissimilar. In many newer churches, the style of ministry is one that more accurately reflects the student culture than the traditional church does. As such, these churches have a much higher number of students connecting in the primary worship service—and can have a more difficult time helping students see the value of a worship service designed just for them. Often the service designed for students in new churches is not too unlike the primary worship service. The traditional church struggles with almost the exact opposite problem. Students connect much easier in the student worship time and struggle to find value in the primary worship service of the church. The dynamic of new churches means the values that are placed with each of these student ministry leaders is changing drastically as a result of their own context.

Gone are the days of free pizza. Students don't just show up with the promise of a T-shirt or triangle-shaped food. There is far too much competing for their attention, and plenty of other people willing to buy it. The fact is, intentionality is key when leading students to engage with the group.

As student ministry leaders, we need to be aware of the shape of our culture and be willing to embrace new means of reaching students. We need to take whatever steps are necessary to reach students. Because it's not just attendance that's at stake; it's the very gospel saturation of this culture itself.

# NOTES

1. Patrick Gillen, student pastor to high school at Prince Avenue Baptist Church in Athens, Georgia. Personal interview conducted on June 29, 2014.

2. Alex Murashko, "Modern Youth Ministry a '50-Year Failed Experiment,' Say Pastors," *The Christian Post*, July 28, 2011.

3. Barry Shettel retired in 2009 from Prince Avenue Baptist Church in Athens, Georgia.

4. As of this writing, Deana Dickerson is the middle school director at Community Presbyterian Church in Danville, California.

5. Deana Dickerson; all comments are from an email response, June 2, 2014.

6. Ed Stetzer, "'Dropout and Disciples: "How Many Students are Really Leaving the Church?'" The Exchange, a blog at http://www.christianitytoday.com/edstetzer/2014/may/dropouts-and-disciples-how-many-students-are-really-leaving.html.

7. See Thomas G. Bandy, "Clergy Anger & the Urgency of a True Spiritual Life," at http://www.ministrymatters.com/all/entry/4253/clergy-anger-the-urgency-of-a-true-spiritual-life.

8. "Lifeway Research Finds Reason Adults Switch Churches," December 2006 survey by Lifeway Research; http://www.lifeway.com/Article/LifeWay-Research-finds-church-switchers-move-to-larger-more-contemporary-church.

9. Polly House, "Millennials: Hard Questions Need Answers," Facts & Trends, April 1, 2013; http://factsandtrends.net/2013/04/01/millennials-hard-questions-need-answers.

10. Thom S. Rainer and Jess W. Rainer, *The Millennials* (Nashville: B&H, 2001), 74; as cited in Jess Rainer, "Family Topped List, April 2, 2013 at http://factsandtrends.net.

# 2

## THE ESSENTIAL OF

# YOUTH WORKERS KNOWING THEIR ROLES

Knowing one's role is essential in organizations, businesses, schools, athletic teams, and even ministries. Organizations have bosses, supervisors, and employees. Businesses have CEOs, CFOs, and CIOs. Schools have presidents, principals, professors, teachers, support staff, and students. Athletic teams have coaches, assistant coaches, trainers, and players (and each player knows or should know his or her role).

There's no doubt that when members or employees know their individual roles, a form of synergy and effectiveness is displayed and demonstrated before everyone. Church and Christian ministries are no different. Those within churches and Christian ministries have their roles as well. They include clergy and laity. There are obvious differences of how churches and ministries are structured, compared with papal authority where one person has absolute authority over a church. Intuitively we default to the Catholic Church as the quintessential example when it comes to this structure, but my guess is that some have been exposed to non-Catholic churches that had a facsimile of papal rule or one person who was (or has) the sole authority over a congregation. I personally find a lot of fault and potential damage with this structure. Anyone who is the sole authority is setting themselves and their congregation up for disappointment at best and failure at worst. There must be a consigliere, or counselor, somewhere in the mix, and hopefully this advisor falls well within the qualifications of being able to give spiritual advice and direction.

I think the Scriptures are clear that within the structure of the church, both local and global, there should be a plurality of spiritual leadership. This is exemplified in current denominational-like episcopal rule, where the authority lies in the hands of a few men; presbytery, where authority is delegated to a few individuals selected by the congregation; and congregational rule, where authority is a democratic process of the entire local assembly.

# THE ROLE OF THE YOUTH WORKER: AN UNDER-SHEPHERD

So let's consider the role of the youth worker. This person should assume the role of shepherd over a young flock. First Peter 5:4 uses the term, "chief Shepherd" to describe Christ Himself. We now find ourselves in the role as under-shepherds of the Chief Shepherd. Our "flocks" will be a younger and more vulnerable flock, but our role as a shepherd is in no way diminished or marginalized. A plurality of shepherds in any flock is not only effective and efficient; there is biblical evidence that making a big flock seem small is simply good management.

Exodus 18 gives us some strong conventional wisdom from the mouth of Moses' father-in-law (who Moses obviously got along with, as evidenced in vv. 8 and 24). To paraphrase verse 14, outspoken Jethro raised some pointed questions toward his son-in-law: "What are you doing? Why are you doing everything? Why is everyone else just standing around?" The result of this exchange was a fine-tuned organized structure to deal with millions of people. In fact, Numbers 1:3 indicates that not only was gender considered in a census, but also age. And with that age (twenty years old) came adult responsibilities like heading up his family and the requirement of serving in the military.

Now in our modern culture, student ministry has a relatively short history. Mark Senter notes,

> Not until the late eighteenth century is there a concerted effort to minister to young people within the context of the church. The Sunday School was first. Then came the Young Men's and Youth Women's Christian Associations. Throughout the nineteenth century individual churches in a wide variety of denominations provided activities for their youth. . . . But why . . . ? During the 1800's a

process of secularization began to decrease the influence which the church and home had previously exerted over young people. The 1859 publication of Darwin's On the Origin of Species symbolized the change. No longer was a Christian understanding of the world the environment in which young people were being raised . . . Parents felt like they were losing control."[1]

## THE EMERGING PSEUDO-MODERNISM AND OUR FACE-TO-FACE RESPONSE

Now being well into the twenty-first century, we are deep within postmodernism, with all its lack of meaning and truth. It has become the acceptable DNA for our culture. What is before us is what one writer calls pseudo-modernism. "The new pseudo-modern cultural product can't exist without us being in the on the act . . . it's a far more intense engagement than anything literature can offer, giving the illusion of controlling, managing, running the show."[2] Pseudo-modernism is posited with banal and narcissist expressions like Likes on Facebook, tweets, blogs, selfies, and texts. No longer does our culture just critique expressions, it creates those expressions, with an ever pressing and futile demand to get others to see it. This preoccupation with social media and technology is how all this is incarnated with students.

When it comes to social media, youth workers prefer face-to-face. In student ministry, we can't always expect our students to conform to our platform of communication but in order for us to be heard, we need to be sensitive to their ways of communication. To be relevant and have opportunity, we certainly can't ignore or dismiss student platforms of communication. I think we take advantage of those platforms, and turn them into those face-to-face relationships. With this sociological characteristic of technology in the background, it's going to take those adults who look beyond student idiosyncrasies and embrace them for who they are, not necessarily for what we want them to be.

## ACTING AS AN UNDER-SHEPHERD

Life change is the end game, but that change can only come from the work of the Holy Spirit in one's life, while we are mere facilitators. For some, this role will be more than just being a concerned volunteer. It truly is the role of being a shepherd. A website from the United Kingdom listed some interesting characteristics of sheep and shepherds:

1. Sheep are foolish.
2. Sheep are slow to learn.
3. Sheep are unattractive.
4. Sheep are demanding.
5. Sheep are stubborn.
6. Sheep are strong.
7. Sheep are straying.
8. Sheep are unpredictable.
9. Sheep are copycats.
10. Sheep are restless
11. Sheep are dependent.
12. Sheep are the same everywhere.

Then it concluded: The shepherd is a sheep.[3]

I'm making an assumption that herders in the United Kingdom know something about sheep. Perhaps there are young faces that come to mind as you read through the list.

But what about the shepherd? Our UK friends address this with the clarity of a shepherd on a Scottish hillside.

1. The shepherd is patient with his sheep.
2. The shepherd knows his sheep.
3. The shepherd values his sheep.
4. The shepherd loves his sheep.
5. The shepherd observes his sheep.
6. The shepherd feeds his sheep.
7. The shepherd leads his sheep.
8. The shepherd speaks well of his sheep.
9. The shepherd pursues his sheep.
10. The shepherd rests his sheep.
11. The shepherd perseveres with his sheep.[4]

The age group known as adolescents needs those adults who feel called to them, just like any other age group that draws people to minister to them. So while the precise term of youth pastor, elder, or bishop is not mentioned in the Scriptures, a younger audience is identifiable and even recognized. Consider these admonitions from the Scriptures:

> The imagination of man's heart is evil from his youth.
> (Genesis 8:21)

He has been a warrior from his youth. (1 Samuel 17:33 NASB)

Do not remember the sins of my youth. . . . You are my trust
from my youth. (Psalm 25:7; 71:5)

Remember now your Creator in the days of your youth.
(Ecclesiastes 12:1)

I remember you, the kindness of your youth. . . . This has been
your manner from your youth. . . . Moab has been at ease from
his youth. (Jeremiah 2:2: 22:21; 48:11)

It is good for a man to bear the yoke in his youth.
(Lamentations 3:27)

Let no one despise your youth, but be an example to
the believers. (1 Timothy 4:12)

Flee from youthful lusts. (2 Timothy 2:22 NASB)

# THE SHEPHERD'S CALL

The concept of a calling is an important one. For those in vocational student ministry, calling is everything. Calling trumps all other reasons for going into student ministry. If a person cannot articulate their calling into student ministry (or any ministry for that matter), they should seriously consider doing something else. In other words, you should be able to describe the events, people, and promptings of the Holy Spirit that led you into student ministry.

For some, youth ministry may be just a cool job . . . to hang out and work with teenagers while offering timely sage advice. Others may be in student ministry because someone said that they are athletic, funny, or just good with kids. These are certainly good attributes to have but if these are the only reasons, then we think you are in student ministry for all the wrong reasons. We hold a much higher view of student ministry and that's where calling must be considered. It is this calling that separates those who are in student ministry based on what people have said, versus those who are in student ministry based on what God has told them.

In *Joan 'n' the Whale*, John Duckworth illustrates this truth in his story "The Call":

> There was a Sitter, and there was a Stander. The Sitter was smil-
> ing contentedly, reading a book as he sat at a sidewalk café. His
> sunglasses, Panama hat, tropical-print shirt, Bermuda shorts, and
> spotless white running shoes matched his mood of permanent

leisure. An umbrella kept him in the shade; on the table at his elbow sat a tall glass of iced tea—and a shining white telephone.

Yawning, he slowly turned a page in his well-worn book. He was about to take a nap when he heard a voice.

"Hey!" cried the voice. He looked up. It was the Stander, and she was approaching his table. He frowned, but only for a moment, and went back to his reading.

"What do you know?" the girl greeted him, putting her hands on her hips. "Is that really you? Long time no see!"

"MMMM," went the Sitter, not looking up.

"So what have you been doing all this time?" the girl asked.

The Sitter nodded toward his book, which he continued to read. "Studying, of course," he said proudly.

The girl scratched her head. "Studying? Well, I guess that's—" Glancing across the street, she gasped. "Hey!" she said. "What's going on over there?"

"MMMM?" the Sitter murmured.

"An old man just fell down in the crosswalk," she said urgently. "Come on, we'd better go help him!" She ran off, leaving the Sitter reading in the shade. Slowly he turned a page; it was his only movement.

A minute later the Stander returned, panting from her dash. "Well," she said between breaths, "he's okay." She frowned. "Hey, how come you didn't give me a hand?"

Irritated, he looked up from his book. "Because I'm waiting, of course," he said.

"Waiting for what?" she asked.

"For the Call," he replied, nodding at the phone on the table.

The Stander shook her head. "What's the—" Just then she happened to look down a nearby alley. "Look!" she cried. "That kid just snatched a lady's purse. Come on—we can probably catch him!" Off she ran again, and the Sitter just sat.

Two minutes later she was back, huffing and puffing. "Hey," she said. "What kind of neighborhood is this? People falling in the streets, kids snatching purses . . .What's the matter with you? Why didn't you come with me?"

The Sitter lifted his head and glared. "Because I didn't get the Call!"

"What Call?" the girl asked, exasperated.

"The Call," he answered, looking skyward.

The girl threw up her hands. "I don't—" All at once she noticed something else down the street. "Oh, did you see that?" she asked, putting her hand to her mouth. "That car just took a left and plowed right into the motorcycle. Now, come on! Don't just sit there; we've got to get help!"

The Sitter sipped his iced tea. "I'm sorry," he said, unconcerned. "But I'm just not called."

The girl started to run in the direction of the accident. "What are you studying, anyway?" She shouted at him over her shoulder.

"First aid," he said placidly and returned to his reading.

Three minutes later the girl was back, so exhausted she could barely stand. "I've got to use your phone," she asked, gasping for breath.

"What?" the Sitter cried, suddenly alert.

"I've got to call an ambulance for that guy," she panted and reached for the shining white telephone.

The Sitter leaped from his chair, wrestling the phone away. "You can't do that!" he said, his eyes panicky. "Why, the Call could come at any time! I might get the Call any minute now!" Whatever the call or wherever the mission or whoever the group of people, we are to enter that calling with a sense of divine mission.[5]

So one's call to student ministry is important. In his book *Working the Angles*,[6] Eugene Peterson declares that ministers have abandoned their call. What many are doing, according to Peterson, has nothing to do with pastoral ministry. It has morphed into something like shop keeping…keeping customers happy, luring customers from competitors, and using the right packaging to keep customers shelling out more money. For whatever reasons, we have moved from the very essence of shepherding this young group of students. The spiritual dynamic that so many teenagers are missing, is embodied in the spiritual resources that those who are called to this ministry possess, including critical basics of intercessory prayer, the clear directives of Scripture, spiritual guidance, Holy Spirit intervention, and an often overlooked aspect of ministry: presence. Simply being there (preferably in person) for someone speaks more than words. It is that presence of the shepherd that brings the stress level down in a stressful situation. Presence of a shepherd can signal that things will work out. Presence of a shepherd signals that if the situation has reached its tipping point, the shepherd will be there to help pick up the pieces and attempt to put things back together. In good situations, presence signals admiration and approval from the shepherd. In this demographic of student ministry, there are many students who are silently screaming for someone to notice. A good shepherd notices (and lets them know they noticed).

One's calling may be considered a bit ambiguous and subjective. While there may be some room for embellishment and subjectivity, there should be some concrete elements to one's calling into student ministry. My personal experience with a calling into student ministry was a mixture of process, people, proclamation, and preparation. The process was being a pastor's son. That gives one a whole different perspective on vocational ministry when you not only live it but you also see behind the scenes. The expectations, pressures, schedules, dealing with human nature, living a transparent life with all the victories and defeats of others, and always being on "call" are all a part of vocational ministry. So I was immersed in ministry, whether I liked it or not.

This could have been a deterrent but God had other plans. Frankly, who would want a lifestyle like that?! I was fortunate to be in a church (where my dad was on staff) where they took student ministry seriously. It was the involvement of a youth pastor and youth group that channeled my spiritual journey that included questions, skepticism, and searching into a personal faith in Christ. It was from that point in my life that my aspirations (of working construction, making lots of money, driving a sports car, or maybe being an ocean biologist with a great tan year round . . . random) were changed from doing what I wanted to do, to consider what God would have me do for others. With that paradigm shift in my heart and mind, came a love for students and ministry. The template had been set before me, when it came to student ministry. So the process continued with the people of student ministry who were major players in my young life.

At first, I wondered if God had the right person. But to continue this calling, I needed to strive to gain the skill set for student ministry. This is where the proclamation and preparation came into play. The proclamation was the continual reminders in Scripture and the preparation was getting as much education (formal, informal, and experiential) that I could take advantage of and could afford. The process, people, proclamation, and preparation continually confirmed this calling into vocational student ministry. And that calling continues in the context of college students today.

Now I would be the first to say that callings come in different shapes and situations. For some, it could have been a single event (i.e., a sermon in a church service or a mission trip). It doesn't necessarily need to be a bright light, voice of God, quasi-conscious type of experience. While it is possible for it to be something like this, it could also be in a quiet moment of contemplation between you and God the Father. For others, this call could have come via a person (i.e., a parent, pastor, spouse, or spiritual friend) who challenged or encouraged you. Then there are those who go through a process, with a combination of a number of factors. For those who are in process, often it is a moment in time where they have simply been ignoring God's call into vocational student ministry and have been going down another path. Then something happens in their lives that makes it clear that they have been avoiding God's call and need to make a course correction (i.e., a promising athletic career that ends with an injury, a broken relationship, a dead-end job . . . stories like these are fascinating).

Regardless of your experience, you can identify and describe your calling. We have the privilege of sending out graduates all over the country to student ministries in local churches and Christian youth organizations. These ministries all have a checklist of qualifications and skills they are looking for.[7] These qualifications and skills are important and should never be marginalized. But the first matter that is of concern for these employers of ministry is the matter of calling. Important? Yes. Some schools of thought hold to the idea that to be the pastor of a church is the highest calling God could give. A look at Scripture will reveal that the youth minister is of an equal calling.

Oswald Chambers raises the bar on the calling of God:

> We are apt to forget the mystical, supernatural touch of God. If you can tell where you got the call of God and all about it, I question whether you have ever had a call. The call of God does not come like that, it is much more supernatural. The realization of it in a man's life may come with a sudden thunder-clap or with a gradual dawning, but in whatever way it comes, it comes with the undercurrent of the supernatural, something that cannot be put into words, it is always accompanied with a glow. At any moment there may break the sudden consciousness of this incalculable, supernatural, surprising call that has taken hold of your life—"I have chosen you." The call of God has nothing to do with salvation and sanctification. It is not because you are sanctified that you are therefore called to preach the gospel; the call to preach the gospel is infinitely different. . . .
>
> If a man or woman is called of God, it does not matter how untoward circumstances are, every force that has been at work will tell for God's purpose in the end. If you agree with God's purpose He will bring not only your conscious life, but all the deeper regions of your life which you cannot get at, into harmony.[8]

# FOUR ELEMENTS OF THE CALL TO MINISTRY

## THE COMMAND

Four aspects need to be considered for this call to ministry and shepherding among students (or any age group for that matter). First there is *the command*, which is found in Scripture. Galatians 1:15 says, "Even before I was born, God had chosen me to be His and called me" (NLT). The word *call* means to summon. So each of us has to answer and qualify this calling. As an educator, I am looking for evidence that one's call is followed up by gaining the necessary education, training, and experience to develop these ministry skills. If one has no desire or shows no effort in improving their knowledge and skills, I would doubt their calling. This calling is a strong motivation to pursue and fulfill that calling—which includes learning as much as they can.

At a recent gathering of seasoned veterans of our graduates in student ministry, there was some thoughtful critique of our current student ministry courses that showed wisdom and experience, which included the discipleship process, dynamics of multisite ministries, assessing the needs of students, ecclesiology, and how it relates to Christian youth organizations, the concept of gratitude, earning the right to be heard, subcultures on campuses, equipping student leaders, volunteering, servant evangelism, recruiting and training lay staff and maximizing mission trips. These student ministry graduates also evaluated, small group ministry, partnering with parents, conflict resolution, sustainable student ministry, networking, building a team, and church culture. Their substantive and robust list shows deep thought and evaluation of those who take student ministry education seriously and reflects a strong commitment to one's calling.

## THE NEED

The second aspect is *the need*. Tom Beaudoin, an author who is a theological combination of Baptist, Catholic, and Pentecostal, describes the reasons for the plight of adolescence today:

> There are plenty of reasons . . . to feel deeply sad. . . . When a generation bears the weight of so many failures—including AIDS, divorce, abuse, poor schools, recessions, youth poverty, teen suicide, outrageous educational and living expenses, failure of government and religious institutions, national debt, high taxes, environmental

devastation, drugs, parents that need to be parented, violence, unstable economic security, premature loss of childhood—how can suffering not be an important part of one's identity?[9]

It doesn't stop there. The very core of our society, God's plan for mankind, and the biblical institution . . . the family is being transformed. Families with the original mom and dad are becoming scarcer. Fractured families are becoming the norm:

- The United States is the world's leader in fatherless families.
- Tonight, some 24.7 million children (approximately 33 percent of all children) will go to bed in a home where their father does not reside.[10]
- The percentage of children living apart from their biological fathers (by race) remains high: African-American children: 57 percent; Hispanic children: 31 percent; and Caucasian children: 20 percent.[11]

So one does not have to look far when it comes to the need of student ministry.

## THE PROVISION

The third aspect of a calling is *the provision*. Typically we default to financial income, so let's address this first. Many admonitions are found in the New Testament, including 1 Timothy 5:17, 18; 1 Corinthians 9:9, 14; Luke 10:7, 8; and Matthew 10:10. If you happen to be in a vocational role of student ministry, I'm sure you thank God daily for the opportunity to minister professionally. I have been in this professional role my entire adult life and I don't take it lightly.

Of course a reality check needs to be expressed here: if you choose vocational student ministry (as well as most vocational ministry positions), you are choosing a modest lifestyle. If you're not good with this, then you might want to consider something else. We have seen God provide the financial side of things so I could focus on the call to student ministry. Have there been times when I was distracted by finances? Yes but the distraction was due to the lack of finances.

While one will not get rich in ministry (I know there are rare exceptions), I think the local ministry organization should demonstrate a commitment to the individual and his or her family, while the minister should focus on the task at hand, namely their ministry. Have there been times where we did not see a paycheck? Yes. More than once. That is distracting. But even when we went without, God provided (at one point in our ministry, it was a nine-month experience)—sometimes in the form of anonymous cash filled envelopes, side jobs, material gifts (appliances, clothes, food, cars, etc.), but regardless of how it came, we knew where it came from.

Another kind of provision can appear in the form of employment outside of professional ministry. A good job can provide the funds necessary to provide for one's family, while giving the individual the freedom of time to minister to students. When one is the primary breadwinner, the noble thing is to do what you can to meet those financial needs. While my primary job was in the context of a youth pastor and executive director (Youth for Christ), there were times where I simply needed to work more to have the extra funds to take care of my family needs. So whether it was painting, being a basketball referee, speaking in public, doing commercial lawn care, or being a human participant in in a medical research project, it was a temporary necessity.

Provision can also come through the actual setting. A call to ministry will eventually direct you to a location or situation that will provide a platform to do ministry. Many times it's in a church context and there's certainly some relative security there. It could be in a Christian organization, camp, community center, group home, etc. With this context, comes your student ministry. With direction from God, He will guide you through the details that will enable you to fulfill this calling.

## THE ASSISTANCE OF OTHERS

The fourth aspect of provision is the people needed to carry out your calling. Some would call this human resources but I would say that this is an invaluable aspect of provision. You can't do this alone. Some would say, "Well I'm married. Doesn't that help?" That certainly helps; a supportive spouse in student ministry is critical A married couple can have an incredible experience of joint ministry together. (And husbands typically will develop friendships with each other as will wives.) But the people needed to do this ministry will need to be developed beyond just the two of you. This will take intentional recruiting of others who are like minded, when it comes to this call to student ministry. In some instances, they will come knocking on your door. In other situations, you will need to knock on their doors. But regardless of how they come, love, train, encourage, and minister to them.

# CONCLUSION

We take this role of the youth worker as a shepherd seriously. It is a role that is equal with another ministry role. For one to ignore this call to student ministry and do something else, would be an endeavor in frustration. For one to be in student ministry without being called to shepherd this young flock, would be an endeavor in frustration. "There are an endless number of symbols of belonging all around us. We join clubs, teams, sororities, fraternities, unions, guilds, churches, synagogues, organizations, and political parties...We mark our tribes through labels, tattoos, piercings, colors, symbols, music, language, and style, and this is just the surface of an array of ways we find to belong, to fit in, to be insiders."[12] The role of shepherd is reserved for a small group of people. It is not an attempt for inclusiveness or exclusiveness. The group gets smaller when you discuss student ministry. This is not a deterrent. It is the common thread that is woven in throughout all of us in student ministry.

---

# NOTES

1. Mark Senter, *The Coming Revolution in Youth Ministry* (Wheaton, Ill.: Victor, 1992), 53, 54.

2. Gary D. Robinson, "What Comes after Postmodernism?" May 27, 2010; at http://www.breakpoint.org/features-columns/articles/entry/12/14560.

3. Andy Hinton, "The Characteristics of Sheep," March 24, 2012 at http://aletheuo.org.uk/2012/05/24/the-characteristics-of-sheep/.

4. Andy Hinton, "The Characteristics of the Shepherd," December 7, 2011, at http://aletheuo.org.uk/2011/12/07/the-characteristics-of-shepherds.

5. John Duckworth, *Joan 'n' the Whale* (Old Tappan, NJ: Revell, 1987), page 47. Copyright © 1987 by John Duckworth. Published by Fleming H. Revell. Used by permission. All rights reserved.

6. Eugene H. Peterson, *Working the Angels: The Shape of Pastoral Integrity* (Grand Rapids: Eerdmans, 1987).

7. Real example: I am looking for a relational guy with great energy to add to the team. He would report directly to me but have oversight and leadership in either the junior high or high school ministry. He needs to have youth ministry experience—not necessarily someone in a mega church, but someone who has proven in their church that they have the capacity and drive to grow a ministry. Lastly, "fit" is very key with us here, as we literally do "life" with the people we are on staff with. Our staff is incredibly close—but a super fun group of people to hang with. As far as a youth guy we are looking for the following things: (1) a godly man, (2) a role

model for teens, (3) stability (4) consistency, (5) great work ethic, (6) ability to follow leadership, (7) maturity, (8) a dynamic speaker, and (9) a visionary leader.

8. Oswald Chambers, *My Utmost for His Highest* (Westwood, N.J.: Barbour and Company, 1963), 201.

9. Tom Beaudoin, *Virtual Faith* (San Francisco: Jossey-Bass, 1998), 107.

10. U.S. Census Bureau, Current Population Survey, "Living Arrangements of Children under 18 Years/1 and Marital Status of Parents by Age, Sex, Race, and Hispanic Origin/2 and Selected Characteristics of the Child for all Children 2010." Table C3; as cited by the National Center for Fathering at http://www.fathers.com/statistics-and-research/the-extent-of-fatherlessness.

11. U.S. Census Bureau, Current Population Report, "Family Stucture and Children's Living Arrangements, 2012"; at http://www.fathers.com/statistics-and-research/the-extent-of-fatherlessness.

12. Erwin Raphael McManus, *Soul Cravings* (Nashville: Nelson), entry #15.

**3**

## THE ESSENTIAL OF

# DEFINING THE STUDENT PASTOR

Allow me (Rich) to acquaint you with who I am and part of my own journey. The Lord was so gracious in allowing me to be born into a family where both my father and mother were mature in their faith and knew God had called them both into ministry.

Both of my parents had given their lives to Christ in their early teenage years. They both were highly involved in their local churches and in Christian camping during their teenage years. Both of their mothers taught children and youth in their own churches. While my dad's father was not consistently attending church at that point in his life, my mom's father was strongly involved in teaching Sunday school classes as well being involved with Christian Endeavor (the largest youth ministry organization during the late nineteenth and early twentieth centuries).

## MY PARENTS AND YOUTH MINISTRY

Even before they met, both of my parents had approached their senior pastors about starting "youth groups" in the churches where they attended. They saw the excitement of their local Youth For Christ rallies and wanted to have this in their own church. When they met and wanted to date, the only place my mom's father would let my dad take his daughter was to the YFC rallies in Binghamton, NY. Ah, let's hear it for the late 1950s. They were married a few years later.

So when I showed up in 1963, I was born into this ministry-minded, godly home. My dad was in seminary finishing his graduate program while mom had just finished her undergraduate degree in Christian Education (this was the equivalent degree of today's youth ministry degree). They were leading the youth group at their church as they were preparing for the overseas mission work of church planting.

Yes, I was also born into a youth ministry! The first child of Dick and Daneth Brown was passed around among the students and there are pictures to prove it. Over the years the Lord redirected my father and instead of growing up a missionary's kid in the jungles of Peru, I grew up a pastor's kid in a small farming town in central New York.

# THE GEEKY YEARS...COLLEGE...AND THE CALL

Fast forward through the geeky years and into college. While attending Liberty University, I had absolutely no clue what God had planned for my life. I wanted to know His plan but if you had asked me back then if it included ministry, the last thing I would have said was I was going to be a preacher. That was just not happening.

In the beginning of my sophomore year, God revealed to me what I was to do. He began to put in me the desire for Christian ministry. I first wondered if it was overseas mission work, but then when I heard a professor speak on the need for youth ministry, particularly a foreign concept to me called a "full-time youth pastor," my heart literally began to race. While our church had a youth group, led faithfully each week by my youth leader, Larry's role was not seen as a pastor. He was a volunteer. His intention was to be a senior pastor but his role in my home church was not the one I had just heard described by the speaker. Even though I had grown up in church and my father was a pastor, this concept of a pastor specifically called to students was brand new to me.

Within the next three to six months I realized God had called me to be a youth pastor. Seeking godly wisdom, seeing how God designed me, and getting involved in my home youth group over break were all contributing factors. But the two most significant factors that confirmed my calling was taking my first youth ministry course and later that summer beginning to preach each Wednesday night. My youth leader graciously allowed me to plan events, develop a midweek meeting, and teach the lessons. It was during that summer I became hooked. The writing and delivering of weekly youth ministry lessons sold me. I wanted to do nothing else in my life other than connect God and His Word to adolescents and adolescents to God . . . and nothing has changed since!

As I continued through college and worked through my youth ministry degree, God led me to a beautiful young lady from Michigan. During the growing friendship I listened of her aspirations to be in some form of counseling as a ministry as I shared my aspiration of being a youth pastor. As the friendship turned deeper into romance, I listened with great eagerness as she shared from "the list" which she wrote before we ever met. In the top three priorities of who this mystery man was, she wanted someone who would be a youth pastor. Hello! He's right here! We were best friends then and are best friends to this day. And while that story may sound "old school" to many, I praise the Lord so much for the partner He provided for me. Jesus and Janet—the two easiest decisions of my life.

## ROCKING MY WORLD

The next twenty years were spent serving in local church student ministry. During this time I turned down over ten opportunities to become a senior pastor because I knew God had put my focus and heart on students. Yet in the early summer of 2001 my world began to be rocked.

My youngest sister was in the middle of the very same youth ministry program that I had graduated from years before. During this summer she was one of my ministry interns. Upon her recommendation, I had invited her favorite youth ministry professor to be my camp speaker. It was at this time I met Dr. Steve Vandegriff. Over the course of the next two years, God used Steve to reconnect me to my alma mater and subsequently into the world of academia.

While this move was from God, it was the most difficult and painful decision I ever have made. To leave the "hands-on" weekly ministry of middle and high school students in order to teach college students about youth ministry tore me up. I literally grieved for over three years. During my first year teaching, while in the class, one of my students asked me what I missed about being a youth pastor. I just stood there quiet . . . and then I just wept. I mean I actually broke down and started to cry. It was an awkward moment for all of us, to say the least! Yet over the years I have realized I still work with students, college students, and this is legitimate student ministry. Honestly, I am now with students more than I ever was as a local church student pastor in the classroom, in my office, and in our home. I know I am exactly where God has intended me to be, yet I am not fully "over it." When high school students visit the classroom during recruiting days, my own students have made the comment how they see me "come to life" because I still love that age group. As I tell my university students, the day I "get over it," out of integrity I should step down as a professor of youth ministry.

It is with this background and current framework that I co-write this book. In this chapter and others (chapters 4–5, 9–12), I will share out of my life and out of God's Word. I want you to feel you are seated in my classroom, as I have written in much the same style of how I teach. Yet I also want you to feel we are seated in a busy coffee shop having a wonderful discussion, as my writing style is also conversational. Early in my career I remember reading many youth ministry books while in my office during a quiet morning, just craving some mentorship from those older in ministry. I am honored beyond words to hopefully encourage you in some way. I hope you will enjoy our conversation.

# FOR STUDENT PASTORS AND THOSE WHO HELP THEM

I had been in my very first youth pastor position for just two weeks when I was asked by the father of one of the middle school students, "So Rich, what are you going to do when you grow up?"

I immediate blurted out, "I want to be a youth pastor."

I must have seemed like such a rookie to this father. After all, everyone in the 1980s knew that a youth pastor was to become a senior pastor. Doing youth ministry was the road to the big show.

This chapter is devoted to the student ministry professional who believes God has called him to the role of student pastor. While I understand there are many seats on the "youth ministry bus," both in professional and volunteer positions, I will focus this chapter on the role of youth pastor. As you read this, you may not currently be in student ministry. Maybe you are serving in student ministry but in a different role than pastor. You may be in the position of student pastor but are not sure this is really what God has intended you to do and/or do not fully understand what the position even involves. You may even be reading this book and have no desire to be involved in student ministry.

Whatever the case, please do not dismiss this chapter. I desire this chapter to be a blessing to the body of Christ, and I pray the Lord may use it as He sees fit. He may use this chapter to call you into this role. Maybe you are a volunteer, a parent, or a church leader and this chapter will assist you to better understand the biblical role and responsibilities of a student pastor. God may speak to some of you who are preparing for this role or who are currently in this role. There may be something you read that will assist you in realizing the importance of your calling and help further prepare you to shepherd the flock of God. So read, enjoy, and may this chapter be a resource to you, no matter where you sit on that noisy bus we call student ministry.

As the topic proposes, this chapter will seek to define the student pastor and describe some of the essential duties the Scriptures assign to such an individual. While I understand among our readership there will be a multiplicity of ages, ministry experience, denominations, traditions, and church political structures, my desire is simply to move right to the Word of God and seek what Scripture teaches about God's church.

When I begin teaching similar information on this topic with my students, I show a video clip of a high school student surrendering his weapons. Then I ask two things, starting with me: let's (1) lay down our weapons of our own backgrounds, opinions, and experiences about church leadership and (2) thoroughly seek God's Word as the source of truth. I want you to carefully think and test everything you read but I urge you to think using the Scriptures as your source (1 Thessalonians 5:19–22).

# THE ROLES AND RESPONSIBILITIES OF A STUDENT PASTOR

## 1. WHAT IS THE POSITION?

Within the first generation of the church, the apostles ordained elders to lead the church. The first mention of this leadership paradigm is when Paul and Barnabas finished their first missionary campaign and "appointed elders for them in every church" (Acts 14:23). Below is a list of basic presuppositions of pastoral leadership that I understand as taken from the New Testament; they are foundational to this section:

- The elders were the leaders of the local church.
- Each local church always had a plurality of elders. There is never a mention of "the pastor" (one pastor or one elder) of a specific church. Leadership was in community.
- While there appears to be some elders who held more authority in leadership than others (i.e., there were leaders of leaders), there was cooperation among the leaders. They seem to have functioned as a team of leaders.

- There is no mention of the specific pastoral titles in the New Testament that are used in the church today. For example, there was no senior pastor, discipleship pastor, worship pastor, and student pastor. However, simply because these roles are not mentioned does not make them "wrong" or "unbiblical" roles, as these roles today are fulfilling biblical principles which were in the New Testament church.

- It appears there were teaching and nonteaching pastors (1 Timothy 5:17).

- The New Testament eldership (pastors) was male in gender.

One cannot imagine more prominent figures in the establishment of the church than Peter and Paul. Peter was the apostle to the Jews, while Paul was the apostle to the Gentiles. These men carried tremendous authority and help us to understand biblical church leadership and church organization. From the beginning of the church, Acts 20 and 1 Peter 5 both teach that the *elders* were also called *overseers* ("bishops" in 1 Timothy 3:1 AMP) and *shepherds* (where we get the word "pastor"). As one studies these pastoral Scriptures, one sees these three roles are interconnecting and these terms are interchangeable. A pastor cannot pick and choose what role he is to fulfill. This issue of three titles for the same pastoral office can also raise two questions: 1. Why would three titles be given for the same pastoral office? 2. Would the use of three titles become confusing? We will look into both in detail.

First, *why would there be three titles given for the same pastoral office?* The reason there are three different titles for the same person is because each title had a specific rationale. (I have put a descriptive word next to the biblical title.) By analyzing the Pastoral Epistles, Acts 20, and 1 Peter 5, one discovers the three pastoral roles are:

Elder (maturity)<br>
Don't let anyone look down on you . . . but set an example . .<br>
. watch your life and your doctrine closely.<br>
(1 Timothy 4:12, 16 NIV)

Overseer or Bishop (managing)<br>
Keep watch over yourselves and all the flock of which the Holy<br>
Spirit has made you overseers.<br>
(Acts 20:28 NIV)

Pastor or Shepherd (ministry)<br>
Preach the word . . . do the work of an evangelist.<br>
(2 Timothy 4:2a, 5d)

In Acts 20 and 1 Peter 5, Paul and Peter speak of and directly to church leadership. As you study the two Bible passages, look for the words *elder*, *bishop* (or *overseer*), and *shepherd*.

> From Miletus, Paul sent to Ephesus for the elders of the church . . . Keep watch over yourselves and all the flock of which the Holy Spirit has made you overseers. Be shepherds of the church of God, which he bought with his own blood. (Acts 20:17, 28 NIV)

> To the elders among you, I appeal as a fellow elder and a witness of Christ's sufferings who also will share in the glory to be revealed: Be shepherds of God's flock that is under your care, watching over them—not because you must, but because you are willing, as God wants you to be; not pursuing dishonest gain, but eager to serve; not lording it over those entrusted to you, but being examples to the flock. And when the Chief Shepherd appears, you will receive the crown of glory that will never fade away. (1 Peter 5:1–4 NIV)

While it is apparent that each pastor will have a certain strength, giftedness, and/or skill set, which may lean toward relationships, teaching, or administration, the pastor must fulfill all three roles. He must guard his godly lifestyle (elder) as he oversees the ministry (bishop) and clearly teach God's truth and love God's people (pastor).

As you study some other passages you can see these three roles and responsibilities are also integrated into the same leaders. First Thessalonians 5:12–13 (NIV) describes the church's relationship to its leadership as the leadership fulfills their responsibilities to the people: "Now we ask you, brothers and sisters, to acknowledge those who work hard among you, who care for you in the Lord and who admonish you. Hold them in the highest regard in love because of their work. Live in peace with each other."

*Work hard* is one's maturity of the faith (elder), *over you* is one's managing responsibility (overseer/bishop), and *admonish* is one's relational and instructional ministry (pastor/shepherd). Note the people were to *respect* their leaders and *hold them in the highest regard*. When leaders do their jobs well, operating as servants and not masters, and the people respond to their leaders in respect and love, *living in peace with each other* is very possible.

Another Bible chapter where all three pastoral roles integrate is Hebrews 13. I personally think that verse 7 is about how to treat past leaders and verse 17 is on how to treat present leaders. As you look at these two verses, the three roles stand out as well:

Remember your leaders, who spoke the word of God to you. Consider the outcome of their way of life and imitate their faith. (v. 7)

Obey your leaders and submit to them, for they are keeping watch over your souls, as those who will have to give an account. Let them do this with joy, and not with groaning, for that would be of no advantage to you. (v. 17)

## THE THREE PASTORAL TITLES: PASTOR, OVERSEER, ELDER

The second question about having three titles for the same pastoral office is: *Would the use of three titles become confusing?*

Regretfully there does appear to be confusion over the use of the three titles given for pastoral ministry. I would contend that it is directly out of this confusion that much conflict and even gridlock has arisen within many churches. Whereas in the New Testament we have seen these three titles all "refer" to the same person, in more recent times these three titles became three different roles. Some churches have elder boards but the elders are not pastors. Some churches have pastors who are not on the elder board. Some denominations have bishops who oversee church districts but do not oversee or pastor specific churches. The confusion typically may come down to two questions: *Who is in charge of the ministry of the church,* and *What is the role of those on pastoral staff?*

I have witnessed this confusion in the various church ministries I served as student pastor. In one church, I was on the board but it was the nonpastor elders who had the "upper hand" as the pastors were the paid staff to do the work. In another church I was not on the elder board. After years of being in the church I respectfully approached my senior pastor and spoke about my role using the previously mentioned Scriptures. The response was, "Yes, pastors and elders were the same in the Bible but the times have changed." I understand churches will have their own opinions on church polity but I believe this confusion is either due to ignorance and/or an unwillingness to follow the scriptural model (as just noted in the recent quote). At the end of the day, I was never seeking power; I just wanted the youth pastor to be seen as a legitimate pastor and a legitimate part of the team of leaders.

With the above as foundation, it is my biblical conviction the student pastor is part of a team of pastors for the local church. The student pastor is to be called of God, to be ordained by godly men, and to meet the specific qualifications given in 1 Timothy 3 and Titus 1. He is to be a legitimate pastor. While he is not the senior or lead pastor, he is to be the shepherd and overseer to the student ministry of that particular church. With these three biblical pastoral roles defined, I would contend the student pastor should be that overseeing church leader whom God uses in the lives of today's students. But before moving into what his role is, let's take a look at some wrong perceptions that some (including student pastors) may have.

## 2. WHAT ARE THE PERCEPTIONS?

*Some see the student pastor's role as:*
- A *student care provider* (one who keeps the students in attendance).
- A *security cop* (one who keeps the students at attention).
- A *social director* (one who keeps the students in activity).

*Some think that in terms of attributes the student pastor must be:*
- A culturally cool pastor (someone who has it all: sharp-looking, played college ball, was in the top five on a reality talent search show, has over one million hits on social media videos, was a drummer in a band, and has the best-looking spouse known to mankind).
- An internship pastor (someone using student ministry as training ground toward real pastoral ministry).
- A minor league pastor (someone not considered a legitimate pastor).
- A youthful pastor (someone who is close in age to the students so as to "relate").

Before moving on, I want to submit to you a few questions. Please read through these and give a thoughtful answer:

1. What is the higher goal of ministering: relating or influencing?
2. Back in high school, who was your favorite teacher, coach, staff person, etc.?
3. Did he or she "effectively relate" to you?
4. What was his or her approximate age?

When I throw these questions out to my residential students, the overwhelming age group they choose are adults who were at least in their forties and older. No, her math teacher may not have known all of the current hip-hop songs nor have seen all of the latest movies, but her math teacher cared for her and influenced her. So while the church has long believed an effective youth worker and/or youth pastor needs to be in their twenties so as to be some kind of cool, the deeper consideration is to have a pastor to students who has a faith worth following, organizational skills to do the job well, thorough in the Word, and a will to nurture students and their families. Here are two more questions for you to consider:

1. Can you think of any disadvantages to youth pastors who do not stay long in student ministry . . . or in a specific ministry?
2. Can you think of any advantages to youth pastors who do have longevity in youth ministry . . . or in a specific ministry?

## 3. WHAT IS THE PURPOSE?

From Acts 20; Ephesians 4:11–16; the Pastoral Epistles; Hebrews 13:7, 17–38; and 1 Peter 5:1–4, one identifies who a pastor is and what he is to do. But to narrow this down to what the purpose is, I reflect back to the three roles of pastoral leadership. While he must be a man of character and demonstrate maturity (his elder role), I want to emphasize the other two areas of the calling: his ministry (the shepherding role) and his managing (the overseeing role).

*The Student Pastor's Role as Shepherd.* Consider these elements of a student pastor acting as a shepherd: instructing, relating, and guarding.

Within his *pastoral role of instructing*, the student pastor is to effectively teach students the Word of God (1 Timothy 4:13–16; 2 Timothy 3:14–4:5; Hebrews 13:7) so they will

- grasp godly belief (doctrine), which should lead to godly behavior (application).

- know how to serve others (Titus 1:16; 2:7, 14; 3:1, 8, 14).

Within his *pastoral role of relating*, the student pastor is to effectively build healthy relationships with those he serves:

- He is not to be simply a *buddy* (just about the relationship).
- He is not to be simply a *boss* (just about the rules).
- He is to be a *balance of both* (both leader and friend) as Jesus gave example (John 1:14; 13:13).

Within his *pastoral role of guarding*, the student pastor is to effectively protect the ministry in which he serves (Acts 28:28–31; 1 Timothy 4:12, 15–16; Hebrews 13:7):

- This includes safety issues.
- This includes doctrinal issues.
- This includes integrity issues.

*The Student Pastor's Role as Overseer.* Consider these elements of a student pastor acting as an overseer: equipping and leading.

Within his task of *equipping*, the student pastor is to effectively prepare (equip) both students and adults to do the work of God (Ephesians 4:12–16):

- He is to mobilize the people for ministry.
- He is to train the people for ministry.
- He is to provide opportunities for people to minister.

Within his task of *leading*, the student pastor is to effectively provide leadership to the ministry of God (Hebrews 13:17; Romans 12:8):

- He is responsible to God as a steward and will give account.
- He is to govern with diligence. While this refers to the gift of leadership, the principle is the same for those called leaders.
- He is effectively to move the ministry forward in fulfilling the Great Commission.
- He is to live a life worthy of being followed (which goes back to the principle of eldership).

Reflecting on what you have read, there are two more questions for you to consider: (1) *Of the three roles—shepherd, elder, overseer—where do you think student pastors are the strongest/weakest?* (2) *What type of ministry implications does a glaring weakness have?*

## 4. WHAT ARE THE PRIORITIES?

As I entered my second decade in student ministry, I did a personal evaluation of my own calling and the priorities of one being a "full-time" youth pastor. From that first month in ministry when I was asked what I would do when I "grew up," followed by ministry transitions due to church financial reasons, to that specific situation where I continued to hear in board meetings, "You are just a youth pastor," this first decade of being a student pastor was not what I expected. Although secure in what God had called me to do, I took the time to go right back into Scripture and see what God said were the priorities of a pastor. I tracked down every text that spoke of the elder, pastor, and overseer. I cannot tell you just how much I needed this time of refreshing.

While I was firmly committed to my daily time in the Word, this additional study reconfirmed who I was as a pastor and rekindled my fire to be His leader the way He intended me to lead. By organizing a layout to who these New Testament leaders were and their various responsibilities, I found such great freedom to see God's "job description" of one in pastoral leadership. As you read this backstory, you may now more fully understand my commitment to a biblical foundation of pastoral leadership. The following list simply helped me organize my own ministry and communicate to others my priorities. This may encourage you as well to see what a student pastor should be focused on and what truly matters.

While there are so many details and responsibilities that go into the daily and weekly life of one who is in ministry, I would see that everything we do should fall under one of these five priorities:

- *Personal* walk with Jesus Christ (1 Timothy 4:15–16).
- *Present* God's truth (2 Timothy 4:2–4).
- *Pastor* the flock in gentleness and care (1 Peter 5:2–3).
- *Prepare* the volunteer leadership team (staff) and students to be competently involved in ministry (Ephesians 4:11–12; 2 Timothy 2:2).
- *Provide* vision and direction for a Great Commission ministry (2 Timothy 3:10–11; Colossians 1:25, 28–29).

One additional thought on priorities has to do with time management. While some pastors take off Monday, I decided to take off a different day of the week and was in the office on Monday. Early in ministry I had developed a template of a weekly schedule. The "to do" list was divided into ministry categories, yet the three main headers were: Overseer / Pastor/ Elder. Every ministry category and every line item fit under the three roles which God had called me to fulfill.

# THE RELATIONSHIPS OF A STUDENT PASTOR

Effective ministry must take place in the context of relationships. Most of us are well aware of this. Yet when I refer to relationships in this context, I am referring to intentionally building and guarding healthy relationships with those around us in our ministry. As you read through these various pointers, please understand these listed items will not represent everything that could be accomplished under each category. You may come up with many more, as I hope you will.

## 1. TO THE THOSE IN AUTHORITY
### (Lead/Senior Pastor, Church Board, Others)

In building healthy working relationships, the student pastor:

- Must recognize he is under the leadership of the senior pastor.
- Must understand he is under the leadership of the senior pastor and act accordingly.
- Must develop a healthy relationship with the senior pastor.
- Should be realistic about his expectations of the senior pastor.
- Must communicate to the senior pastor that he is praying for him.
- Should take a genuine, personal interest in the senior pastor.
- Should be open to being mentored by the senior pastor.
- Should seek to be a shepherd to the senior pastor as well.

In building healthy working relationships, both pastors have needs. Among those needs:

- The student pastor wants to be treated like a professional, and the senior pastor wants to have the student pastor act professionally.
- The student pastor wants respect, and the senior pastor wants reliability.
- They both must understand each other's spiritual gifts, strengths, personalities, etc., and must learn to respond accordingly.
- They both must be committed to communication and feedback.
- They both should provide an open door policy yet respect the other's schedule.

As you know, healthy relationships take work and need attention from both parties. Yet while I cannot guarantee another's willingness to reach out and respond to me, I can guarantee my own reaching out and response to them. "If possible, so far as it depends on you, live peaceably with all" (Romans 12:18).

Study the following table of contrasts, which I refer to as the "Simple Dos and Don'ts of Ministry Relationships." While the context is between the student pastor and lead pastor, these principles go well beyond this particular relationship.

## SIMPLE DOS AND DON'TS OF MINISTRY RELATIONSHIPS

| DOS | DON'TS |
|---|---|
| Publicly support | Never say anything positive |
| Privately encourage | Ignore him altogether / passive-aggressive |
| Invite him to attend events | Expect him to attend |
| Provide just enough information | Provide too little or too much information |
| Build a defense against criticism | Have an open ear to criticism |
| Know when to use him in crisis | Want him to be your constant hit man |

## 2. TO THE CHURCH

Our love and connection to our local church is imperative to a successful ministry. In addition, a wise leader needs the reminder that we are not making disciples of and to ourselves; we are making disciples of Jesus Christ—disciples who should be firmly committed to their local church. What exactly does that look like?

- The student pastor should be able to publicly and positively affirm his church.
- His philosophy, goals, etc., should be similar to the church, and he should support his church.
- He should be involved in the life of his church.
- He should be an obedient donor to his church.
- He should positively communicate with his church.
- He should love his church, and the church should never have to question this love.

In light of this relationship to one's church, when my college students and I begin to discuss a possible church hire, I raise a question they must ask themselves even before they agree to take the ministry position being offered to them. "If you were not paid to be there, would this be the church in this community that you would attend?"

## 3. TO THE LEADERSHIP TEAM

Chapter 4 will speak much on this subject but for the sake of this context, here are some valuable points to consider:

- The student pastor should publicly and positively affirm each leader.
- While he may be closer to some, the student pastor should treat each one alike and fairly.
- He should value those on the leadership team as gifts from God and equals in Christ.
- He should treat them with respect (respect their time, families, etc.).
- He should place them in the precise positions of ministry.
- He should give them the proper education and resources to succeed.

## 4. TO THE PARENTS

I cannot stress how imperative it is to have strong relationships with the parents of students. Chapter 5 will provide specific focus to understand parents and working with parents, yet we should recognize this issue even now. Provided below are the exact instructions and directives I gave to the leaders in my last church at the Adult Leaders Retreat before the start of the school year. I was committed to intentionally create a culture of valuing parents and working with parents. (On a personal note, I did not know at the time of delivering these instructions I would be entering my final school year as a student pastor. Each of these principles and goals were accomplished before my transition to the university. As I reflect back on these steps taken, I am so thankful how our team fulfilled these steps.)

How student ministries leaders can be family friendly:

- Develop a relationship with the parents.
- Affirm the parents about their youth.
- Thank the parents for letting their youth come to the ministry.
- Don't engage in "parent bashing" with their child.
- See the role as builder between child and parent.

How student ministries can be family friendly:
- Provide safe and wholesome events.
- Do not "overschedule" so many events (especially when families want to have family time over holidays) or be out super late.
- Have lots of handouts and communication.
- Return from trips on time.
- Provide parent meetings, classes, family events, etc.
- Give talks and lessons with the students on how we can have strong families.

## 5. TO THE STUDENTS

For all of the previous mentioned groups of relationships, they all center on this special group of people. It is about the students. If we do not have a healthy relationship with our students, we have no student ministry. While much of this topic will be covered under the Nurture section (in the next chapter), please note these practical principles:

- The student ministry leader should love his students.
- He should affirm his students.
- He should respect every student.
- He should protect his students.
- He should be the adult with his students.
- He should be consistent with his students.
- He should keep his word.
- He should keep confidence with his students (when it is appropriate).
- He should involve his students.
- He should provide an environment that fosters relationships, growth, and ministry.

# WRAPPING THIS UP

You and I have the opportunity to work in positions where we can influence for eternity the most spiritually fertile age group of humankind. Keep that in perspective when you want to walk away. When you are tired, discouraged, misunderstood, and just want to quit, remember Who called you and Who you are seeking to please. Keep in mind the admonition Paul gives to Timothy when he writes, "You then, my child, be strengthened by the grace that is in Christ Jesus" (2 Timothy 2:1). What a calling!

I leave you with the two Scripture verses I have based my life on since high school. May these words impact you even more than they have impacted me

> Him we proclaim, warning everyone and teaching everyone with all wisdom, that we may present every man mature in Christ. For this I toil, struggling with all his energy that he powerfully works within me. (Colossians 1:28–29)

# 4

## THE ESSENTIAL OF

# DEVELOPING EFFECTIVE LEADERS

Y ou are faced with an immediate decision the moment you step into a new student ministry position . . . who is going to work within the ministry? You only have a few options.

*Are you going to lead the ministry solo?* After all, you are the professional, right?

*Are you going to have a few hard working adults join the ministry with you?* This way, you can trust them, possibly control them, and make sure everything goes just the way you desire.

*Are you going to bring in many adults and develop a team?* Yet in doing this option it just may take much work and you may have to give up some control.

Before we continue on, I urge you to think through these three choices. Look back in your own past. What choice did you make in a similar situation? What style did you choose and how did that turn out? Next, look around you and consider the choice that others have made in similar situations. How did that turn out? I trust you can see the wisdom in bringing in many adults to develop a team that will be able to effectively meet both the task and relational ministries that go into an effective student ministry.

As we begin to look into the essential of developing an effective ministry team, I sincerely believe many presuppositions need to be considered. With all the differing criteria, this list could never be comprehensive, but allow me to share seven:

1. The key leader needs to understand that the ministry is bigger than he is.
2. The key leader must acknowledge the ministry is about the glory of God and not some type of personal fulfillment, ego, or agenda.
3. The key leader must see himself as a servant and not a master.
4. The key leader must be a clear communicator to the team.
5. The key leader will build an effective leadership team by focusing on building effective individual leaders.
6. The key leader must have the wisdom and guidance to develop these individuals into an effective team.
7. The key leader needs to have a large and long-range perspective rather than a small and immediate one.

With these areas in mind, let's go back to our opening scenario. Okay, new leader, where do you start? Before I present this, I want to provide some context. During the late 1990s, while living in the Seattle area, I knew God was leading me from one ministry to another. As a thirty-five-year-old youth pastor, I prayed to the Lord to give me insight and wisdom like no other time as I entered into what I believed might be my last youth ministry. I felt like the athlete who was entering his last season. I wanted to finish strong; leave it all on the field with no regrets. While I had always sought the Lord for His wisdom throughout the years in church work, this time I just sensed more urgency. "Lord, if this is my last youth ministry, please give me Your wisdom."

The following suggestions are what the Lord gave me and I can truly say I greatly benefitted from these. I guess I should have prayed with such urgency in my early twenties, right?

## WHAT IS THE HISTORY AND CURRENT SITUATION?

Much of the following information should be gathered even before one makes a decision on saying "yes" to the ministry position. After all, they are looking at your past ministry history so why not look into theirs? Seek the following information with tact, grace, and maturity. This is not some kind of "gotcha" game; rather, it is to assist you in making an intelligent decision. I would even ask the potential church if I had permission to speak with the previous youth pastor. Please note that their reaction and answer to this request does speak volumes. The following are just some questions that I used to find out some of the background of the previous student pastor:

1. Has there been a youth pastor(s) previous to you?
2. If so, what is the history?
3. What were the wins and the losses?
4. What did he bring to the ministry?
5. What was his personality like?
6. What was he most known for?
7. Why did he leave?

Then as the process of you entering the position becomes closer to reality, consider the following questions as they pertain to the leadership team. Some of these questions can be answered by the "inner circle" of those who are at the church, such as the search committee, various pastors, and leaders, etc., while some of these questions would be answered more appropriately by the specific individuals themselves:

1. Was there an adult leadership team previous to you?
2. If so, what were the various roles and responsibilities?
3. Were those involved pleased with this role of involvement?
4. Did they feel overused or underused?
5. Did they feel confident and competent in ministry?
6. Were they previously in the ministry before the departure of the youth pastor?
7. Who helped the student ministry through the transition between youth pastors?
8. Are they planning on staying involved?
9. How involved do they want to be?
10. Are they open to new adults joining the team?

In my opinion, these current leaders will make or break your ministry at this church. There may be some current leaders who need to transition out, but please take note on what to do when you first arrive. You only get one chance at a first impression!

Here is a suggested process for evaluating and choosing student leaders from among the current ministry team:

1. Publicly affirm the current leaders and thank them for a job well done.

2. Privately go to each one to express your gratitude as well. Be sincere and be specific as to some of the areas of positive contribution.

3. You must think like Nehemiah! As he gathered people around him to perform the task of rebuilding the wall, his cry was, "Then I said to them, 'You see the trouble we are in, how Jerusalem lies in ruin with its gates burned. Come, let us rebuild the wall of Jerusalem, that we may no longer suffer derision'" (Nehemiah 2:17). Notice the pronoun is plural, not singular. Communicate your commitment to building and empowering a team!

4. As best you can, have your first meeting where you storyboard the entire history of the youth ministry. What were the wins and losses, dreams and fears? Talk about the health of the student ministry and don't focus on individual personalities. You may want to prepare a survey in advance in addition to this step.

5. Share your vision of what you would like to see God do in the lives of the students. Stay away from speaking so much of the program but focus on building the people.

6. Begin to find out who wants to stay onboard and in what capacity.

7. Have everyone go through your application process. This will set the precedence and priority of this important process from the beginning. (I realize you may want to "grandfather" the current ones in but having them go through the process gives you an objective look at each person individually. More work at the front end may save you serious grief later on.)

# BECOMING A LITTLE INTROSPECTIVE

You may recognize the pastoral priorities from chapter 3, "The Essential of Defining the Student Pastor." While the list was crucial to that particular section of material, I think you may find the reminder quite helpful again for this context as these can be seen as the baseline of pastoral leadership. Here is a little more context to these five priorities.

During the winter of 1993, I arrived at the introspective age of thirty. While I actually embraced it, thinking that maybe the adults in church would see me as a legitimate adult, this birthday can make any one of us step back and become quite contemplative. At this time I asked myself, "Do I truly see myself staying in student ministry throughout my thirties?" After all, many of my youth worker friends had left youth ministry for other pursuits. But as for me and my house, the obvious answer was yes! It was also during this time that I was in the middle of a very discouraging and draining ministry. While I will leave the church political landscape alone, let's just say I was in one of those ministries where I was under much scrutiny and criticism from key lay leaders. With these two life conditions before me, I went right to my Bible and drew up what I believed were my five most important priorities in student ministry. In other words, what does God say is my pastoral job description? Here, as a reminder from the previous chapter, are the five pastoral priorities: (1) *personal* walk with Jesus Christ (1 Timothy 4:15–16); (2) *present* God's truth (2 Timothy 4:2–4); (3) *pastor* the flock in gentleness and care (1 Peter 5:2–3); (4) *prepare* the volunteer leadership team (staff) and students to be competently involved in ministry (Ephesians 4:11–12; 2 Timothy 2:2); and (5) *provide* vision and direction for a Great Commission ministry (2 Timothy 3:10–11; Colossians 1:25, 28–29).

As you look through these priorities, consider this question: When it comes to our priority of relationships, which should come first, the students or the leaders? To be honest, during my early years of youth ministry, I would have answered "the students." While I believed in the strong value of building a leadership team, time with students was my priority. Yet as I entered my second decade of youth work, this perspective changed. Yes, both then and now I believe in spending time with students, just like I value spending time with their parents, other church leaders, etc. However, building the leadership team became my highest relational priority. I will even go so far as to say the strength of your ministry is your leadership team.

In *The Youth Builder*, Jim Burns writes, "Perhaps the most important (and most overlooked) aspect of youth ministry is building a dynamic youth ministry team. In fact, we would go so far as to say that beyond your programs—and even beyond the students themselves—your most precious commodity is your volunteer team."[1]

# WHY DEVELOP A LEADERSHIP TEAM?

Let's be honest. Building an effective leadership team takes significant time and much hard work. I raise the following reasons as to why youth leaders fail to build a leadership team: (1) *Leaders do not see the need for it.* (2) *Leaders do not take the time to do it.* (3) *Leaders do not know how to do it.*

I will admit it. Been there and done that. But even early on in ministry I did seek to overcome those barriers. In my own innocence and inexperience, I did somewhat see the need, I did somewhat take the time, and I did somewhat know how. The desire was there. This may be true for you as well. Maybe you will relate to me as I mention four other obstacles to building a leadership team that I personally struggled with and had to work through:

1. I wanted to be seen as a hard worker and not lazy (delegation may appear lazy).
2. I wanted to be seen as a good employee (I was worth the salary).
3. I was told by many in the church that they were paying me to do the work.
4. I was told by the church board that they hired me knowing that the church would grow; so therefore, my salary would be justified (my hire would pay for itself).

As you can see, none of these reasons was because I did not want to build a team. These were due to a church mindset of years gone by that we hire pastors to do ministry, contrary to Ephesians 4. I also had the real-life situation of being quite young in my first positions where the church body was much more "seasoned" than I was. (You know your congregation is older when the giving is much larger the Sunday after the Social Security checks are mailed out.) But I had to overcome these through using Scripture and humbly teaching what the Bible teaches as to the pastoral role of building leaders and equipping people for ministry.

I believe one can see the reasons for developing are both biblical and practical. Note the following biblical examples used to teach team leadership.

# BIBLICAL EXAMPLES

There are so many biblical examples of leaders developing leaders throughout Scripture for various causes and in various contexts. The Lord is an organizational God who has called His people to position themselves in such a fashion in order to effectively do His work. Out of the many examples available in Scripture, I will take a brief look at two Old Testament leaders.

## LOOKING AT MOSES (EXODUS 18)

Many sermons have been preached and material written on the classic Old Testament encounter between Moses and his father-in-law, Jethro. Moses was in great fatigue as he was handling a large number of court cases. When his father-in-law came to visit, the two entered Moses's tent and began to catch up on the events of the past few years. You know, things like Moses confronting Pharaoh, ten plagues, God delivering the people of Israel from Pharaoh, just basic father-in-law and son-in-law conversation (Exodus 18:7–11). Afterward Jethro went to sacrifice to the Lord and to have a meal with Moses and the elders of Israel.

The next day, though, he observed the overwhelming situation that Moses faced on a daily basis.

> When his father-in-law saw all that Moses was doing for the people, he said, "What is this you are doing for the people? Why do you alone sit as judge, while all these people stand around you from morning till evening?"
>
> Moses answered him, "Because the people come to me to seek God's will. Whenever they have a dispute, it is brought to me, and I decide between the parties and inform them of God's decrees and instructions." (Exodus 18:14–16 NIV)

Moses thought he was doing God's work by doing it all himself. The response from Jethro surely must have shocked Moses, yet it was this wisdom that brought stability, and some could even argue became the foundation of many executive and legal structures in later nations.

> Moses' father-in-law replied, "What you are doing is not good. You and these people who come to you will only wear yourselves out. The work is too heavy for you; you cannot handle it alone. Listen now to me and I will give you some advice, and may God be with you. You must be the people's representative before God and bring their disputes to him. Teach them his decrees and instructions, and show them the way they are to live and how they are to behave. But select capable men from all the people—men who fear God, trustworthy men who hate dishonest gain—and appoint them as officials over thousands, hundreds, fifties and tens. Have them serve as judges for the people at all times, but have them bring every difficult case to you; the simple cases they can decide themselves. That will make your load lighter, because they will share it with you. If you do this and God so commands, you will be able to stand the strain, and all these people will go home satisfied."
>
> Moses listened to his father-in-law and did everything he said. He chose capable men from all Israel and made them leaders of the people, officials over thousands, hundreds, fifties and tens. They served as judges for the people at all times. The difficult cases they brought to Moses, but the simple ones they decided themselves. (vv. 17–26 NIV)

There are some key points to consider in the wisdom provided by this older man that every wise leader should adhere to:

- Point people to God and stop trying to be "the man" (v. 19).
- Teach the people how to live to please the Lord (v. 20).
- Select capable leaders from the various "tribes" (v. 21).
- Choose leaders who fear God and have integrity (v. 21).
- Develop an organized infrastructure (v. 21).
- Do not completely back away from being involved but get involved when necessary (v. 22).

## LOOKING AT NEHEMIAH (NEHEMIAH 2)

There was trouble in Jerusalem in 445 BC. The city walls of Jerusalem had lain in ruins for years. Ezra had rebuilt the Jewish temple a few years earlier but the city walls were still in desolation. If this continued on, how long would it be before the temple would be demolished once again?

God put His burden of restoring the city walls in the heart of a man named Nehemiah, the cupbearer to King Artaxerses of the Medo-Persian Empire. Chapter 2 of Nehemiah gives a beautiful example of God's pattern of restoration as God uses a team. It was through this wise and persistent leader that a team was developed and the project was completed in fifty-two days (Nehemiah 6:15). Taking a brief look of Nehemiah 2:17–20, we see:

- Nehemiah saw the distress of Jerusalem (v. 17).
- He acknowledged this as a reproach to the Lord God (v. 17).
- He established a committed team of single-focused people (vv. 17–18).
- The people did something about the problem (v. 18).
- The people faced opposition (v. 19).
- The people put their faith in the Lord God (v. 20).
- The people put their faith into action (v .20).

# PRACTICAL REASONS

## PREPARING FOR MINISTRY

This is so obvious I don't know where to begin. Taking the priority of pastors to the church body, we as leaders are commanded in Ephesians 4:11–16 to equip God's people to do "the work of the ministry," thus effectively "building up" (v. 16) the body of Christ. For those of you in the key leadership position in a student ministry, your responsibility is to develop (equip) people to do the work of student ministry. Consider the following groups of people who are edified as a result of effective leaders being developed:

- the individual students
- the youth pastor
- the specific adult leader
- the student ministry as a whole
- the specific church body as well as the universal church

And all of this is part in the fulfilling of the Great Commission command to make disciples (Matthew 28:19).

## BENEFITS FOR THE STUDENT AND THE STUDENT LEADER

When you effectively build up this team, certain benefits automatically take place for all involved in the ministry. The following will focus on the two areas of the students and the student pastor. I would encourage you to ask your leaders to list their own benefits and then together develop a list of the benefits of the student ministry, your local church, and the fulfilling of the Great Commission.

There are several benefits for the student:

- The student learns to relate to a variety of adults.
- The student watches and interacts with a variety of godly role models.
- The student learns there are adults who are not "paid" who want to spend time with them.
- The student sees how those in the body of Christ are supposed to work together ("many members . . . one body," 1 Corinthians 12:12).
- The student knows there are adults in their church who love them, love their church, and love the Lord Jesus Christ.
- The student knows there are more adults than the student pastor who can serve God.

Finally, for every adult the student connects with, each adult gives them one more reason to be connected to their church, especially after graduation from high school.

There are also many benefits for the student pastor:

- The student pastor receives the needed workers to carry on an effective ministry.
- Creative ideas, vision, and strategy can be birthed and put into action with the perspectives of others.
- More gifts and talents are used for one common purpose.
- The personal influence of the student pastor can extend further with others at his side (thus causing the group to "stay small" as it gets larger).
- The student pastor shares the joy and the burden of ministry with others.
- The student pastor fulfills the biblical command to produce internal leadership (2 Timothy 2:2).
- The student pastor enjoys much-needed relationship and guards against ministry loneliness and isolation.
- The student pastor has built-in accountability as he is watched by his leaders.

# HOW TO DEVELOP A MINISTRY TEAM

The obvious question is, "How do I get an adult from outside the student ministry integrated into leadership within the student ministry?" This section in leadership is what will make or break you in ministry. You may have good intentions in developing a leadership team but good intentions left alone will not get the job done. You must proactively seek out and develop leaders.

Within this section we will cover how you can find potential leaders and transfer them into powerful leaders. A strong leadership team starts by developing strong leaders. Using the acrostic LEADER, here are six steps to developing effective leaders:

Look for potential leaders.

Expose to the student ministry.

Apply to join in the ministry.

Directly involve in the ministry.

Equip for the ministry.

Review at the end of the year of ministry.

## 1. LOOK FOR POTENTIAL LEADERS

Three questions typically surface among student pastors as they look for potential leaders. The first question is "Who should I look for?"

### Who Should I Look For?

Sadly, many student pastors—and especially young student pastors—limit their potential pool because they have a narrow view of what a great youth worker would look like. For example, their stereotype would be a right-out-of-high school, totally cool gamer, who is in a Christian rock band, is in the middle of a six-year junior college plan, drives a sweet car, and can eat large burritos in one bite. They rarely consider someone beyond thirty, someone who is a parent of teenagers, someone in a professional career, and even someone who eats with their mouth closed.

I believe student pastors who limit their pool of potential adults have a very small vision of student ministry and are only hurting themselves and the potentiality of what God can do in the lives of the students. Maybe they limit this because "older" adults intimidate the leader so he surrounds himself with people the same age and/or the same interests. Please, do not make the mistake of King Rehoboam (1 Kings 12:8) and surround yourself with people you grew up with who are your age. You must broaden your view of who can be a great youth worker.

For example, consider some of the benefits of each of these groups: *College-age students* have great enthusiasm, the ability to relate, and time; *young married couples* can provide the same benefits as those of college age but also some maturity and stability; *thirtysomethings*, with their smaller children, can be taken seriously by older adults in the church; and *fortysomethings*, as parents of youth have tremendous youth ministry wisdom. How about those who are older? Yes, you could invite some in their fifties or even sixties to join the team. They have great life experience and wisdom, and they have more time!

### How and Where Can I Find Potential Leaders?

The second question student pastors ask as they look for potential leaders is "How and where can I find potential leaders?" Here are seven resources for locating potential leaders.

> 1. *Have your students provide you with suggestions.* Personally, I found this resource quite helpful. The students may know a number of adults we do not, and they have a good understanding of which

adults may connect with them. This is a great positive for you to be able to tell an adult that your students want them to consider serving in the student ministries. In addition, many of our own students suggested their parents. Now that came as a shock to a few parents but I loved it!

2. *Have the current adult leadership team come up with potential names.* Similar to the students, your current leaders will have many connections that personally you may not, especially if you are newer to the church. This connection may be from within their adult fellowships, their personal friendship groups, or even acquaintances of mutual friends.

3. *Have your current leaders speak with potential leaders.* This step of leadership reproduction was actually one of the responsibilities within our leaders agreement form. I asked each leader to reproduce themselves during their year of ministry. They were to be proactively looking to bring another adult into the leadership team of the student ministry. This is a very effective means of bringing in new potential leaders. It is one thing for the paid youth leader to invite new adults aboard, but I believe it is entirely more significant for one volunteer to invite another potential volunteer aboard. The potential leader may feel much more relaxed and honest with their questions about the ministry to the current volunteer than they may with the student pastor.

4. *Ask your church leadership (pastors, board, etc.) of anyone they are aware of whom they would recommend for the ministry.* How significant for the student pastor to say to an adult, "Our senior pastor recommended you to work in our student ministry." Think of the message this can send to the potential leader. The potential leader surely will be blessed to know senior leadership values them and believes they are important to such a high place of influence. This also puts the student pastor in greater partnership with the senior leadership as together we strive for the success of our church's student ministry.

5. *As the student pastor, you personally ask potential leaders to consider serving in the student ministry.* I found this to be very effective. As the leader, you of all people know what you are looking for both in the character and the responsibilities of the team you are called to build. Always be on the lookout for adults who have a heart for God and a heart for students.

6. *Search out the local colleges (both Christian and secular).* This can be a gold mine if you are in the right geographical setting. College-age

students can give much life and energy to your ministry. Many are away from home, have previously been involved in a student ministry as a teenager, and are looking for a church to call home and a place to serve.

A few words of caution when using this resource, however. First, college students may be hard to depend on. Since this may not be their home church, they have marginal accountability, and it is easy for them to come and go, while leaving you high and dry.

Second, because of the transitory nature of these individuals being in college, be cautious about using them in relational ministry such as core group leaders, discipleship, etc. I found them more suited for task-oriented ministry, such as games, worship, events, etc.

Third, in relation to the transitory nature of college students, ministries may become dependent on local college students, so much so that their ministry opens itself up to being crippled and/or even shutting down when the out-of-area students return home.

Finally, heed the biblical command through Acts (and in 2 Timothy 2:2) for each church to develop its own leaders. My humble opinion of leaning too heavy on "outside" leaders is that it actually impedes potential leaders, especially parents, within your own church from getting involved since "the local college students have it covered."

7. A final resource would be to *consult a few trusted leaders currently serving in the student ministry.* Together you are building a potential list and will review the names together. Doing this creates a positive screening and vetting of various potentials, both in regard to the positives of the potential leaders and any concerns. There may be some serious issues with some potential leaders of which you are not personally aware. As Proverbs 15:22 states, "Without counsel, plans fail, but with many advisors they succeed." While this step is not meant to be critical, keep in mind your job as pastor is to guard the flock.

I must add that the group of leaders you use in the final step may not be all of your current leadership team. Actually, this may be very harmful if this intense vetting process were open to all the leadership. I would encourage you to have your own sense of an "inner circle" of leaders that you appropriately trust their godly wisdom and integrity to keep such a process positive and private.

*What about the Public Appeal?*

The third question student pastors ask as they look for potential leaders is, "What about the public appeal?"

Based on personal experience, I would be cautious about relying on the traditional "Sunday Morning Begging and Pleading" announcement. You want to be able to regulate who gets involved in the student ministry, so when you come across desperate and sound like you will take just about anyone, that is just about what you will get! In addition, consider the precious overworked servant who feels guilty if she says "no" to any appeal?

Further, what about the nonbeliever who has been attending your church and "wants to help kids"? And what about the person who wants to get involved for other motives other than serving students and making disciples? When you politely tell them "thank you but no," their immediate comeback may be, "But you told us you needed help and help has arrived!" Public appeals may place you in a position you do not want to be in. I would publicly announce our Potential Leadership Informational Meeting in the worship service, church bulletin, and other communication venues but this was much different than the public appeal.

In addition, it is very tempting to ask people already busy in other church ministries to consider joining your leadership team. After all, they are probably proven as faithful and responsible leaders. But while this may be true, is this wise? I believe if you do this, do so with respect for the other ministry and with integrity. Before asking "Sam and Joan" to leave their children's Sunday school class to join the "absolutely amazing student ministry," I strongly recommend you first talk to the leader of that ministry before making any contact. Basically, ask that leader's permission and his or her insights. Remember, you need to build bridges to the other ministries, not blow up the bridges. We must strive to be one church.

## 2. EXPOSE TO THE STUDENT MINISTRY

*How to Introduce Prospective Leaders to Student Ministry*

The second step to developing effective leaders is to expose people to the student ministry. This can be done in various ways. You can talk the ministry up to the potential leader. You can show them some of your ministry video clips, have them visit your social media sites, give them some of the ministry materials, and show them the youth center. You could even have them meet a group of students in a very unassuming manner.

But probably the most effective is simply to have the potential leader visit a weekly meeting and one of your events. If you have two weekly meetings such as a traditional Sunday morning and Wednesday night, it may be wise to have them visit both meetings. My rationale of asking the potential leader to visit both weekly meetings was one meeting was designed for outreach and the other for discipleship. This gives the potential the chance to see the entirety of the weekly ministry. In addition, having them visit one of your events shows more of your relational emphasis to the ministry.

While they are visiting, assign them to one of your adult leaders who can act as a subtle host. This could be similar to a job-shadowing experience. This can provide a very relaxed atmosphere for the potential leader to engage in the midst of the ministry but not feel lost or overwhelmed. This benefits the potential leader both relationally and structurally. The hosting adult leader can explain to the potential leader what is taking place, why certain areas of the ministry are done the way they are, and/or what went wrong and should have happened instead. It also provides the potential leader the freedom and opportunity to ask questions.

### Two Cautions

Be cautious that your current leaders do not go around introducing this potential leader as someone entering the ministry. Could you imagine the awkwardness and even damage of one of your leaders walking up to the ninth-grade guys and blurting out "Hey everybody, this is Larry! He is this amazing guy and is going to be your new core group leader!" This not only puts the potential leader in an uncomfortable and assuming position, but it also does the same to the student pastor.

Another area of caution would be using the potential leader in a significant place of ministry while he or she is simply visiting. For example, it is one thing to be at the registration area with a host, but it is another to give the potential leader a responsibility on his or her own. Not only do they possibly not know what to do, but it is once again highly assuming and not appropriate at this stage.

### A Sunday Workshop . . . with a Full Lunch

One approach that worked well for us when I was a student pastor was to host a Prospective Adult Leaders Workshop. This was done in the late spring, during the height of our inviting season. All the potential leaders we have been talking to in our personal invitations came, as did some new ones who responded to our general invitation. This was a seventy-five to ninety-minute afternoon meeting held approximately one hour after the Sunday worship service. I made sure our leadership team was there and would spread out among the lunch tables during this gathering.

We provided a complete catered meal. This took away one excuse as to why folks could not come. During this time we sought to build simple rapport with everyone in attendance. We would show some digital pictures and/or video files of recent student ministry events. This visually demonstrates the ministry and is not about programs or events but students. Next, I would walk through a basic overview of the need of student ministries, our ministry's mission, vision, and strategy, and how one can get involved in the ministry. This would follow with some of our leaders giving their own stories of how God brought them into the student ministry and how God has blessed them through their service to Him.

There was no massive emotional appeal or a high-pressured guilt trip. We simply had a response card for each one to fill out; we thanked them for coming and had application packets available for those who were interested. If they had not yet visited the youth ministry, we encouraged that step at this time. While this is not the only way to have potential leaders exposed to the ministry, I must say I wish I started this process at the beginning of my career and not toward the end!

## 3. APPLY TO JOIN IN THE STUDENT MINISTRY

This is where many youth ministry leadership teams are won or lost. As I see it, asking the prospective leader to formally apply is the part of the leadership process that separates healthy youth ministries from the unhealthy ones.

### Benefits of an Application Process

Here are some of the benefits of a strong application process: (1) The leader is assuring the parents he is proactive in guarding the flock; (2) The leader is seeking to make sure he knows who he is getting; (3) The leader is able to determine whether this person is truly a good fit for the ministry and where the person could best fit in; (4) The student leader is helping the potential leader become aware of the requirements before the person commits to the ministry; this brings about a well informed and intelligent commitment from the potential leader. Finally, (5) the leader is demonstrating to the candidate an atmosphere of professionalism and excellence.

The very act of taking time to complete the form also reveals something about the candidate. Very few people like filling out forms. Those who do show their interest. If a person cannot take the time to go through the application process, can the leader sincerely count on them to be faithful when ministry gets monotonous and laborious?

### A Three-Step Application Process

There are many different ways an application phase can be done. I would strongly suggest you read various student ministry books, research numerous student ministry websites, and speak with seasoned youth pastors as to their own application process. The book *Youth Ministry Management Tools* has some of the best and most comprehensive information I have ever read on this subject.

As one model, here is my own personal tried-and-true application strategy. The goal was to have our new leadership team in place before July 1, as we promoted the students to the next grade at the beginning of the summer. Thus, summer camp was the initial major event with the new leaders in place with their small groups. To prepare for this target date, each potential leader would go through three phases. This process was explained in a step-by-step handout, but below is a simple description of each phase.

1. *The Interested Phase* (two weeks, completed sometime in April or May). Each potential leader was asked to spend time seeking God for His direction, and also to seek out godly counsel as to this opportunity. They were to carefully read through all the materials in the packet. Then they were to observe the ministry up-close by attending two of the weekly student meetings and an event. Finally, the potential leader was to attend the spring Prospective Adult Leaders Workshop as previously described. After they had completed these four steps, they were to look through the application packet, which included a staff process sheet, a listing of adult leaders qualifications, a spiritual gifts test/survey, a philosophy of student ministries booklet, and an application.

2. *The Inquiring Phase* (two to four weeks, completed sometime in May or June). After the potential leader had read through and filled out all the needed forms, we would meet for a formal interview. It was during this time they would step into the ministry on a trial commitment. As they were observing, they were to be thinking and praying as to which age group and in what capacity they saw they were best designed by God to serve. Each one would also attend and participate in the appropriate adult leadership meetings.

At the conclusion of this trial period, the potential leader and I would set up an appointment to go over the application. A key question we would seek to answer was, Does this adult sense the Lord's direction to serve with us and in what capacity? If both the individual and I sensed clarity from the Lord, he or she would fill out the agreement form. They would then move into the third level as they have officially joined the ministry team.

3. *The Involved Phase* (twelve months, July—June). During this time each one agreed to begin their yearlong commitment to the student ministry. They agreed to attend the Adult Leadership Retreat, the monthly leadership meetings, as well as the specific responsibilities each one had agreed to fulfill. At the conclusion of the year, there would be a review to see if we both would want to continue or move in a different direction.

You may have noticed there was a one-year commitment. While I understand many ministries may have a different time commitment, I was very comfortable with this approach. The majority of leaders would stay on board for many annual commitments, but this allowed for a healthy "off ramp" as some had new seasons of life (i.e., having a child, taking care of an elderly parent, etc.). Others realized student ministry was not their fit. Still others just needed the freedom of a short-term commitment. Finally, it provided me with a natural way to move someone who may not be best suited within the ministry to a different ministry.

There were no shortcuts with this process. While it may sound legalistic, it certainly served us well. I remember many in the church making comments as to why it was so difficult to get involved serving in the student ministry while all they had to do for other ministries was just show up and they would immediately be plugged into duty. My answer was simple. Student ministry is typically the most demanding and draining ministry within the church. We need intelligent and godly decisions from both parties before having people enter the ministry.

The timing of these three phases was crucial. As already noted, by using this model the new team is in place as the students move into their new department, new grade, and new small group. The intention is then to use the summer as the relational and structural preparation time so by the end of the summer, everything is in place and everyone should be comfortable with their roles and relationships. This way one can start the school year off strong.

## 4. DIRECTLY INVOLVE IN THE MINISTRY

A key step to developing effective leaders is to directly involve a new leader in the student ministry. Again, the summer can be a great place for the integration to begin. Now the new leader is becoming involved within his or her role. This was where the inquiring phase starts to transition into the involved phase. As your new leaders are moving ahead, make sure you are not leaving them alone. Bring them alongside veterans who will be able to assist them in his or her roles. This is especially helpful within small groups. Consider having the new leader who is still in the inquiring phase sit within a group as a silent observer led by a veteran. Once the new leader is within the direct involvement stage, you may want to consider combining two of the small groups so that the veteran leader can observe the new leader facilitate the group. This will provide the new leader with the opportunity to have some coaching from the veteran.

Much of this description has been focused on the relational side of ministry (what I titled the shepherd roles). But what about those who take on various task side of ministry (what I titled the support roles)? The principles stay the same. Have the new leader come alongside an existing leader in that support, or task position. For example, if you are having adults step into your creative arts team, then simply have them connect with current leaders in that particular ministry. Yet what if you are having someone come in to develop a new area of ministry? For example, you may want to start or upgrade your ministry's social media, but there is no current ministry leader in that role. The new leader is the leader of that ministry. Then either you personally need to provide him or her with support and direction or have someone else assist the leader. Whatever you do, never leave a new leader alone. This is not fair to them and can lead to frustration and failure.

Each leader should have a specific written job description that is explained and agreed upon before the commitment. This should describe the leader's role, the expectations, the legitimate time commitment this role will take, their commitment to the role, and your commitment to them.

Some of the roles you may want to consider utilizing in student ministry are as follows:

## ROLES FOR THE SUPPORT AND SHEPHERD TEAMS*

| FOR THE SUPPORT TEAM | FOR THE SHEPHERD TEAM |
|---|---|
| • Worship<br>• Drama<br>• Promotions/Social Media<br>• Events<br>• Hospitality/Guest Services<br>• Refreshments<br>• Recreation<br>• Database (Office Assistance)<br>• Host Homes | • Discussion Groups<br>• Discipleship Groups<br>• One-on-One Discipleship<br>• Teachers<br>• Campus Group Leaders |

\* These are only examples. Other roles may exist for your specific support and shepherd team.

### 5. EQUIP FOR THE MINISTRY

This area is so crucial to the development of the healthy team. This is the feeding and leading side of ministry. Whereas the success of the *Directly Involved* stage depends on the mutual cooperation of both the youth pastor and the youth worker, the *Equipping* stage depends on the youth pastor. This is your Ephesians 4 responsibility! As I look into 1 Thessalonians 2:6–12 (NKJV), I find the heart of Paul revealed:

> Nor did we seek glory from men, either from you or from others, when we might have made demands as apostles of Christ. But we were gentle among you, just as a nursing mother cherishes her own children. So, affectionately longing for you, we were well pleased to impart to you not only the gospel of God, but also our own lives, because you had become dear to us. For you remember, brethren, our labor and toil; for laboring *night and day, that we might not be a burden to anyone, we preached to you the gospel of God.*
>
> You are witnesses, and God also, how devoutly and justly and blamelessly we behaved ourselves among you who believe; as you know how we exhorted, and comforted, and charged] every one of you, as a father does his own children, that you would walk worthy of God who calls you into His own kingdom and glory. (italics added)

Notice the discipleship and equipping roles are labeled within the context of parenting. Paul identifies himself in a maternal role as the relational parent (vv.7–9) and in the paternal role as the instructional parent (vv.10–12). As shepherds, we are to be about both the relational and instructional roles with the ones we have spiritual oversight. While never perfect at this, my heart's desire was to bring both of these aspects to my ministry team.

## Your Relational Role

Here are a few examples of each role. Under your *relational* role:

1. *Create a "family" atmosphere among your leaders.* No matter how big or small your leadership team is, create a family. This starts with you, so you take the initiative.

2. *Connect with your leaders.* Write them encouragement notes and do coffee or lunch with them. (Obviously there should be an above-reproach approach when it comes to men with women.) Other ways to connect are to have them in your home, go to their home, spend personal time with them, and be their authentic friend. Again, so much of what you do may be determined by the size of your leadership team, but you need to have connection points with each one in some way and your leadership team must be connected with each other. Finally, a great leadership teams plays together and prays together.

3. *Congratulate your leaders both publicly and privately.* While it may sound simplistic, I made it my goal to connect with each leader and personally say thank you for their service after every event or meeting we had. It may sound like this is over the top but I would rather err on the side of showing personal care and gratefulness. Those leaders knew they were loved.

## Your Instructional Role

Here are some approaches to use under your instructional role:

1. *Provide the individual leader with the resources for personal student ministry development.* In the 1980s, leaders had books, cassette tapes, magazine and journal articles, and seminars. Look at us today with the explosion of the Internet and electronic reading devices. We are truly blessed with so many resources. Provide your leaders with the actual resources or give them the information where they can find these resources on their own. Consider having a resource center in your office full of resources: game ideas, dramas, event ideas, curriculum, various youth ministry books, etc. I was old school with the bookcase for my leaders to stop by and grab what they needed. Speaking of old school, I still have the original set of *Youth Specialties Ideas* periodicals, years of *Youth*

*Worker Journals*, vintage authors like Josh McDowell, and cassettes...lots of cassettes.

2. *Provide the team with the resources for group youth ministry development.* Consider providing each leader with a professionally designed notebook, complete with section tabs. I wish I would have incorporated this team notebook concept much earlier in ministry. I highly recommend you consider implementing such a tool. Include all ministry materials, student rosters, attendance records, training material, leader's meeting notes, and other items had a place to be stored.

### *Opportunities for Preparing Your Youth Leaders*

Commit to having consistent youth leader meetings. The first Sunday afternoon of the month worked well for us. You choose what works best for your team. The monthly youth leader meeting consisted of all support and shepherd leaders from both middle school and high school departments. During this ninety-minute meeting, there was a time for: (1) *celebration* (fifteen minutes to celebrate areas where God was working in the students); (2) *instruction* (thirty to forty-five minutes of leadership development); (3) *communication* (thirty to forty-five minutes for each department to go over logistics for their specific ministries). Planning was done outside of this meeting by those specifically charged with those responsibilities; thus, we had more time for equipping and for group prayer.

Another opportunity for instruction happens when the team members go to youth conferences or conventions together. Or possibly bring an outside speaker to your own group. Maybe join alongside other youth ministries and put on your own seminar or workshop. One may also have professionals in your own church body or community who can give insights into the world of adolescents from their professional perspectives. A few suggestions would be to incorporate educators, police officers, counselors, and social workers.

### 6. REVIEW AT THE END OF THE YEAR OF MINISTRY

As opposed to having the "sign up until Jesus comes" commitment, I encourage you to consider a termed commitment. You have already noted my one-year approach. I know other youth pastors who ask for a two-year commitment. Either way, make sure you provide a safe landing place for the journey to end. Hey, even sports teams have the end of the season! This allows the leader to have a natural place to step out if needed and also allows you a natural place to let someone go.

Either way, end the school year with an interview with each of your leaders. During this meeting, thank them for serving, point out their contributions to the team, ask them how you can serve them more effectively, and then discuss any areas that need to be dealt with (both positive or negative). I tried to make sure my leaders understand this review was not something to get stressed over! So many of them have reviews built into their jobs where that was the annual time for the boss to clobber them. This should be just the opposite for us in the Lord's work. We are about building people, so use this as a constructive time. Some youth ministries even have a specific form or survey to be filled out by the volunteer before the meeting.

As this personal meeting winds down you are looking at two options:

1. *Renew the leader for another year of youth ministry.* Is it your desire to maintain them with the ministry? Maybe so, but see if this is also their desire. They may need a break or a change in responsibilities and/or ministry departments. This review is a great place to find this out.

2. *Release the leader and help them find another place of ministry.* This is not meant to be negative. Maybe student ministry is just not the right fit. Maybe their ministry passions are more in another area in the church. Sadly, maybe they are struggling with some personal wounds, unhealthy issues, or even sin, and need to seek spiritual restoration. No matter what the issue, this review provides both of you the natural exit ramp to make this happen. It is better this exit takes place than the leader stays within the student ministry where some harm may occur. It is better to lose a leader than lose the ministry.

# A STUDENT LEADER'S REWARDING RELATIONSHIPS

There are so many resources on leadership. Many of you have read and listened to wise and talented authors and speakers, such as John Maxwell and Andy Stanley. My contribution is a simple one. The intent of this chapter is to assist the leader with the developing of a leadership team primarily made up of volunteers. I realize you may be looking for more than this and I say seek on!

Some of you are seasoned veterans who already have much of this information in place in your own ministries. May I encourage you to consider mentoring others around you? Some of you may have paid leaders. While this may look somewhat different in your context, I do believe many of these principles can apply to your context.

Looking back on my own years of serving in the local church, of all the relationships that were the most rewarding and the deepest, it was by far the relationships I enjoyed with our leadership team. To this day we stay in contact through social media and other venues. Many of them are still involved in ministry. Odd as it may sound, in my early twenties I wanted to be the leader that the students turned to. Yet as I matured, what gave me such reward was watching the students turn to their leader for spiritual counsel or attention. And to know the leader would represent God and His Word to these students was a continual blessing. The retention rate among the leadership team was absolutely astounding. I owe so much of this to the thorough process described in this chapter, but also to the relationships we treasured. These leaders became family to my wife and me as together we sought God and worked together for the furtherance of the gospel (Philippians 1:27).

Communicate with your leaders. Respect your leaders. Love your leaders. Value your leaders. Invest in your leaders. Lead as you want to be led. And when you are hitting the wall, look into the eyes of our Master and remember He is the Great Shepherd. Love Him and please Him.

---

# NOTE

1. Jim Burns with Mike DeVries, *The Youth Builder* (Ventura, Calif.: Gospel Light, 2002), 156.

# 5

# PARENTS—THE OTHER SIDE OF THE STUDENT MINISTRY

There has been a new emphasis in ministry on the most important people in a teenager's life . . . their parents. Parents are the key influence and influencers in the lives of our teenagers.

I have an advantage of having three adult children (somewhat of an oxymoron). They are all married with children. I can say with all gratitude and credit to a loving and patient God that my kids have not embarrassed us beyond recognition. Instead they have become kids anyone would be crazy proud of. Currently, our two sons are in the military (one is a war veteran who served in Iraq and Afghanistan and the other is Special Forces. I'd like to tell you what he does, but then he would have to eliminate me). My daughter has the toughest job of them all. She is a homemaker (four little girls to look after is no small task) and married to a pastor.

All three have been fruitful and have multiplied. It really doesn't get any better than that (as far as I'm concerned). And we went through the raising of three teenagers while being in full-time student ministry. So I have been on the parental side of this equation as a parent with teenagers. With that said, for some reason, past student ministry has overlooked this critical segment of adults . . . maybe not knowingly or with intention, but the perception has been there.

There has been a renewal of family ministry, with an emphasis on homes and parents, and no one is going to argue against that. Another emphasized topic has been dads being the head of the household and being responsible for the spirituality of their family. No one is going to argue with that biblical mandate, but one must consider a social problem in our modern culture, and that is number of fatherless families both physically or emotionally absent (see chapter 2, page 48). So the nuclear family that consists of original parents is becoming more of an ideal than a reality.

This is the harsh reality that youth pastors and leaders will have to address. Part of this reality will include youth leaders finding themselves in surrogate parental roles. Another spin-off of this family theme has been an emphasis on parents being responsible for the education of their children. No debate here. (Homeschoolers tend to resonate with this thought at a level and involvement that others may not as enthusiastically embrace.) The bottom line is that parent(s) can and should be the biggest influence upon their kids.

## NECESSARY PARENTAL STRATEGIES

While parenting may be relatively easy in preadolescents, it becomes a trickier relationship when those preadolescents enter puberty. Parental influence remains important, and several strategies are important. The first is *prevention*: making decisions for one's children, anticipating problems or dangers, and determining their schedules, friends, and interests. Parents do their best to raise their kids, and for the most part, during the preadolescent years children believe parents can do no wrong. The second strategy could be described as *engagement*, especially during the adolescent years, when teenagers often think their parents can do no right (this is fueled by the fact that teenagers are beginning to think for themselves). Without this parental engagement (in the lives of their teenagers), teenagers are susceptible to all kinds of influences (not all of them good ones). The engaged parent can act as ballast for all the wrong influences. (Part of the challenge in student ministry is to encourage teenagers to give their parents something to brag about.) There are incidences where a parent has done all the right things—including affirming kids for right choices and accomplishments—and their teenager still goes off the rails.

So a third strategy of *intervention* may need to be implemented. Intervention can be as subtle or intimidating as a face-to-face conversation with a parent, or it could be as aggressive as physically removing a teenager from a detrimental situation or individual. Hopefully a parent does not have to resort to this more aggressive approach but frankly, there are societal influences and lifestyles that might have gained a foothold in the lives of our kids, and parents have reached an impasse that requires action.

The wise student leader will walk with parents through these difficult times and have an understanding of the strategies that are needed to get their adolescent through adolescence. A student leader can mention to parents individually or together those influences that should be considered for intervention, including anything drug related, under-age drinking, and immoral relationships.[1] Intervention by a social worker or counselor can be daunting for any parent. Rehabilitation is by far the most time consuming and most expensive. This strategy takes place when a person has "crashed and burned." Any good parent never wants to get to this stage, but there are times where we have to pick up the pieces of a broken young life and help them rehabilitate within the walls of a loving home with loving parents.

# YOUTH LEADERS AS PARENTAL RESOURCES

Parenting teenagers is no easy task, and youth pastors and leaders need to be a strong resource that lends itself to parents.

The youth pastor or youth worker needs to be in the parents' corner, and I think I can say with almost 100 percent certainty that most youth pastors and leaders are in the parents' corner.

For a long time, we have dismissed any input on the subject of parenting from youth workers who weren't parents. So we've created this unofficial parental gap, between those with kids and those without. I have dismissed that perspective. Youth workers who are not parents themselves still can recognize good parenting and they can recognize bad parenting. Why? Because they had good or bad parenting during their own adolescence. Any former minor can look back with better than 20/20 vision and clearly see elements of both good and bad parenting, whether they have their own kids or not.

The other thing that youth workers and leaders bring to the table is a current and progressive understanding of what teenagers are going through, both in the cultural world, as well as in their relational world. In fact, I would go one step further and suggest that these want-to-be parents (who are looking ahead) are already planning on what their parenting skills will look like and what they will not look like. There are tremendous pressures on the kids within a blended family (which is becoming more commonplace), especially when you get into the subject of firstborns being in the same house, for both male and female. (I'm a firstborn, and when another firstborn moved in, it wasn't a good relationship.) Add to that the sheer numbers of children, as well as a brand-new parent . . . along with the stress of schedules and finances—it's not easy. Being raised in a blended family of seven kids, I know the challenge of having brothers and sisters learning to somehow get along with each other, as well as pleasing Mom and Dad. Before I was even close to being a parent, I was already identifying those parenting practices that I wanted to implement and those I wanted to avoid, based on my current family situation.

# ABOUT YELLING

One of those practices was yelling. I've always sensed that yelling was counterproductive (when it came to parenting teenagers) and was in fact, detrimental both relationally and psychologically. Research has been done that not only implicates the practice of yelling, but it also indicates it is counterproductive. The consequences of yelling have been equal to corporeal punishment. According to a research paper that appeared online in the journal *Child Development*, authors Dr. Ming-Te Wang and Sarah Kenny found that "adolescents who had experienced harsh verbal discipline suffered from increased levels of depressive symptoms, and were more likely to demonstrate behavioral problems such as vandalism or antisocial and aggressive behavior." In other words, it can be damaging to students who are still developing. It gets worse.

> Significantly, the researchers also found that "parental warmth"—i.e., the degree of love, emotional support, and affection between parents and adolescents—did not lessen the effects of the verbal discipline. The sense that parents are yelling at the child "out of love," or "for their own good," Wang said, does not mitigate the damage inflicted. Neither does the strength of the parent-child bond. This verbal shouting included shouting, cursing, or using insults.[2]

While I did not have this peer-reviewed research paper at the time of my parenting, I had already decided that I would not be a yeller with my own kids. I saw the resentment and strained relationships that festered within my own family, along with other siblings of mine, picking up the same practice but still with the same reactions and consequences.

Now, if a train, plane, or automobile is coming at your child, it's time to yell. But in the setting of your own family, it's one of those practices that should have strict limits and narrowly defined circumstances. I figured all this out before I was a husband and a parent. My guess is that many nonparent youth leaders are making their own list, even now. They might have some inexperienced advice that could benefit our parenting skills with teenagers.

## GET A GRIP

From a psychological context, teenagers are beginning to become independent from their parents. It's a slow process that typically starts in middle school and ends when they finish high school or college (though some have what is called a delayed adulthood or extended adolescence, which often is an excuse for the struggling adolescent to avoid adult responsibilities). Sometimes this process is seamless, but most parents see adolescence as a turbulent transition. Regardless, teenagers are beginning to separate from their parents. Some parents can't handle this; others handle it incorrectly. Instead of loosening their grips on their kids, they tighten their grips. Instead, parents should begin to loosen their grips appropriately and in a timely manner. Do parents want their kids to be dependent on them into adulthood? (I'm sure there are some "Mommy Dearest" types out there; but for the most part, the answer is no.) The parent's job is to prepare them for adulthood.

During adolescence, parenting needs to modify itself to compensate for the young adult inside of a teenager's body. Once the son or daughter is eighteen, the parent needs to shift his role from parent to advisor. I'm convinced that if parents embrace this new role, they will be included in much of their kids' lives as they move through their own adulthood.

## IT'S COMPLICATED

I'm all about the family context, but frankly we tend to hang out with those closest to our age. To amalgamate everything into one big happy church ministry at the exclusion or elimination of age-segregated gatherings is a step back into the Stone Age. It is certainly idealistic. *Wired* magazine has even alluded to this gathering of teenagers by looking at comments by Microsoft researcher Danah Boyd in her book *It's Complicated: The Social Lives of Networked Teens.* Boyd seems to reinforce this social dynamic (among teenagers). While her research focuses on the online socializing of teenagers, she makes a provocative observation. According to reporter Clive Thompson in *Wired,*

> What [Boyd] has found, over and over, is that teenagers would love
> to socialize face-to-face with their friends. But adult society won't let

them. "Teens aren't addicted to social media. They're addicted to each other," Boyd says. "They're not allowed to hang out the way you and I did, so they've moved it online." The result, Boyd discovered, is that today's teens have neither the time nor the freedom to hang out. So their avid migration to social media is a rational response to a crazy situation. They'd rather socialize F2F, so long as it's unstructured and away from grown-ups.[3]

As one of our pastors said, "Tear down the silos and work in the barn." In other words (to stay with the farm analogy), the various animals have their stalls, but they are all under the same roof. Sure we have times to get everyone together, but not everything is done together. When was the last time you went to a family reunion? You don't mind them, but you don't go to one every weekend; and when you do go to a family reunion, you do age-appropriate things. I can do everything I could do when I was fourteen . . . for about two minutes. I don't want to and cannot do everything that everyone is doing at a family reunion. Teenagers don't always want to be with adults; adults do not always want to be with teenagers; and teenagers don't always want to be with children. It's just not human nature. God designed us that way. "When I was a child, I spoke like a child, I thought like a child, I reasoned like a child. When I became a man, I gave up childish ways" (1 Corinthians 13:11).

This problem might not have occurred if during the past thirty years parents stopped dropping off their kids at church and expecting the church to teach their children all they need to know about faith and, instead, discussed what they learned at church as a family at home and built on the teaching they received from church teachers and ministers. The youth worker's job is to build on the foundation that parents have built, and help cultivate and reinforce what parents have built into their children. The youth worker is to help/aid the parents in giving them the essentials that a teenager needs in order to stand alone in his or her faith. What does that look like? It's a picture of a teenager who begins to make the right decisions on his or her own—without prompting from parents—regardless of the potential social consequences.

# TO BE (INVOLVED) OR NOT TO BE (INVOLVED)

To strengthen the parental variable in our equation, youth workers and leaders need to determine a couple of things. First, determine the level of involvement parents should have in youth ministry, and second, the level of instruction and guidance the parents will need (in order to nurture the faith of their teenagers). The involvement level varies but it is not a guarantee. I do not think that the biological ability to have kids is an automatic pass into student ministry involvement. Parents should go through the same vetting process that any other volunteer goes through.

Obviously the level of involvement needs to be compatible to the level of qualifications. For example, I would suggest that student ministry involving youth room arrangements, food preparation, group chaperoning, transportation, etc., does not require a background check for parents who want to contribute at this level. Now if a parent desires to be involved in a teaching or small-group leadership role, the vetting process should be more in depth. So there should be some discerning as to the degree of qualifying, when compared to the task or role in which parents want to be involved.

Instruction also needs to give consideration as to what topics need to be taught to parents that would give the skill set needed to maneuver with their kids through adolescence. Those topics should include:

- What's going on in the mind of a teenager;
- adolescent behaviors and lifestyles;
- the psychology of teenagers;
- effective parenting skills;
- pop culture;
- ways to spiritually connect with teenagers;
- transitioning from middle school to high school, and then to college; and
- dealing with conflict and rebellion

You don't have to look very far to find those websites, conferences, and resources that address these topics. Student pastors and leaders should act as facilitators of these timely subjects and make parents aware of their availability. I have personally been involved in many parent seminars, and I have seen the desperation and hope in the eyes of parents who are grasping for anything that will help aid them in raising their teenagers. I have also seen the "stock value" of those youth pastors and leaders skyrocket because they took the initiative to plan and organize such an event.

With regard to the level or amount of instruction and guidance parents need, youth workers and leaders can act like guides and advisors. Parents of teenagers are looking for ways to connect with their teenagers. We can recommend the usual parent informational meeting but it needs to go beyond that. This needs to be more of a churchwide effort and not limited to the student ministry. Some would suggest that parents should have an open door to any and all student events. I don't have a problem with that but I think we also need to do what would be best in facilitating teaching opportunities and candid interaction. In other words, teenagers need space.

Still, parents should be encouraged to be involved in student ministry in appropriate and beneficial ways. What does that look like? Parents are parents to all the students . . . not just their own when they volunteer. As youth leaders we should jump on those opportunities that get their parents involved. At the same time, youth leaders have to discern what is best for the youth group. So compatibility and need are factors that should be included.

On a micro level, parents are not only looking for ways to connect with their teenagers, but they are also looking for ways to connect with their teenagers on a spiritual level. This can and should be a direct involvement as well as some delegation. Direct involvement should include nurturing a climate at home that easily discusses spiritual matters. This climate allows for open and honest questions, opinions, disagreement, and even doubts. And when there is a gridlock of differences of opinions, house rules should apply (i.e., no explosive arguing; living in harmony at home trumps opinions; kids should always consider parental preferences over theirs; while living at home, house rules are house rules, whether a family member agrees with them or not). If at any time a teenager can't live with the house rules, they can find work and another place to live.

It is critical that parents do what they can to create a safe environment, one that is free from judgment, verbal attacks, but has two-way conversations. If that safe environment is not perceived by teenagers, I can guarantee that several things will happen: they will go somewhere to people who will listen; they will simply give answers that they think their parents want to hear; they will avoid saying anything and simply keep their thoughts and opinions to themselves. I think this safe environment is a direct result of parental intentionality. Direct involvement can include encouraging teenagers to become more involved in their church and youth group. It could include a mission trip or community project. I've had the opportunity to go on several mission trips with my own teenagers and there is nothing better than to see your own teenagers working hard to help others in need, as well as serving God and His people. This is a highlight of my student ministry vocation.

Direct involvement needs to include helpful materials that would help facilitate conversations about spiritual matters. This might look like special curriculum or activity suggestions that would stimulate conversations. Along with direct involvement, there will be a need for some delegation. This is where student ministry can be a positive reinforcement for parents. This delegation could be described as spiritual midwifery (i.e., 1 Samuel 1–3, when Hannah left Samuel with the priest, Eli). Daniel 1 is another example of training and education outside of the home context (even though brought about by unfortunate political developments). In this case, in the middle of obvious conflicts of lifestyle and beliefs, Daniel became a great example of a teenager asking permission, and then using a term of respect . . . please. Exodus 2 is the familiar story of Moses and Pharaoh's daughter, yet in an ironic but providential arrangement, Moses's mother ends up raising her son but in a completely different world.

As my own kids went through their adolescent years, the church and youth group became more important in their lives. As a parent, I was thrilled that the spiritual dynamic was being addressed, within the context of a church and youth group, with youth leaders who had their best interest at heart. That has been very reassuring to me, and I'm sure there are a countless number of parents who feel the same.

## THE BOTTOM LINE

In his profound book *Raising Adults*, Jim Hancock makes the following comments based on research:

> There's a lot of evidence that kids listen to adults before they listen to their peers. You'd think this isn't true because of the mythology around peer pressure. The truth is, kids gravitate first to older people who accept and value them and with whom they feel safe. If no one like that is around, then they look to peers for relationship, affirmation and support.[4]

Hancock gives a strong affirmation to the parents' role and credence to those youth workers who are nearby. Youth workers are on the same side as parents, he says.

Sure I'm biased in my opinion of the validity of student ministry, and one could argue this position is simply one of job security. I would be the first to argue that methods do change according to the cultural climate, and some methods become archaic. However, our culture has catered, targeted, influenced, manipulated, brainwashed, and marketed our teenagers. I'm convinced that parents are encouraged and thrilled that there are those who make their kids the focus of their calling and ministry. Student ministry in its traditional and modern sense has been a viable, effective, and blessed methodology. Countless numbers of teenagers have been influenced for the faith by organized student ministry, in conjunction with parents. While we may not agree with what this looks like, when it comes to student ministry partnering with parents, we know that effort, instruction, experimentation, and cooperation needs to be a part of the equation.

The apostle Paul had a pretty good attitude about those with whom he did not see eye to eye: "Some indeed preach Christ even from envy and strife, and some also from goodwill: The former preach Christ from selfish ambition, not sincerely, supposing to add affliction to my chains; but the latter out of love, knowing that I am appointed for the defense of the gospel. What then? Only *that* in every way, whether in pretense or in truth, Christ is preached; and in this I rejoice" (Philippians 1:15–18 NKJV).

Let's challenge parents *and* teenagers. Proverbs 22:6 says, "Train up a child in the way he should go; even when he is old he will not depart from it." Colossians 3:21 says, "Fathers, do not provoke your children, lest they become discouraged." Proverbs 23:25 says, "Let your father and mother be glad; and let her who bore you birth rejoice." Proverbs 28:7 says, "Young people who obey the law are wise; those with wild friends bring shame to their parent" (NLT). The antonym of "shame" is "pride." In other words, we need to encourage teenagers to do whatever it takes, in order to make their parents proud. In the meantime, I will continue to promote, push, ponder, perfect, pursue, and practice student ministry, with engaged parents who feel the same way. For those of you without your own kids, take heart and take notes. For those of you who have your own kids, take courage and take advice.

# NOTES

1. Other influences that parents should consider worth their intervention include crime and bodily harm to self or others.

2. "Yelling Doesn't Help, May Harm Adolescents, Pitt-Led Study Finds," September 4, 2013, at http://www.news.pitt.edu/news/yelling-doesn-t-help-may-harm-adolescents-pitt-led-study-finds. Summary of study by Ming-Te Wang and Sarah Kenney, "Longitudinal Links Between Fathers' and Mothers' Harsh Verbal Discipline and Adolescents' Conduct Problems and Depressive Symptoms," later published in *Journal of Child Development,* vol. 85 (May/June 2014): 908–23.

3. Clive Thompson, "Don't Blame Social Media If Your Teen Is Unsocial. It's Your Fault," *Wired* December 26, 2013; http://www.wired.com/2013/12/ap_thompson-2/.

STUDENT MINISTRY

# ESSENTIALS

PART 2: NURTURING

# 6

## THE ESSENTIAL OF

# UNDERSTANDING TODAY'S STUDENTS

## (WHAT HAPPENED TO MY CHILD?)

As most parents—and student leaders—well know, teenagers are *not* like their childhood selves. Prior to the teen years, parents will usually dote on their kids. Children do and say cute things. Then, before parents know it, puberty sets in. All of a sudden, those kids are changing.

Sometimes the changes are for the better, but often those changes irritate parents, and even frighten them. That sweet compliant little child morphs into someone parents don't recognize. Parents often wonder if this child of theirs was accidently switched at birth.

The changes at times can be funny, but they also can create stress and uncertainty for teens and their parents alike. And they often will influence the teens' interactions and attitudes in youth gatherings at school and church. This should influence your ministry programs and relationships with the kids in your group. Here are the changes that come during middle school and high school years

## THE CHANGES ARE A COMING

### PHYSICALLY

The physical changes begin for the "tweenager"— a child between childhood and adolescence. This is when most kids experience rapid and dramatic growth.

I remember a family vacation when our older son was sitting in the backseat of our car. When we left home, his head was below my view in the rearview mirror. Three weeks later, he was eyeball to eyeball with me in the mirror. His growth spurt was evident to relatives and friends who hadn't seen him in a while, but it was even more evident to us.

Some kids, of course, have a growth spurt during their early teens. They may even experience actual growing pains. The pace of their growth can be so fast that their bodies get sore. The teenagers' hands and feet first reach adult size, making them clumsy. Try watching a middle-school basketball team warm up and notice that the teens lack coordination and grace. They knock over full drinking glasses, small pieces of furniture, knickknacks, and then stumble over pets and small children, simply due to these newly discovered appendages that they haven't figured out how to control.

The traditional onset of puberty has been redefined on both the beginning and the end. For girls, puberty begins around age eleven, while guys start puberty around twelve. The early onset of puberty, in particular with girls, has been as early as seven years old. A study published in the journal *Pediatrics* found that 23 percent of black girls and 10 percent of white girls began puberty by age seven.[1] The reasons behind this include obesity, diets high in meat and junk food, gender, and race. There is also evidence that puberty might be initiated neurologically due to stressors. It appears that preteens experience some of this stress, which is reserved for their adults. But due to this exposure physically, preteens' bodies react by prematurely developing. Their bodies are reacting in order to deal with untimely and highly unsettling stress.

This certainly has implications when it comes to student ministry, particularly with a consideration of student ministry to late elementary grades, or even a focused ministry to grades four to six.

## EMOTIONALLY

Emerging teenagers begin to develop a sense of personal identity and self-worth. Parents can help them find their niches, those things they do well or in which they have a strong interest. If a teenager shows interest in a team sport (basketball, volleyball, hockey) or an individual sport (skateboarding, snowboarding, tennis), the parents should allow their teenager to go as far as their interests will take them. This can be a relationship-strengthening experience between parents and teenager. Parents can make their teenager aware of good camps or conferences, help them with the costs, get them there, buy equipment, and cheer them on. Obviously, this is predicated by what is wholesome, right, and within reason.

Of course, teenagers are fickle; they change their minds and get bored easily. And parents hope that sooner than later, their teenagers will find some things that will give them their identities. As parents help to facilitate teenagers in their pursuits, this strengthens the parent/teenager relationships. This is all a part of teenagers striving for independence, yet still depending on their parents for the time being. Youth leaders can help teens in this transition by encouraging appropriate independence while accepting a healthy dependence on their parents, demonstrated by respect, honor, and obedience.

In the midst of these feelings of self-worth or its flip side, insecurity and uncertainty, there is often a feeling of being self-conscious. Even teenagers who are gaining more confidence have one paramount concern—and it's not global warming, not the war on terror, and not the price of gas. It's how they look! They are self-conscious of how they look and present themselves. Because of their self-consciousness, *they fear ridicule*. Sarcastic peers target awkward teenagers for verbal abuse. Bullying tends to target the weakest of our young for whatever reasons . . . none being valid reasons.

With the advent of advanced technology, especially social media, self-conscious teenagers have become the targets of bullying in the online world too. While an online presence is somewhat nonconfrontational, in a teenager's mind it is now and loud, with clever but often cutting words that are used in bullying situations. It can be subtle or blatant. So even in a cyber-bullying situation, a teenager's fragile self-esteem can be fractured in this expressionless and sometimes anonymous attempt to hurt a self-conscious teenager.

Adults can act as counterbalances by offering genuine praise and encouragement. In spite of the significance of peer groups in teenagers' lives, adults are able to exert extraordinary influence with simple yet sincere compliments. Author Jim Hancock exhorts us to use caution and discretion in our compliments. He puts it this way, "Be cautious about praising things that children have nothing to do with, i.e., You're so pretty; You're so tall; What big beautiful eyes you have! Kids who get praise for things outside their control or acts of God, become suspicious of people and nervous about their own self-worth. Looks do change."[2]

## SOCIALLY

Emerging teenagers do everything enthusiastically. And the adults in their lives must be characteristically enthusiastic. Parents and adults must infuse enthusiasm in whatever they do with teenagers—and the teens will follow anywhere!

Most teens are enthusiastic but often fluctuate between being friendly and moody. So when adults think they have a solid relationship, teens may turn their backs on adults without warning; or when parents think they have them figured out, their teens go off with wild-eyed ideas. So go with the flow when maneuvering among teenagers.

Along with moodiness comes developing crushes and hero worship. As one who has raised three teenagers, I am thrilled when the youth leaders are the heroes in my teenagers' lives. I'd like to be their hero, but I know my teenagers would have a difficult time admitting that I could fulfill this role. Later on this hero role could happen, when the peer group isn't so prominent in their lives. In the meantime, I'll yield to youth ministers and youth leaders. When dealing with the prevention of "crushes," the modus operandi is to show equal attention to everyone. As a student leader, be sure you give equal and undivided attention to the good looking and the not so attractive, the athletic and the nonphysical, the popular and the not accepted, the rich and the poor.

## MENTALLY

Believe it or not, teenagers are beginning to think. At this time, teenagers move from the question of What to the question of Why. This can be unnerving for parents and for those who work with teenagers. I'm sure my parents wondered if my brain cells as a teenager were functioning, even minimally. My sarcastic mouth with "why" questions, often got me in more trouble than I care to remember.

The "why" question cannot be ignored. Teenagers are learning to define their tastes, values, and preferences. So they ask Why a lot. Of course, parents and adults don't always have the answers. So be honest with them and admit, "I really don't know."

This shift from nonthinking to opinions and beliefs is a great opportunity for adults to assist young people in the shaping of their tastes, values, and preferences. Some young people have moved into their adult lives with a love for alpine experiences and the great outdoors because I led them into those experiences. Other young people have pursued particular careers and ministries after I introduced them into specific professions and ministries. Still others have enrolled in Christian colleges and universities after I talked to them about those particular schools. Many young people have given their lives in the service of Christ because I introduced them to Jesus. This may sound arrogant, but it's not meant to be. I simply want to point out that ordinary people can have a tremendous influence in helping teenagers shape their tastes, values, and preferences.

How can adults help teenagers think? One way would be to challenge them to think for themselves. Help them realize that MTV, BET, VMAs, Latin Fusion TV, MuchMusic (Canada), or any part of the music industry doesn't think for them. Yet it does try to shape their thoughts according to its lyrics and subtle messages. These messages form beliefs that could be coined as the MTV Statement of Faith. It consists of four ways of thinking and living that include "Whatever"; "Keep it real"; "Stay true to yourself"; and "Follow your heart." To help students with their thought processes, student pastors must get beyond their beliefs to the reasons behind them and then provide a biblical response for the student to follow. Here is the underlying meaning of this musical Statement of Faith that students need to consider:

1. "Whatever." It doesn't matter (see Colossians 3:25). You don't matter. When one says "Whatever," he or she is saying "Who cares?" "Whatever" takes nothing seriously. It often has no standards of behaviors and says, "Don't judge me." It disrespects authority.

2. "Keep it real" (see Colossians 3:17, 23). The statement is an excuse to do whatever you want, as long as you are sincere and believe in it. It allows one to stay in the status quo. It says, "You can do what you feel is right." This contradicts the Scripture's command that teens and adults should "do everything in the name of the Lord Jesus" (v. 17).

3. "Stay true to yourself." (See Jesus' call to deny yourself in Matthew 16:24; Mark 8:34; Luke 9:23). Being "true to yourself" is a call to do what makes you feel good (i.e., self-gratification and self-glorification). This message removes the teen (or any who embrace the message) from any rules or any authorities. It is to do what is right in one's own eyes (Proverbs 30:12). This message also disregards the need for change.

4. "Follow your heart" (see Jeremiah 17:9; Isaiah 44:20; Mark 7:21–22; Titus 1:15). This is an excuse to indulge oneself. Often it means to follow shallow or unreliable feelings that are masked under the term of "love." It becomes an excuse not to think. It can make one emotionally dependent.

Thinking requires hard work, time, and research. The Scriptures have some things to say about thinking. They give young people an explicit grid by which to measure their thought lives. For example:

- "For as he thinks within himself, so he is" (Proverbs 23:7 NASB).
- "Therefore, prepare your minds for action" (1 Peter 1:13 NASB).
- "Finally, brothers and sisters, whatever is true, whatever is noble, whatever is right, whatever is pure, whatever is lovely, whatever is admirable—if anything is excellent or praiseworthy—think about such things" (Philippians 4:8 NIV).

We could reword the Philippians verse without losing its meaning: "Whatever is false, whatever is dishonorable, whatever is wrong, whatever is impure, whatever is ugly, whatever is of a bad reputation, don't let your minds think on such things." Without question, a believer's thought life is where the spiritual battle begins and is constantly fought.

## IDEALISM

Teenagers' expectations of others are off the charts. For whatever reasons, they idealize the perfect parents, the perfect churches, the perfect teachers, and even the perfect world to live in. They think that the grass is greener on the other side of the fence. Unfortunately, no one or no thing can live up to their expectations. As a result, they become disappointed, even cynical of their parents, their teachers, their churches, and the world they live in.

For those living and working among teenagers, do not take their criticisms too seriously. Address them in even-tempered discussions. Teenagers need to know that no one is perfect—and neither are they. They need to be objective rather than subjective when people fail them. Parents and other adults will disappoint them one time or another, but that is not a justifiable reason for teens to wipe them off the radar screen. A teenager's cynicism that's brought on by idealism needs to be channeled into something productive and not just be an empty emotion. During Paul's ministry, the Berean believers were "examining the Scriptures daily to see if these things were so" (Acts 17:11). What a great idea for teenagers to dig into the Scriptures for themselves. First Corinthians 3:7 says, "So neither he who plants nor he who waters is anything, but only God who gives the growth." Regardless of parents' and adults' efforts, they still need the God factor. Without the Lord being involved, nothing of significance will happen.

Finally, teenagers need to be part of the solution and not just observe the problem.

- "As we have opportunity, let us do good to everyone, and especially to those who are of the household of faith" (Galatians 6:10).

- "Let each of you look not only to his own interests, but also to the interests of others" (Philippians 2:4).
- "I want you to be wise as to what is good and innocent as to what is evil" (Romans 16:19).

## ARGUMENTATIVE

Parents have told me that their teenagers argue for the sake of arguing. Exactly! Teenagers are argumentative. Remember, they're beginning to think, so arguing is their version of verbal thinking. Some adults and parents are threatened when teenagers question and argue. As unnerving as this may be, it can actually be a positive thing. Teenagers need help in distinguishing between arguing as an exercise in thinking and arguing as an exercise in trying to convince someone to their point of view. So how do you tell the difference? If a teenager wants to hear my opinion or my side of the story . . . that's an exercise in thinking. If they have no desire to hear my side of an argument . . . that's nothing more than arguing for the sake of arguing. It is highly unlikely that a fourteen-year-old is going to convince me in an argument. But if I sense that they want to hear my side of things, there's a possibility that I just might see it their way. As long as it is an exercise in thinking, adults shouldn't be too concerned. But when they try to persuade a parent or adult to their point of view— that's when the sparks may fly. So let them know up front that you're happy to hear their side of things, but that you have just as strong feelings as they do, no matter what they come up with.

One way to keep the volume level down at the household table is to avoid emotionally charged topics—those subjects that make a parent's face turn red and the neck veins bulge out. Emotionally charged issues include curfew, dating, friends, clothes, hair, social media use, cellphone use, and music. All parents have strong opinions about certain matters. What fosters a combative atmosphere in the home is that parents argue, many times, against the peer group. For example, the daughter may say, "Amy's parents let her stay out past midnight."

At this point, the parent must argue principle and not argue against peer pressure. If the parent argues peer pressure, the parent loses. If the parent argues principle, he or she has a sporting chance.

What is the principle behind not staying out late with Amy? Things tend to deteriorate after midnight!

First Peter 3:15 says, "Always be prepared to give an answer to everyone who asks you to give the reason for the hope that you have. But do this with gentleness and respect" (NIV). Notice two key words that describe the way the parent should respond: *gentleness, respect.* Responding to argumentative teenagers on peer pressure questions is difficult. If the parent blows up and verbally rips them to shreds, the teen will be reluctant to bring up the subject again. Sadly, when this happens, teenagers take their questions elsewhere—to friends, schoolmates, teachers, or employers. But the parent needs to know who their teen's friends, schoolmates, teachers, and employers are.

One more point about arguing: pick your battles carefully. While you want to help shape your teenagers' thinking, you don't want to drive them to exasperation. Ephesians 6:4 says, "Fathers, do not provoke your children to anger, but bring them up in the discipline and instruction of the Lord." *Provoke* can mean to embitter, exasperate, or irritate. There is nothing wrong with having strong feelings and opinions about some matters, and wise teenagers will stay away from those matters that stir up their parents. But when they begin to "push the envelope," parents need to decide if this is worth fighting over. Does it really matter how they wear their hair? Keep principle in mind. If it's principle, argue away. If it's not, lighten up. Remember, teenagers will have questions about many things. Do what you can to keep the communication lines open between you and them.

Teenagers must understand that a boundary may seem unreasonable or an issue may seem insignificant to them, but if it's a hot-button issue with their parents, teens need to obey their parents. The old adage "while you live under my roof" may not resonate with kids, but it still makes sense while they remain on their parents' "payroll." In the meantime, parents should pick their fights carefully and selectively. And those fights should be few and far between. Parents may have to yield some minor battles while they fight the critical ones. When it's a life-and-death matter, figuratively or realistically, then "fight the good fight," stand in the way, be a prude, be stubborn, old, and boring.

## SELF-CENTERED

Teenagers tend to be self-absorbed and have a self-centered focus. Everything that happens to them seems to be unique and exclusive. They exclaim, "I can't believe this happened to me!" or "No one has it as tough as I do!" They don't realize that whatever has happened to them has happened to thousands or millions of others—and that some teens on planet Earth do have it tougher than they do.

Parents and youth workers need to show teenagers that they can learn volumes from other people's experiences. Introduce them to stories of those who have gone before, the experiences they faced, and the lessons they learned. Point out how other individuals are unique, just as they are unique.

# A TEEN'S IMAGINARY AUDIENCE

Teenagers have an imaginary audience; they think they are always on stage. As a result, they are overly concerned about their appearance and behavior. Now you know why it takes teenagers so long to get ready. "Everyone" will be watching them, or so they think. Remember, they are beginning to think. So in their thinking processes, they think that everyone is concerned about them. Of course this isn't true, except in their own minds. This imaginary audience usually diminishes with age. As teenagers mature and celebrate birthdays, the imaginary audience becomes less and less a factor in their lives.

What are adults and parents to do? First of all, they need to be sensitive about teens' public exposure. This is something that needs to be avoided, or at least, parents should know how much their teenagers can handle.

Second, public criticism and ridicule should be avoided. There simply is no place for this when working or living among teenagers. Third, never point out physiological features, no matter how innocent this may seem. Don't put up with it on an occasion. Parents and adults must have a zero-tolerance policy. Don't remind a teenage girl that she has a complexion problem. She already knows. Don't remind a teenage guy that he is skinny. He already knows. Stating facts like this fractures any opportunity for a meaningful relationship with this teenager.

Finally, avoid labels. The problem with labels is that teenagers tend to live up or down to their labels. A teenage guy that's been called "dumb" or a "retard" just might live down to that label. A teenage girl who has been labeled "easy" or a "ho" just might live down to that label. Instead, give teenagers labels they can live up to—hard workers, sensitive, friendly, thoughtful, smart.

I had a teenager in my youth group whose name was L. B. (not his real initials, of course). He was one of those teenagers who didn't know he was goofy even though other kids were making fun of him. L. B. was frumpy, red-haired, and a bit outgoing. It was my practice to give equal attention to all my teenagers, and I gave special attention to L. B. He even tried to morph himself into me by cutting his hair the way I did. That's scary! Later, our family moved to Alberta, Canada, and I lost touch with L. B.

Then one day L. B. called me. It had been almost ten years. Yet he talked to me as if I was still his youth pastor. He was a truck driver and had taken a job that would take him to Edmonton, Alberta, where I lived. This trip would be a "dead-head" trip (meaning he will go up fully loaded but come back empty). He probably wouldn't make any money on it, but he wanted to see me. So we connected at his drop-off location. When he stepped out of the eighteen-wheeler, I couldn't believe how big he was. L. B. was no longer a frumpy, nonathletic kid, but he was a muscular 6-foot 8-inch man. We embraced and had a great weekend together.

We talked about what had taken place in his life. When I last saw him, he was just going into high school. He had gotten bigger and stronger, and discovered a love for football. He started every game on the defensive line. "I love hittin' people, Pastor Steve," he said with a grin. Then after high school, he became a US Army Ranger. During that time, the United States had a problem with a drug lord in Panama who was thumbing his nose at us. So in December of 1989, President George H. W. Bush approved Operation Just Cause, and the US Army invaded Panama and captured General Manuel Noriega, a military dictator and drug trafficker. L. B. was one of the soldiers who helped capture him. As he was parachuting down at night, gunshots whizzed past, barely missing him.

"What'd you do?" I asked. "I shot back. I liked shooting guns, Pastor Steve," he said with that familiar grin. As I listened to his amazing story, I was in awe that this once-upon-a-time teenager in my youth group had made a blip on the "historical radar screen." You never know the positive impact you may have on any teen!

# LATE ADOLESCENCE AND THE MOVEMENT TO ADULTHOOD

This chapter began by noting that physical changes signaling puberty may start as early as age seven. So when is late adolescence and the movement toward adulthood?

Traditionally late adolescence has been between ages eighteen and twenty-two, but now late or delayed adulthood has extended that age. The adult markers that signaled adulthood (i.e., finishing school, employment, marriage, moving out of the parents' house) are being delayed. Some have this extended adolescence going into the late twenties and even early thirties.

Any ministry-minded individual would see this demographic as an opportunity of spiritual need and ministry. I agree. I disagree that this should be an emphasis for those in student ministry. While spiritual needs cross all generations, socially and practically, this age group of extended adolescents should not be included in the ministry portfolio of student leaders and pastors. Regardless of the reasons for this delayed adulthood (bad economy; high employment rate; parents facilitating this extended adulthood; lack of initiative or work ethic; etc.), extended adolescents should be in a motivated fast track to a transition into adulthood, while at the same time achieving some of those adult markers.

# TWO FINAL AREAS

Two final areas bear some greater focus, because they will be crucial to the teen's future role as an adult, and perhaps as parents themselves. Let's consider the teen's development in the areas of making decisions and growing spiritually.

## DECISION MAKING

Ever wonder why fast-food restaurants are so popular with teenagers? It's because teenagers have difficulty making decisions. They go to the counter (or drive-through lane) and order by numbers. The only thing they have to decide on is a number between one and ten and whether to place the order as a super-size or value-size order. Take them to a restaurant where the menu is in cursive, and what do they look for? Burger and fries.

Okay, maybe this is a bit overstated, but what about picking out clothes? What they pick out may seem bizarre to most parents. But adults and parents need to keep in mind that the major difference between an adult and a teenager in the decision-making process is one word: *experience.* Not that adults are necessarily smarter than teenagers, but they certainly are more experienced. Students need help in making decisions. Here are some questions for students to consider before they make significant decisions:

- Is there a conflict or command in the Scripture about this matter?
- What do other people say about it, especially parents or friends who have your best interest at heart?
- Is the Holy Spirit giving you any leading and direction?
- What would help you the most spiritually?
- Do circumstances line up?
- Are there any negative, harmful, or irreversible consequences?
- Once you've made the decision, can you make it work?[3]

A biblical example of a decision maker is Joshua, who made his decision explicitly clear: "Now therefore fear the Lord and serve him in sincerity and in faithfulness. Put away the gods that your fathers served beyond the River and in Egypt, and serve the Lord. And if it is evil in your eyes to serve the Lord, choose this day whom you will serve, whether the gods your fathers served in the region beyond the River, or the gods of the Amorites in whose land you dwell. But as for me and my house, we will serve the Lord" (Joshua 24:14–15).

Have you noticed that teenagers are quick to mouth off? They vocalize the way they see things without any consideration of personal involvement. There's a lot more talk than walk. One day as I was walking on a high school campus, I met a student who had a "Save the Whales" button on her jacket. "What have you done to save the whales?" I asked. "I bought this button!" she said. Wow, talk about involvement!

So how can adults help teenagers as they prepare to make important decisions about their future? Adults must find ways to get teenagers involved in meaningful work. Talk with them about serving others, going to the mission field, or doing evangelism. The next step would be the application of these subjects. Look around. I'm sure there are service opportunities staring them in the face. Take students on a mission trip. Make it an arduous experience, one they will never forget. Or plan an evangelistic event that your teenagers can get excited about. Provide walk with the talk.

## GROWING SPIRITUALLY

The fact that God is a personal God is appealing to young people. But here's the catch: teenagers must move from parental faith to personal faith. I would never want to minimize the faith of parents influencing their teenagers. Parental faith gives teenagers the opportunity to commit to a personal faith. While parents are anxious about their teenagers' faith, the young people themselves must make it their own personal faith.

What does personal faith look like? It begins with a teenager making decisions on their own that are spiritually based. It develops when their spiritual decisions are made and followed even in front of peers. Personal faith continues when those decisions have influence on their future involvement in the kingdom of God. This personal faith is galvanized and codified when they feed themselves spiritually and are self-initiated, when it comes to maintaining their spiritual walks. Scripture explains it this way:

> Though by this time you ought to be teachers, you need someone to teach you the elementary truths of God's word all over again. You need milk, not solid food! Anyone who lives on milk, being still an infant, is not acquainted with the teaching about righteousness. But solid food is for the mature, who by constant use have trained themselves to distinguish good from evil. (Hebrews 5:12–14 NIV)

# A BIBLICAL PERSPECTIVE OF IDENTITY

The biblical concept of self in the Christian is one of the most important issues in ministering to a young person, or any other person for that matter, to discover and establish their self-identity. If our faith is in Christ, then our identity is in Christ. There are a number of characteristics that can be discovered with personal Bible study.[4]

The question "Who am I?" may or may not be a question that a teenager consciously asks himself. But it underlies some of his most basic actions and emotions in the process of self-identity. He is bombarded with this question from all sides, and the answers are varied. In science class, his teacher may declare him the result of an accidental arrangement of atomic elements. Marketers view him as a potential customer. The IRS sees him as a future taxpayer. Politicians see him as a future voter. The sociologist views him as a member of society.

A young person's identity does not depend on pure psychology, human goals and achievements, or societal labels. Each young person's identity and worth—and ours as well—comes because we are held in high esteem by a sovereign God who has informed us of sin and forgiveness.

# IS THERE ANYTHING ELSE?

Overwhelmed? Don't be. All parents and youth workers go through the trials of trying to understand what is happening to their teenagers and how to deal with them. Honestly, I was nervous when my three kids approached their teen years. Being a youth pastor, would I do a good job of parenting my own teenagers? Now that my kids have moved through their teenage years, I can honestly say that I enjoyed those years. Did we get it right all the time? No. But it's nice to look back and see that my kids didn't mind being around dear old dad and mom. We included them in as much as we could. We got involved in their lives. We helped them pursue their dreams. We got on them when they messed up.

The irony in parenting is that you don't become an expert until your kids are grown. From this vantage point, I can look back and see what my wife and I could have done better—along with what worked and what didn't.

The teenage years are only seven years long (give or take a year or two due to various maturation levels). These years are pivotal in the morphing of a teenager into a responsible adult. As a parent, take advantage of the time you have. As a student ministry leader, enjoy your role in partnering with church and parents to help teens grow in esteem and perspective through the power of God's Word and the Holy Spirit.

# NOTES

1. Amanda Gardner, "Study: More U.S. Girls Starting Puberty Early," as cited at Health.com. See http://www.cnn.com/2010/HEALTH/08/09/girls.starting. puberty.early/index.html.

2. Jim Hancock, *Raising Adults: Getting Kids Ready for the Real World* (Colorado Springs: NavPress, 1999), 55.

3. Based on the book Gary Friesen and J. Robin Maxson, *Decision Making and the Will of God* (Sisters, Oreg.: Multnomah, 2004).

4. Neil T. Anderson lists thirty truths about our identity in Christ. See Anderson, *Victory over the Darkness,* 2nd ed. (Eugene, Oreg.: Harvest House, 2000), 51–53.

# 7

## THE ESSENTIAL OF

# INTERGENERATIONAL STUDENT MINISTRY

Okay, the title of this chapter may sound like an oxymoron—intergenerational youth ministry—but think about it: What can be more normal than other generations being a part of ministry to young people/teenagers/students/adolescents/whatever? I'm not trying to get back to "back in the day" days, nor am I trying to sound culturally relevant, even though anyone who knows anything about youth ministry would know that being culturally relevant is a youth ministry mantra. So let's sound culturally relevant while suggesting some "back in the day" common sense.

## COME TO TERMS

Intergenerational ministry has been defined as "transformational relationships: connecting elders and young people and all ages in-between; finding common ground, mutual interests, and places where we 'fill each other's gaps'; building a warm, healthy community. Sometimes, these things can only happen by intentionally creating the appropriate conditions. Other times, it is simply a matter of intentionally recognizing the possibilities in an existing environment."[1] Angie Clark defines it this way: "Intergenerational ministry is ministry that crisscrosses generational lines. It is allowing for ministry of (1) children to adults, (2) teens to children, (3) children to teens, (4) teens to adults in addition to the usual, adult to teens or adult to children. It is not only allowing this kind of interaction, but encouraging it and giving opportunity for it within the church structure at as many levels/ministries as possible."[2]

Contrary to these definitions, many churches tend to segregate the generations, from children to teenagers. Now I would be the first proponent to that kind of ministry segregation. It should be done and done well. But within those segregated groups, other generations need to be integrated into leadership and participation. On the flip side, there needs to be ministry that includes a coming together of the generations. T. Scott Daniels writes that "other church analysts and church leaders are seriously questioning age-specific ministries in at least two ways. First, rising evidence shows that ministries that are not intergenerational may not be as pragmatically valuable as they first seem. Recent studies by George Barna and Mark DeVries suggest that the short-term gains received through age-specific ministries are not consistent over the long haul. Their separate studies indicate that young people raised in age-specific ministries often don't remain in the church after they become adults. Likewise, people who attend age-specific congregations tend to stop attending church altogether when they 'outgrow' their current church."[3] Mark DeVries says it even more succinctly: "Are we connecting our kids to nurturing relationships that will last them after they complete their teenage years, or are we simply exploiting them as public relations tools to make our ministries appear successful?"[4]

There has been much debate on the attrition rate of students leaving the church when they begin college and never returning. There are obviously enough stats to raise alarm regardless of which survey you cite, but to put the blame solely on youth ministry is biased and skewed. Let me weigh in on this ecclesiastical issue with a probable solution. One way to lower the attrition rate among wayward college-age students is to have a vibrant and active college student ministry. This is the link that is missing in many churches between high school and adulthood. The modus operandi for many churches is to utilize their college students as volunteers and workers within the church (at best) or morph them into some adult church group (at worst). College students need to be ministered to, as well, and they still like to have fun, date, do adventurous things, and be challenged . . . similar to . . . youth ministry.

We need to connect our youth with adults during their high school years and beyond. As DeVries writes, "Unless we are making intentional, focused efforts at connecting kids with mature Christian adults in the church (not just their youth leaders), we are more like the vultures preying on kids at rock concerts and less like the spiritual leaders praying that their children's lives would be founded upon eternal things."[5] So somewhere along the way, some purposeful merging of the generations needs to take place, usually in some main church gathering or service. When it comes to "big church," leadership needs to strive toward having parts of the service, from time to time, to "speak" to their younger generations. Something that is said or done or performed or sung needs to catch the attention of the younger, more scrutinizing audience, no matter how minimal it may be. Something needs to resonate with this younger generation, something that they recognize. If you attempt this, there may be a "rub" with some folks. So be prepared.

# A FOCUS ON THE FAMILY

Some common sensibility to intergenerational youth ministry has to include the importance of family. Moms and dads, uncles and aunts, cousins, grandparents—every family member has an important role and most have embraced it, whether for a moment or a season or a lifetime. Yet Western culture can limit these vital interactions. Take mobility. We are everywhere and we go everywhere. Why? Because we can! In many situations, employment determines where we go and what we do. The downside is the distance we've put between the ones we usually trust the most . . . family.

I am no one to talk here. When my wife and I married, we moved from Florida to Southern California. My family was in Florida and her family was in Wisconsin. Now when there are no kids in the picture, this isn't a bad idea. It was just the two of us, no in-laws to run to, just each other. But when kids entered the picture, the absence of extended family became more noticeable. And of all places that I decided to move, was to Edmonton, Alberta, Canada . . . another country! We did all we could to remain connected, but 2,300 mile road trips (one way) got real old real quick (and expensive). So involvement and influence from extended family members was sporadic at best. Whether it's two thousand miles or five hundred, family has been distanced from each other. So anything that comes close to a facsimile of family members is always a good thing.

On the youth ministry side of things, intergenerational means including as much family as possible. I don't mean necessarily doing stuff where the entire family is welcome. I know there have been some good "college tries" here but frankly, sometimes young people need their space as well as their place to simply be teenagers. But I am saying that having parental and grandparental types who are best described as matriarchal and patriarchal in their demeanor, would go far in effectual ministry among young people. Their involvement can be regular or seasonal. But whatever the involvement, it is needed and should be wanted.

# REAL AGE

Now let's be honest, in most church youth ministries, age and maturity are not always top on the priority list of desirable characteristics. It can sometimes be described as more of "young and dumb." This needs to change. It does not have to be one or the other. It really should be a combination of age *and* maturity. Youth ministries need the age, maturity, experience, wisdom, and resources of an older generation. Youth ministries paradoxically need the youthfulness, enthusiasm, energy, technical savvy, and entrepreneurial spirit of a younger generational leader. Even the research says that generations can work and cooperate together. Paul Taylor of the Pew Research Center explores this perceived generational battle in his book *The Next America*, in which he concludes that the generations have more in common than differences; that includes the value of intergenerational cooperation.[6]

Age is relative and unavoidable. Some people under forty are old because they think in old ways. Their age of mentality has caught up with their chronological age. If you begin to think old (or in old ways), then you are old, no matter what chronological age you are.[7] I work in a very fast-paced Christian university (Liberty University), where the founder of the school, Dr. Jerry Falwell, was chronologically an older man (in his seventies). But if you hung around campus long enough, you knew that he never thought old. Things progressed, ideas were exchanged, decisions were made, decisions were changed, and initiative was encouraged. Under this founding president, visions come to fruition . . . everything remained on track and on Message . . . as a direct result of his tutelage and his ageless thinking. Dr. Falwell (who joined his Lord in 2007) was the quintessential example of a patriarch who does not think old and did a most effectual ministry among young college students.

Maybe you've met some vibrant women and men like that in your own church or ministry. When you interact with them, you wish you had a dozen more like them. I had an individual who was on the board of directors with Youth for Christ. He was always thinking of ways to do business so he could make more money to help financially support our ministry (when you're in the support-raising ministry, you really love guys like this). He was fast moving, not afraid to ask, not afraid to give, not afraid to interrupt, not afraid to take a risk, and not afraid to identify with a ministry to teenagers and help make it happen. And he was well in his seventies, playing golf, body surfing, deal making, when he was overtaken by a debilitating and eventual fatal stroke. That one hurt. He was always a source of encouragement. With him, the glass was always half full.

# AN EASY BUTTON

To make it easier for other generations to be involved in youth ministry, you have to make it easy for them. In other words, create ministry situations that make it easy for older generations to interact and minister to the young generation. Let's face it. Teenagers can be a bit intimidating. Thanks to the Internet, they are the most intelligent and most impatient generation ever. (It takes Google .08 seconds to find 85,800,000 sites for MTV.) So who wouldn't be intimidated?

Let me give you an example of "easy." Many ministries are now investing in youth ministry via the development and construction of youth rooms and youth centers. Kind of like a community center with a spiritual dynamic integrated into the program. Sometimes these facilities are in the current church building, or a separate building on the property, or a freestanding structure off the property. But a youth center is a way to making it easy for other generations to be involved. Why? You just show up! "Oh yeah, stand over there and play a game with a teenager." In one youth center I was in, the entire youth center was designed for interaction. There were no snack machines or soda machines. You had to ask an adult for something to eat or drink. All the games were designed for interaction, in that a teen had to "play" against someone, usually an adult. So what's hard about that? Stand there and play. Now that's easy. The kids come to you! Not so threatening.

That is what has to be developed . . . ministry situations where the students have to come to you to engage, to interact, to talk. Situations where it's adults who need to be sought out, where adults are in positions of leadership. I was in one church in Tipp City, Ohio (near Dayton), where the church invested in a youth center (The Avenue) on the church property. The attendance of teenagers in the area was overwhelming. I met a retired individual who became the "go to" person for all the skaters who were coming. Retired guys tend to know how to fix things. They may not know skateboard lingo (decks, ramps, rails, grind rails, etc.) but given a little time, they can figure it out. So this retiree got to know a bunch of middle school students who were all about skateboarding, and loved this man, no matter what his age was. Who knows? Maybe he was a surrogate father or grandfather to a bunch of young teenage boys who needed him in that role.

# A COUPLE OF THINGS TO THINK ABOUT

For a more traditional approach to purposeful placement of older generations in youth ministry, there are some other factors to consider. First, recognize a person's spiritual gifting(s), personal skills, and personality. Some would say that spiritual gifting trumps personal skills and personality. I would disagree. All three must fit succinctly. One may be more prominent than the other but not by much. This may be a bit subjective, as far as your own judgment here. Probably your best "ally" is time . . . time to see how they are doing, the reaction of students, and the gaining of rapport (or lack of) with those students. Are they comfortable around students? Are students comfortable around them?

Second, have permission from the teens, specifically for parents to participate. Not all parents are automatically qualified to be involved with your youth ministry, simply because they have teenagers (or were once teenagers themselves). You know who I'm talking about. They're kind of like pseudo teenagers, either reliving their own adolescent years or they are living their adolescent years vicariously through their own teenagers. Here is a "trick of the trade" in youth ministry. Have parents get permission from their own teenagers to work in their youth ministry. That's right, parents get permission. Either their teenagers won't mind, or there is no way during this lifetime that will happen, or involvement will be conditional. Those conditions will vary from a limited amount of time, to a trial basis. Remember, anyone involved among your students begins on a trial basis.

# *PROGRAMMING* IS NOT A BAD WORD

When we are discussing the matter of intergenerational volunteer leadership in youth ministry, the issue of programming needs to be factored into the equation. *Programming* for some youth pastors/leaders is a bad word. It seems too calculated, and not spontaneous. It is perceived as not having much guidance from the Holy Spirit—heavy on human input and light on spiritual insight. Youth ministry is spontaneous by nature and often spontaneity is equated with the leading of the Holy Spirit. I would suggest that this spontaneity can be experienced in youth ministry programming, giving thought and structure before plans are carried out, while allowing the freedom to change it up or even to abandon plans when appropriate. In the meantime, I think it would be foolish to think that everything will work out if we just let things fall into place, without giving leadership and thoughtful direction. Of course there needs to be room for a bit of entrepreneurial and at times cavalier thinking. But it would be difficult to maintain the confidence of parents and adults if this was a consistent and regular modus operandi. Instead, we should consider Holy Spirit leading, while we plan and program. Within that framework, we allow elbow room to experience things that weren't necessarily planned or programmed, while maintaining some resemblance of structure and knowledge of what is supposed to take place.

## WHAT TO LOOK FOR IN INTERGENERATIONAL VOLUNTEER LEADERSHIP

Many times when intergenerational youth ministry is considered, what the student leaders are really asking is, "Where can I get some adults to run small groups, teach a particular class, etc.?" Again, we need to make this as relatively easy as possible. Not everyone is cut out for teaching, though they can be trained. But the teaching/mentoring/discipleship role is typically a paramount need. Here is what *not* to do. Don't advertise. Putting a "Want Ad" on your website or church bulletin is not the best of ideas. Instead, identify potential intergenerational volunteers. Pray for wisdom and discernment here and don't go it alone. Lean on Holy Spirit guidance and spiritual "advisors."

After that, it's time to let them know of the need and to give consideration to your leadership needs. Let me make some suggestions as to what kind of person to look for:

- easily gains rapport with teenagers
- pretty good "reader" of personalities (among teenagers)
- sensitive to teenagers' individual learning styles
- comfortable with their own age
- not easily agitated
- strives toward a leadership style of servanthood
- an ability to listen
- able to make teenagers feel safe around them
- able to forecast potential problems
- recognizes varying levels of spiritual development among teenagers
- open to partnerships with other intergenerational leaders

- not quick to judge
- willing to take directions as well as a confidence in making suggestions
- spontaneity and a sense of humor (always a plus)
- whether a parent or not, they need think like a parent
- their personal faith is growing and transparent

I know what you're thinking: "In a perfect world . . . maybe." This is an ambitious list. So will you get the entire package in every potential leader? Probably not. But you need to see a combination of these characteristics. For any deficiencies, spell out your expectations to your volunteers. Most of the time, any misunderstandings of this type of ministry relationships result from not knowing what your expectations are. So spell them out. The previous list of suggestions would make a pretty good list of expectations. This will go a long way in building a team of intergenerational leaders for your youth ministry.

With the need for teaching or mentoring or discipleship, let's go back to "easy." The most valuable commodity that adults have is time (it used to be money, but many adults would rather give money than time). So respect that. Your intergenerational leaders may not have the kind of time you have to develop and prepare material for discussion groups, teach small groups, whatever. Provide them the tools and resources to do the kind of job you expect.

Another "trick of the trade": give your leadership a start date and an end date (usually a school year). People are reluctant to get involved when there is no end date. Now that doesn't mean that they will only be involved for that year. Usually volunteers stay on much longer. But at least they have the option. Another thing . . . give them the summer off (this is also beneficial to vocational youth leaders). Modify your ministry plans to accommodate this. Everyone needs a break and many times after a break, people are ready to get back into it, with renewed vigor and enthusiasm.

# BOYS WILL BE BOYS

I was watching a news story. It was an animal story. It seems that in Kruger National Park in South Africa, the game wardens had a baffling problem. Someone was poaching their white rhinoceroses. What was confounding was the fact that the poachers were killing the rhinos but leaving the entire carcass behind. Typically, poachers harvested the tail, feet, and of course, the horn. But whole carcasses were being left to rot in the African sun. Besides the legalities, this simply didn't make any sense. Who would do such a thing?

So game reserve officials had an idea: Put up surveillance cameras in locations where the white rhinos would frequent, particularly watering holes, and see if they could capture the perpetrators on videotape. After a few days, and still no suspects or arrests, officials starting reviewing the tape. To their surprise, it wasn't poachers killing rhinos. It was elephants, specifically orphaned adolescent bull elephants. The cruel irony is that these young bull elephants were without older male elephants in their community, victims of poachers who had slain the adults for their larger ivory tasks. So in an *Animal Planet* sort of way, these young bull elephants had formed their own "gang." Videotape captured them ganging up on white rhinoceroses, antagonizing them by tossing logs, spraying water, and then surrounding them and stomping them to death. A fatal attraction of intimidation.

There were no older bull elephants to put them in place, to keep them in check. So these adolescent bull elephants were virtually doing whatever they pleased, from harassing tourists to killing anything that stood in their way. Game officials came up with a novel idea . . . import older bull elephants. They did and the problem disappeared overnight. Older bulls told the younger bulls to "smarten up" and if they didn't, they were disciplined in an elephant sort of way.

The analogy? We have a problem with our teenage guys. Many are out of control, without any direction or guidance from older males in their lives. So they go about their lives, intimidating, harassing, and hurting anyone in their way. There is a vacuum of older male adults to keep them in check and thus student leaders and pastors will benefit from older male volunteers who can be godly examples for teenager guys.

Whether we like it or not, this sociological phenomenon will have a significant impact as to whom we will be ministering. If there ever was a critical mass in intergenerational youth ministry, this would be it. Now before you think I've abandoned the girls, I haven't. But let's be honest . . . girls tend to follow the "leader."[8] So without intentionally sounding a bit stereotypical, we need to address the guys. The problem is critical. Thousands of boys walk the streets with little support from the services of community, school, or even church. It isn't until they become bad that they attract the interest of the criminal justice system. That is when they get any significant attention, but by that time, it may be too late.

In his book *Angry Young Men*, Dr. Aaron Kipnis presents some sobering facts. Adolescent guys are four to five times more "successful" in their suicide attempts. (This is a bitter difference between the sexes, whereas girls tend to rationalize and become emotional, guys are more determined to carry out the threat.)[9] The Center for Disease Control says that nearly 20 percent of all ninth- to twelfth-grade students periodically carry a weapon to school (the majority of them say it is because they feel threatened). Homicide is the second leading cause of death among young people between the ages of fifteen and twenty-four (ten times higher than Canada). Between five and fifteen million children of working parents are home alone after school. More than half of all juvenile crime occurs between 2 and 8 p.m.[10] These facts point to a desperate need for adults to be involved in the lives of teenage guys

With these enormous ministry challenges, where do we start? Let's start with ourselves. Dr. Kipnis explains that guys need to have a sense that you, as a youth leader, are cool. "What is cool? Being direct, courteous, at ease, authentic, egalitarian and most of all . . . your words come from your heart, and the actions you take demonstrate that no matter how challenging or novel your intervention may look, a bad boy can trust that every move is designed for his welfare, not his subversion."[11] After that, it will take intergenerational youth leaders, more specifically, older mature men, to model and talk about true manhood and fatherhood. With fatherless guys (either physically or emotionally absent), this is paramount. The association with others who are involved in more mainstream routines of work, school, church, and family can be a beacon of normalcy for these guys. These guys need attention and affirmation. They have been getting it in all the wrong places and it is leading nowhere. The element of a faith community, with all their spiritual experiences, can be an anchor that keeps them secure in a storm of turbulent life experiences.

The percentage of disadvantaged and disenfranchised guys (and their girlfriends) has risen dramatically. They are no longer a small fringe group of kids. They are more noticeable now. Intergenerational youth ministry needs to be aggressive in connecting them with their churches and ministries. Make no apologies about your church or ministry, or the fact that you desire for them to be a part of it, even if it's simply for their own good.

# THE POWER OF A CHURCH FAMILY ON YOUTH

To bring this full circle, intergenerational youth ministry is nothing new. But for some, it has been abandoned. It needs to be revisited and it needs to be on purpose. An atmosphere of dependence and need on all the generations should be cultivated, with the right people doing the right things in the right places. What better place to foster community among the generations, than within a church family. For within a church family:

- Everyone benefits.
- Weaknesses can be strengthened by others.
- Inexperience will give way to those who have experience.
- Teachers will have students, and students will be taught.
- Spiritual maturity will trump immaturity.
- Mentors will mentor.
- Teenagers will be reconciled to God, when, for the longest time, they have been estranged from Him.

# NOTES

1. Jennifer Griffin-Wiesner, *Generators: 20 Activities to Recharge Your Intergenerational Group* (Minneapolis: Search Institute, 2005), 2.

2. Angie Clark, "Intergenerational Ministry," handout at National Childeren's Ministry conference, Dallas, June 2005.

3. T. Scott Daniels "Don't Fall into the Gap," *Holiness Today.* (January/ February 2007) http://www.holinesstoday.org/nphweb/html/ht/article. jsp?sid=10005078&id=10008264.

4. Mark DeVries, "What Is Youth Ministry's Relationship to the Family?" Richard R. Dunn and Mark H. Senter III, gen. eds., *Reaching a Generation for Christ* (Chicago: Moody, 1997), 485.

5. Ibid., 485–86.

6. Paul Taylor, *The Next America: Boomers, Millennials, and the Looming Generational Showdown* (New York: Public Affairs, 2014).

7. For a fascinating read on the subject of aging, read Michael F. Roizen and Elizabeth Anne Stephenson, *Real Age: Are You as Young As You Can Be?"* (New York: Harper Collins, 1999). You may be younger than you are or, sadly, older than you really are. This book has nothing to do with your spirituality but everything to do with your physical health. You can also explore their website: http://www.realage.com/.

8. "Elsewhere around the country, school administrators, police, and teachers are seeing a growing tendency for girls to settle disputes through violence. They are breaking up fights in which girls are going toe-to-toe and nose-to-nose, just like the boys. . . . Most experts contend that this trend simply is a reflection of society. In other words, girls are more violent because society in general is more violent and less civil. These experts say the same breakdowns blamed for violence among boys are finally catching up to girls. . . . Authorities say this

is symptomatic of a disturbing trend around the county: Girls are turning to violence often and with terrifying intensity. 'We're seeing girls doing things now that we used to put off on boys,' former Baltimore school Police Chief Jansen Robinson said." Lee Vukich and Steve Vandegriff, *Disturbing Behavior: 53 Alarming Trends of Teens and How to Spot Them* (Chattanooga: AMG Publishers, 2005), 47–48.

9. Aaron Kipnis, *Angry Young Men* (San Francisco: Jossey-Bass, 1999), 81.

10. As cited in Ibid., 83, 86.

11. Ibid., 229.

# 8

# DEVELOPING SPIRITUAL FORMATION

The opportunity for spiritual formation is a key element in student ministry that distinguishes the church from social agencies that work with teenagers. Social agencies can play a critical role among teenagers, but spiritual formation is at the very core of what student ministry is all about and can play a vital part in the lives of our youth.

Those in student ministry know that much of what they do appears to be social work (activities, programs, mentoring, family support, safe zones, meeting real physical needs, interventions, counseling, etc.), but it has spiritual dynamic that not only motivates student ministers and volunteers, but also provides a spiritual and moral compass. It is also a biblical mandate.

It would be difficult to overlook the admonition in Matthew 28:19–20. "Go therefore and make disciples of all nations, baptizing them in the name of the Father and of the Son and of the Holy Spirit, teaching them to observe all that I have commanded you." This becomes the lens we look through when it comes to doing what we do in student ministry, as well why we do what we do. Obviously there will be some variance when it comes to points of emphasis for different denominations (denominational distinctives) as well as some theological differences, but hopefully we will see some commonality when it comes to spiritual formation. While our focus group is among students, there's no doubt that spiritual formation is critical at any age, as well as always being in process.

It would be easy to categorize spiritual formation as discipleship. While different ideas present themselves when we use the term *discipleship*, we are striving for a broader approach and much more encompassing involvement when it comes to spiritual formation. This discipleship approach should strive to avoid categorizing spiritual formation as something that is demonstrated only when we are in church or at any other religious or spiritual events or gatherings. Instead, it is this spiritual formation that impacts a student's daily life . . . where it is most needed.

We may overuse the term *relevancy* so I'll suggest another familiar term, *applicable*. Regardless of what synonym you use, a student needs to know that what he or she is taught as spiritual formation will have impact and influence when it comes to the real world that they are living in. While we strive to shape our local ministries to be safe and protected zones for teenagers to be teenagers, we have to prepare our students to be able not only to survive but also to thrive in their real world. The critical ingredient to see this happen is spiritual formation. If we don't believe this, then we need to reconsider our participation in student ministry.

## STUDENT COMPLEXITY

Two aspects of spiritual formation are the characteristics and distinctives of the teenagers themselves. Before we can have any opportunity to minister and disciple teenagers, we must first have a basic knowledge of the inner makings of teenagers. This is in the context of their psychological makeup that includes the social, intellectual, physical, emotional, and spiritual aspects of their complex lives. To add to the complexity of teenagers, there are also groupings within the context of teenagers (clicks or interest groups). Once this has been understood, the youth worker will have a much better approach with their age-appropriate spiritual formation plan.

The youth worker needs to know the world in which teenagers live in order to facilitate spiritual formation. This aspect of student spiritual formation cannot ignore the characteristics and distinctives of the world and culture teenagers find themselves living in. Before we can have any opportunity to minister and disciple teenagers, we must first have a basic knowledge of their world. This is in the context of their world that includes home, school, work, social life, technology, and pop culture in media consumption, all of which make their lives that much more complex. Thus the youth worker strives to get the attention of teenagers in their distracting, entertaining, and often conflicting world of adolescence. With a better understanding—and empathy—for the teens' world, the youth worker will have a more effective approach with their spiritual formation plans.

# THE PREREQUISITE TO SPIRITUAL FORMATION

Before we can instruct and guide students into any spiritual formation, we need to look at the prerequisite for spiritual formation. Before discipleship can take place, the element of evangelism needs to be present among teenagers. Discipleship and evangelism are a part of the same process, and student ministry should reflect a healthy balance of both. Evangelistic methodology becomes a major part of the youth worker's strategy that will complement any spiritual formation and discipleship efforts. The youth worker will need to assess which ministry emphasis bent he or she has when it comes to evangelism or discipleship.

Obviously if one has a good balance of both, that's a good thing. From my vantage point, I have seen students of youth ministry lean more to one side or the other when it comes to discipleship or evangelism. There have been those vocational student pastors who focused on discipleship, so while the spiritual depth was there, the numbers weren't. On the flip side, some students of ministry have focused on evangelism. So while their numbers were strong, the spiritual depth was not. Often it is self-intuitive as to one's bent, but usually a confirmation can come from someone who is close to that individual. Once that has been determined, the youth worker will need to balance out any shortcomings in order to maintain that delicate balance.

This honest assessment (of one's strengths or weaknesses) can have a positive impact on any youth group, with an implementation of student workers using their strengths, while recognizing the strengths and weaknesses of others. The wise student ministry worker will augment any ministry weaknesses with those who resonate with his or her weaknesses.

## EVANGELISM: THE FIRST AND LAST STEP

Evangelism is the first and last step of discipleship. It begins with evangelism and it ends in evangelism. In other words, the end game for the student who has been discipled in spiritual formation will be an awareness of those around him or her who do not have their faith in Christ. This conscious awareness will move the student to somehow engage those who are not of faith in some kind of interaction that will help cause them to become self-aware of their spiritual understanding.

My personal bent is evangelism. So I have had to make a conscious effort to shore up any discipleship or spiritual formation shortcomings. With evangelism being the first and last step of discipleship, it would be the in-between part of this equation that I have struggles with the most. Now for those whose bent is discipleship and spiritual formation, you simply cannot relate. If discipleship and spiritual formation is your spiritual bent and there is nothing more important, demonstration of this is almost second nature. With that said, my spiritual formation efforts included both believers in Christ as well as nonbelievers.

Obviously nonbelievers do not always get it. As the apostle Paul wrote, "The person without the Spirit does not accept the things that come from the Spirit of God but considers them foolishness, and cannot understand them because they are discerned only through the Spirit" (1 Corinthians 2:14 NIV). But I have seen students who were definitely curious; it is something that has a biblical parallel. Acts 8 tells us a great story of curiosity shown by an Ethiopian official who was "seated in his chariot, and . . . reading the prophet Isaiah." Prompted by the Holy Spirit, "Philip ran to him and heard him reading Isaiah . . . and asked, "'Do you understand what you are reading?'" The man replied, 'How can I, unless someone instructs me?' And he invited Philip to come up and sit with him" (28–31).

## SPIRITUAL FORMATION FOR NONCHRISTIANS TOO

The treasurer of Ethiopia was not a student as we know it, in the context of adolescence, but he surely was a student (wanting to learn). We have an incredible opportunity to address the curiosity of students who are not of faith, but still have questions. In some cases, the questions are obvious. In other cases, the questions need to be suggested. The core element here is what the Scriptures tell us. This should be our starting point. It is an incredible experience to walk with a student who is seeking but doesn't always know what they're looking for. Yet, because of a nurturing relationship, we have an opportunity to walk with them, no matter how temporary, and seek answers. The culmination of this journey is seeing this student come to faith in Christ as a direct result of being there at the very beginning of his or her spiritual formation. So I would suggest that nonbelievers can be discipled but his or her starting point is from the beginning as well as limited in spiritual formations, whereas with believers, the starting points should be progressive. Obviously there needs to be a distinction between one who is seeking and searching, in comparison to one who has found the Way.

This spiritual interaction is a quintessential example of discipleship being a journey and not an arrival. The apostle Paul wrote that for believers God "gave us the ministry of reconciliation" (2 Corinthians 5:18). The word *reconcile* means to close the distance between two parties that have been estranged from one another. We typically see the terms *reconcile* and *estranged* referring to divorce proceedings. An estranged husband or wife is separated . . . the person has distanced oneself from the spouse. When the two are reconciled, they are brought back to each other or reunited—in essence, the distance is closed between the two. So if we are doing the ministry of reconciliation, we are helping students who have distanced themselves from God to close that distance. Hopefully, our involvement in this ministry of evangelistic discipleship will shorten that distance and will result in these two estranged parties being reconciled completely.

## SERVANT EVANGELISM

Servant evangelism is one approach that is gaining traction in churches and among students. It's something they can literally get their hands on. I think the balancing part is the giving a cup of water as Jesus described (Mark 9:41), and letting people actually see Jesus in us. Then the next step would be how we move the relationship and experience further to a realization of Christ (what He can do for them and how they can experience it). It may take more time, but I would think that it would also produce fruit "that remains."

Servanthood and evangelism should go hand in hand. There are those as well who tend to raise this ministry involvement to the level of sharing the gospel. Giving a cup of cold water or doing similar humanitarian deeds can facilitate us (as believers) to earn the right or privilege to be heard. So it's not an either/or option. It's both. Ministering among students should include those issues that have been deemed "social justice issues." These issues should fall into a qualifying scriptural grid that includes Proverbs 31:9 (KJV) that identify the "poor and oppressed." Mark 3:5 (TLB) says of Jesus, "he was deeply disturbed by their indifference to human need." Psalm 72:4 says, "May he defend the cause of the poor of the people, [and] give deliverance to the children of the needy." God calls on us to "defend the weak and the fatherless: uphold the cause of the poor and needy" (Psalm 82:3 NIV). There certainly are a number of worthy social justice issues, but in the world of student ministry the focus should be on the moral issues and people who are deemed the underserved, disadvantaged, unprotected, and preyed upon (e.g., the unborn, children who are victims of human trafficking, orphans, and the homeless).

# SPIRITUAL FORMATION AND EVANGELISM WITHIN THE CHURCH...A DELICATE BALANCING ACT

If you believe that discipleship and evangelism are critical parts of any student ministry, then your ministry should reflect a healthy balance of both. Generally speaking, churches (and student ministries) find themselves in one of two categories: the Outside-In Church (evangelism focused); the Inside-Out Church (discipleship focused). The Outside-In Church focuses intentionally and solely on reaching the lost. These are often called seeker-sensitive or seeker-driven churches. Such churches do a great job at evangelism, engaging the community, and applying the Bible to everyday life. Often they grow rapidly. They typically do a poor job at retaining people, discipling people, and getting below the surface biblically. They have high salvation and baptism numbers, but are often focused more on making decisions than making disciples. Their growth continues because the new converts have more relationships with nonbelievers than with those who have been in church a long time.

In contrast, the Inside-Out Church focuses on the believers in the congregation. Their philosophy is that if we are growing believers, then they will reproduce. They do a great job at discipleship, taking people deep in God's Word, and retain attenders better than the Outside-In Church. Their downfall is that they get so internally focused that they never make much of an impact in the community and reach very few unchurched. Most new members are transfer members from the Inside-Out Church up the street looking to go deeper. Also they develop deep, biblically trained people who do not reproduce nor make connections with those in the world and tend to be religious. Biblical application tends to be nonexistent in many cases, because the focus is on deeper understanding and knowledge of Scripture. Inside-Out Churches that are not growing always use the excuse that they are not growing because they are more focused on discipleship. They see a church growing exponentially and instead of praising God for revival, they express doubts that can be characterized by statements like "Well, that church must not be teaching the true gospel," or "churches don't grow like that," or "they must be an entertainment-driven church," or "they are neglecting discipleship."

There needs to be a balance. Are discipleship and spiritual formation most important? Yes! Is evangelism most important? Yes! To me this is not a contradiction. If evangelism is the first and last step in discipleship, then evangelism leads to a response for Jesus, growth takes place through the discipleship process, and in that process the student will get to a point where he or she reproduces (evangelism). By definition, discipleship has a level of reproducing. To be a disciple is to become like the one you are a disciple of. We must be a church that reaches people and a church that believes it is the responsibility of every believer to advance the gospel. We cannot abdicate our responsibility as believers to fulfill the Great Commission. Some don't share their faith because they use the excuse that they don't have the gift of evangelism. We are all called to advance the gospel. Either the Great Commission is for everyone or for some. I believe it is for all. The one with the gift of the evangelist will just do it more easily and reach more people (e.g., Billy Graham).

It is never easy to just open up and begin sharing about Jesus if you know someone is totally against Jesus, but we have to do it and a disciple wants to do it out of love. A compelling passage of Scripture is 2 Timothy 1:7, "For God gave us a spirit not of fear but of power and love and self-control." The Scriptures challenge us to be bold in our faith. We must open our mouths and share our faith. Paul asked, "How are they to hear without someone preaching?" (Romans 10:14).

When we plan events, services, and talks, we should be thinking about both the unbeliever and the believer. The large-group gathering could be considered more of an entry point for unbelievers. Every communicator should ask themselves two questions. First, "What do I want them to know?" Second, "What do I want them to do?" If you cannot answer these questions then you shouldn't present the message. Every speaker of God's Word should present every message with the intent of transformation as the goal. If we are not speaking for transformation then we are just doing an academic exercise.

# PURPOSES AND METHODOLOGY OF SMALL GROUPS

## THE PURPOSES OF SMALL GROUPS

In student ministry, small groups are designed to take each student deeper in their walks with God and provide the strategy for discipleship. These groups really challenge students in their personal faith and time with God. These groups are designed to train students how to feed themselves, how to use their gifts, and how to share their faith. Student ministry is not healthy until you have a consistent flow of students on student evangelism, or reproduction. If your students are not reproducing then they are not healthy. Proper discipleship would suggest that a seventeen-year-old teenager who has been a Christian for eight years should be spiritually reproducing. If a teen has not reproduced his or her faith with anyone, then someone has dropped the ball on the discipleship and spiritual formation end of things.

This again shows how evangelism and discipleship go hand in hand. Student ministry should challenge and empower believers to grow to maturity, serve the church, and share their faith. Student ministries that have large crowds without spiritual growth are partly responsible for the statistics on college students leaving the church. Student ministries that focus on fattening their kids on the Bible without application and without challenging them to evangelism are breeding teens with a consumer mentality. It is critical to constantly ask those around you about how you are doing in both arenas. The pendulum swings back and forth on this, so you need to make sure that you stay in the middle on your focus. Evangelism and discipleship are equally important. Numerical and spiritual growth seem to be correlated. Student ministries grow numerically, plateau for a time in order for spiritual growth to catch up, and then the process is repeated.

## THE METHODOLOGY OF SMALL GROUPS

When it comes to approaches for effective small groups, here are some strategies you can use—practical suggestions for effective small groups:

1. *Make sure the group meets the needs of individuals.* There must be something in it for the individual student.
2. *Base the groups on common interests.* The most basic groups are probably by gender. Have separate small groups of guys and girls. Other groupings could be by sports interests, e.g., skateboarders or team sports. Depending on size you could have small groups by year in school: freshmen, sophomores, juniors, and seniors.
3. *Have some diversity in personality within each group.* This enhances group interaction. The group should have both quiet, compliant kids and outgoing kids.

4. *Gain a commitment from the students to be a part of the group.* This will prevent students from feeling forced into the group. It also gives group members a sense of responsibility.

5. *Assure members that their group will be safe.* Do not allow rude or vicious comments. Members should be able to express feelings without attacking others in the group.

The time frame for small groups is a bit subjective, but I would recommend a shorter time frame (four to six weeks) over a lengthy time frame (months), with an option to extend the small group meetings. Shorter time frames will encourage more students to participate, as well as fostering students to meet more often (than less often). I always want students wanting more, than less. Plus it will give other students the opportunity to join a small group, with the frequency of renewed time frames. If a small group ministry is meeting weekly (for convenience and consistency of scheduling), then youth leaders will need to modify their teaching in order to accommodate irregular attendance. There have been some student ministry practices that include both large and small group, with an individual being the master teacher (teaching everyone), then breaking up into smaller groups for the sake of discussion and better personal interaction. The objective is to somehow make the big seem small.

Here are several basics of managing a small group:

1. *Practice positive nonverbal behavior.* Have strong eye contact and a listening posture as members speak, and have everyone seated at the same level.

2. *Insist on proper communication.* Allow no put-downs and listen when someone else is talking. Everyone gets an opportunity to participate.

3. *Announce the purpose of the group.* Everyone should know why you are meeting.

4. *Choose commitment.* Group members should be there unless there is an emergency or death in the family (or your own). Be on time, stay until the end, and contribute.

5. *Learn to listen actively.* The leader can paraphrase, summarize, and clarify.

6. *Learn to ask open-ended questions.* These are questions that cannot be answered with yes or no, such as "How," "What do you think of . . . ," "What would it be like if . . . "

7. *Be willing to redirect the group* when it goes off track.

8. *Be willing to gently confront* members who are disruptive.

9. *Develop and share leadership* within the group.

10. *Build group cohesion.*

11. *Summarize what the group has accomplished* (closure) and make people aware of the next meeting time and place.

# WHAT DOES SPIRITUAL FORMATION LOOK LIKE?

The expected practices of spiritual disciplines should include daily Scripture reading, prayer, church attendance, and lifestyle choices that do not include partying, drugs, alcohol, or tobacco. Then there's a level of spiritual formation that involves fasting (not just food), the participation in the church ordinances of baptism and communion (the Lord's Supper), the practice of church liturgy, and one that is becoming more difficult (mainly due to the ubiquitous presence of Wi-Fi access to online sources) . . . solitude.

There's no doubt that these practices of spiritual formation are important and will develop an apparent spirituality among students. These practices need to be taught, explained, and exemplified. But there has to be caution here. There should be an avoidance of characterizing these spiritual formations as a legalistic expectation of performance. If this happens, failure becomes something that is frowned upon, discouraged, and shamed.

I attended a conference at Lake Louise in Alberta, Canada, called the Graham School of Evangelism. One of our speakers announced (somewhat tepidly) that he was not 100 percent with his daily devotional time with God. This was the first time I ever heard someone admit that, although my guess was that there were many of us who resonated with his "confession." He went on to explain that while he wasn't 100 percent, he was consciously aware of this and strived to compensate any time that he had neglected with God, not out of guilt but out of simple obedience that is often compensated with forgiveness and grace. It reminded me that with our humanity we have a tendency to do wrong.

So our attention should not be focused on performance. Instead, these spiritual formations should be conveyed as outward expressions of a love for God and wanting to know Him better, as well as loving those who He loves. "The truth is that Christian growth and progress is coming to the realization of just how weak and incompetent we are and how strong and competent Jesus continues to be for us. Spiritual maturity is not marked by our growing, independent fitness. Rather, it's marked by our growing dependence on Christ's fitness for us."[1]

Some qualities that will reflect a vibrant spiritual formation would include *a love for God* (Mark 12:30) that includes regular participation in corporate and individual worship, and has an understanding of foundational doctrines (i.e., sin, the exclusiveness of Christ, the role of the Holy Spirit, the Trinity, etc.). *Faithfulness to God and to others* (Romans 12:1, 2, 10) is demonstrated by keeping appointments and commitments. *Being a student of Scriptures* (2 Timothy 2:15) includes times of Bible study, behavioral change, and using Scripture as a grid for daily decisions. *Prayer* can almost be considered a default quality but this goes beyond regular prayer times. Prayer is incorporated into daily circumstances and is offered freely to others. *Critical decision making* (1 Kings 3:1–15) is another quality that incorporates the Holy Spirit guidance, experience, and reason. *Being a lifelong learner* (2 Timothy 3:14) is a quality that manifests itself in thoughtful questions as well as being a critical thinker.[2] *Being an example of a leader* (1 Thessalonians 2:8) is a quality that manifests itself as a godly example, both in word and deed. Finally, there is a *commitment to a community of faith* (Hebrews 10: 19–25). This spiritual formation values the gathering and fellowship of both the local body of believers as well as the identifying with the church at large, both with local assemblies and those ministries that work outside the walls of local churches.

Identifying and using one's spiritual gifting becomes an effective tool in the ministry of the kingdom. While I do believe that some have the gift of evangelism, it certainly doesn't exclude those who do not from evangelism. It's just a matter of using their gifting regardless, though evangelism may be a bit more difficult for them, both in methodology and motivation.

This can be an exciting experience when it comes to spiritual formation and discovering one's spiritual gift(s). There are plenty of online resources that identify spiritual gifts, as well as provide spiritual gifting assessment tests. These tests may not be an exact science and can be influenced by denominational doctrinal distinctives, but they certainly can give a strong indication as to one's spiritual gift(s). It might be wise to take several assessments to find any recurring conclusions. Beyond assessment tests, it's hard to dismiss the conclusions of spiritually minded people who have observed students and have seen those spiritual gifts in action. If a student has a propensity to help others, that would indicate to me that they have the gift of helps and that servant evangelism is something that comes easy for them.

# SPIRITUAL FORMATION AS A PROCESS

Spiritual formation is a process and continues through an individual's lifetime. The opportunity and challenge we have in student ministry is facilitating that process both in introduction and progression. This window of opportunity is a brief one but regardless of the challenges, spiritual formation is why we do what we do in student ministry. The nurturing of students' spiritual formation is our message, mission, motivation, and mandate.

One final thought: *Spiritual formation is about drawing students to Christ…not us.* Any discipleship program or spiritual formative relationship should always be one that develops students toward Christ Himself. The dependence should be on Christ and not us. While this may sound like conventional wisdom, this sensitive and important relationship can be easily tainted when the student being discipled becomes dependent on their "discipler." Let's remember and practice Paul's perspective, "What then is Apollos? What is Paul? Servants through whom you believed, as the Lord assigned to each. I planted, Apollos watered, but God gave the growth. So neither he who plants nor he who waters is anything, but only God who gives the growth" (1 Corinthians 3:5–7).

---

# NOTES

1. Tullian Tchividjian, "Rethinking Progress, December 30, 2011, *Youth Worker*, http://www.youthworker.com/youth-ministry-resources-ideas/youth-ministry/11662800/.

2. One listing of qualities of a critical thinker can be found on the website studymode.com, http://www.studymode.com/essays/Attributes-Of-a-Critical-Thinker-578696.html. Among the attributes listed are: (1) asks pertinent questions; (2) assesses statements and arguments; (3) is able to admit a lack of understanding or information; (4) has a sense of curiosity; (5) is interested in finding new solutions; (6) is able to clearly define a set of criteria for analyzing ideas; (7) is willing to examine beliefs, assumptions, and opinions and weigh them against facts; (8) listens carefully to others and is able to give feedback; (9) sees that critical thinking is a lifelong process of self-assessment; (10) suspends judgment until all facts have been gathered and considered; (11) looks for evidence to support assumption and beliefs; and (12) is able to adjust opinions when new facts are found.

# 9

# THE ESSENTIAL OF

# BIBLICALLY CENTERED TEACHING

Imagine it's late afternoon on a Wednesday and the students will show within two hours. You still are not sure what to speak on tonight. The game is planned. The food has been purchased. The room is all set up. The band has told you they have their worship set rehearsed and ready to go.

But there you sit . . . and the lesson is just not coming together. Maybe you can pull one out of your file. There is always the option of that sermon website your ministry friends have been telling you about. Or maybe you could just do one of those "open question" talks and ask the students what they want to talk about. They seem to like that one.

You are feeling it. Something is eating you up inside. This has become so old and so dry. Is this all there is? Is there a better way? Just then the AWANA's verse you memorized as a child comes flooding through your mind, something about studying to show oneself approved to God (2 Timothy 2:15). Then another verse comes back to your attention and hits you hard, "Not many of you should become teachers, my brothers, for you know that we who teach will be judged with greater strictness" (James 3:1). Something has to change. But where do you start?

# FIRST THINGS FIRST

In the next two chapters we will be taking a look into some basic principles on lesson development. This chapter will start with the larger picture, and the next chapter will focus on the specifics of the individual lesson. We will be looking into more of the hermeneutical (preparation) side of teaching and not necessarily the homiletical (presentation) side of teaching. There are great resources for both of these elements of biblical teaching available, and I would strongly encourage you to pursue them. There are some timeless classics, such as *Lectures to My Students* (D. L. Moody) and the more recent *Biblical Preaching* (Haddon Robinson). If you have completed various educational courses in biblical preaching or teaching, you may already have these books or others written by noted Bible professors. I have incorporated several of these books into my own classes.

Do not let go of the classics. When you walk into a Christian bookstore, walk by the front display and go directly to the back of the store. This is where you find the classics. As the writer of Hebrews counsels, "Remember your leaders, those who spoke to you the word of God. Consider the outcome of their way of life, and imitate their faith" (Hebrews 13:7).

# THE DEFINITION OF BIBLICAL TEACHING

By no means do I have the direct line from God regarding the exact definition of biblical teaching. But here is one definition. Please read it carefully and process it. I sincerely believe this definition to be based on the Word of God. *Biblical teaching* is presenting and representing God's Word accurately, completely, clearly, and practically both through our words and through our lifestyle.

Please note biblical communication starts with *God's Word*. We are merely His representatives (2 Corinthians 5:20). Teaching the Word *accurately* is seen in 2 Timothy 2:14–16. Teaching the Word *completely* is what Paul reminded the leadership at Ephesus he did for them in Acts 20:27. Paul teaches the Colossians to make sure they speak God's truth *clearly* as they should (Colossians 4:4). And of course the Word is to be taught *practically* for each of us to become more like Christ (2 Timothy 3:16). Finally, Paul admonishes Timothy that we teach with *words and through our lifestyle* (1 Timothy 4:16).

As a student ministry leader, now that you see the very essentials of teaching in this definition, just imagine having a room full of teenagers who were like the audience listening to Ezra about 2,500 years ago:

So Ezra the priest brought the Law before the assembly, both men and women and all who could understand what they heard. And he read from it facing the square before the Water Gate from early morning until midday, as he in the presence of the men and women and those who could understand. *And the ears of all the people were attentive to the Book of the Law.* (Nehemiah 8:2–3 italics added)

# THE PROCESS OF BIBLICAL TEACHING

The process of teaching starts with God as He moves to you to speak His truth in His way.

## IT STARTS WITH GOD

The phrase "word of the Lord" is used 230 times in the Scripture in the NIV. The phrase "word of God" is used 39 times in the Scripture in the NIV. The word we speak must be the Word that initiated with God. As the apostle Peter wrote to his readers in 2 Peter 1:20–21, "No prophecy of Scripture comes from someone's own interpretation. For no prophecy was ever produced by the will of man, but men spoke from God as they were carried along by the Holy Spirit."

Although by no means exhaustive, the following list is a good sample of Bible passages showing God as the initiator of communication to humankind. Take some time and work through these Scriptures.

## THE GOD WHO INITIATES

| TEXT: | DESCRIBE THE SCENARIO: |
|---|---|
| Genesis 1 | |
| Genesis 15:1, 4 | |
| Exodus 9:20-21 | |
| Exodus 19:7; 20:1 | |
| Deuteronomy 8:3 | |
| 1 Samuel 3:1-7 | |

## IT MOVES TO YOU

As one recognizes the truth that teaching God's truth started from God as the initiator, we must now see that God calls people to speak His truth. Some prominent biblical examples are:

- Samuel (1 Samuel 3:4–19)
- Jeremiah (Jeremiah 1:3–5)
- Peter (Matthew 4:18–19; Mark 1:17; Luke 5:10)
- Paul (Acts 9:15)
- Timothy (Acts 16:1–4)

Many of you reading this book may have sensed the specific calling of a pastor and/or a church leader as taught in 1 Timothy 3:1. If you have, I trust you can articulate your own calling and can relate to the calling of the personalities above. Yet others reading this may not see themselves as called into what the Christian community entitles "vocational ministry." Therefore, does this sense of calling and even this content on teaching matter to you? Absolutely! When we come to Christ, we are all His witnesses, ministers, and ambassadors. We are all called to communicate the message of salvation to the lost (Matthew 28:19; 2 Corinthians 5:18–19) and to teach and admonish the saved (Colossians 3:16). This is not a spiritual-gift issue, where one can push back by saying, "I am not called to speak God's message; I am just called to live it." Each believer is called to speak God's truth to the lost, and each believer is called to speak God's truth to believers. Again, do not confuse spiritual gifts and specific ministries with the broader sense of each believer's calling to speak up for the Lord. Therefore, to my "lay worker" friends, do not skip over this chapter. Read it and glean from it. There will be principles you can incorporate into your own life and personal ministries, especially us as parents. In addition, each one of us is called to discern what our leaders are teaching (1 Thessalonians 5:19–22).

## IT IS PRESENTED AS GOD'S TRUTH

The emphasis of biblical communication must be God's Word! Many Bible teachers—myself included—share a deep concern over the shallow teaching and preaching that is taking place within the church. In the midst of our explosion of creative teaching, my concern is whether we've moved away from keeping the Word of God as the emphasis of teaching. For example, I believe in the use of "object lessons" in my own teaching and even have our students prepare such a talk in their communications course. Yet the principle I seek to drive home in class is "Be sure the audience remembers the lesson (the scriptural teaching) of the object lesson."

Another great concern I have is the continual moving away from sound teaching as our culture shifts more into a secular and even anti-God mindset. I do not even need to mention recent "hot topics" as even more social issues may be added to the "redefined" list by the time you read this. As I teach my students: Do not be a Pharisee by adding to the Scripture yet do not be a Sadducee by taking away from the Scripture. Study the story surrounding Jesus being confronted by the Sadducees during the Passion Week.

When questioned about the issue of marriage in the resurrection (by leaders who did not believe in the resurrection), Christ replied with a frank response, "You are in error because you do not know the Scriptures or the power of God" (Matthew 22:29 NIV).

Checkmate . . . end of game . . . boom. Jesus rebukes leaders who do not use the Scripture in its context and leaders who do not know the power of God. What an incisive reply. Also note "the power of God" is seen as synonymous with the Word of God (Hebrews 4:12). How can one say they have the power of God as they take Scripture out of context or ignore the Scripture altogether? Good teachers will stick with the Word of God (2 Timothy 4:2).

Before moving ahead, note the sequence of how we have been given God's truth and think through what this sequence teaches us.

## HOW GOD REVEALS HIS TRUTH

FATHER GOD → JESUS CHRIST → THE APOSTLES → US TODAY

1. The message and authority comes from God (John 1:1–14; 8:28; 14:10).
2. God gave Jesus Christ His message and authority (Matthew 28:18–20).

3. Jesus gave this message and authority to the apostles (Acts 1:1, 8; 2:42).

4. The apostle have given it to the church; now we are to speak this message with authority to others (2 Timothy 2:2; Titus 2:15).

## IT IS PRESENTED IN HIS WAY

It is one thing to speak God's Word, yet it is another to speak it in His way. As already noted, *not* speaking it in His way can happen when we present verses out of context or soften and possibly silence a text in order to be politically correct. Yet there also can be the issue of abusive teaching. Each one of us may know someone, maybe even ourselves, who was deeply wounded by someone speaking the Word yet doing it in a way that was truly not edifying. Instead of the Word being used carefully as a surgeon would use a scalpel, the speaker uses the Word to take a scalp! The old phrase "People don't care how much you know unless they know how much you care" is more than a thought-provoking phrase. Proverbs speaks of confrontation as faithful wounds and yet these wounds are more readily received from someone who cares (Proverbs 27:6). I would value more Christian leaders studying and applying Galatians 6:1–5 before they start wielding the sword of truth like a battle axe instead of a surgeon's tool. As Proverbs 25:11 states, "A word fitly spoken is like apples of gold in a setting of silver."

Another area of caution is for the speaker to know the audience to whom he or she is speaking. Even as I am writing this, I recognize there is the potential of a variety of age groups, educational training, denominational background, and ministry experience. So I am seeking to reach all these readers from different audiences and have each one believe he or she is learning without the feeling of being either overwhelmed or underwhelmed. What a challenge! The issue is obvious—we do not know each other.

As a guest speaker I consult my host to learn about the audience before I prepare my talk. As a professor, I seek to know my students as quickly as possible. Yet the most intimate of ministry relationships would be as a student ministry leader. Knowing the sheep as Jesus taught us to do is paramount to being able to connect the right word with the right student at the right time and at the right level of comprehension. And all of God's people said, "Right!"

As you consider the following four points of communicating God's Word in God's way, please search these Scriptures for yourself. Let your time studying these passages shape you and equip you to be the leader who correctly communicates His eternal truth:

1. Speak God's Word with boldness and authority (Acts 4:29, 31; 9:28; 13:26; 14:3; 18:26; 19:8; 28:31; 2 Timothy 4:1–4; Titus 2:15).

2. Speak God's Word with His power (Acts 1:8; 4:33; 6:8; 7:22; 9:22; 10:38; 19:20; 1 Corinthians 2:4; 4:20; 2 Corinthians 6:7; Ephesians 6:10; Philippians 3:10; Colossians 1:29; 1 Thessalonians 1:5).

3. Speak God's Word with grace and tact (Colossians 4:6).

4. Speak God's Word with the understanding of the spiritual level to whom you are speaking (Acts 26; 1 Corinthians 3:2; Hebrews 5:12).

Finally, remember the power of prayer as you prepare to teach and preach. Have others pray on your behalf. Recall the apostle Paul's words:

> Pray also for me, that whenever I speak, words may be given me so that I will fearlessly make known the mystery of the gospel, for which I am an ambassador in chains. Pray that I may declare it fearlessly, as I should. (Ephesians 6:19–20 NIV)

> Continue steadfastly in prayer, being watchful in it with thanksgiving. At the same time, pray also for us, that God may open to us a door for the word, to declare the mystery of Christ, on account of which I am in prison—that I may make it clear, which is how I ought to speak. Walk in wisdom toward outsiders, making the best use of the time. Let your speech always be gracious, seasoned with salt, so that you may know how you ought to answer every person. (Colossians 4:2–6)

# THE COMPONENTS OF BIBLICAL TEACHING

*Logos, ethos, pathos.* It was the Greek philosopher Aristotle who has been given historical credit for developing the three pillars of public speaking. These can be found in his work, *Rhetoric* (Book 1, Part 2). These three axioms of public speaking have been adopted and modified over the centuries, and I will assume these axioms are not new to the reader. One could make the argument that the apostle Paul even used these three components in the Areopagus on Mars Hill while speaking to the Greek philosophers of Athens (Acts 17:16–34). Allow me to develop and paraphrase these three components to being an effective communicator:

*Logos*—(my word: what I say/how I say it)

*Ethos*—(my life: what I live /how I live it)

*Pathos*—(my passion: what I believe/how I believe it)

Let's examine 1 Timothy 4:12–16 and look carefully to see if any of these three components are present. I would argue all three are present. I would even suggest each verse has one as a dominant theme. As you observe any of them, identify them.

> 12Let no one despise you for your youth, but set the believers an example in speech, in conduct, in love, in faith, in purity. 13Until I come, devote yourself to the public reading of Scripture, to exhortation, to teaching. 14Do not neglect the gift you have, which was given you by prophecy when the council of elders laid their hands on you. 15Practice these things, immerse yourself in them, so that all may see your progress. 16Keep a close watch on yourself and on the teaching. Persist in this, for by so doing, you will save both yourself and your hearers.

I would make the argument for:

- verse 12—Ethos
- verse 13—Logos
- verse 14—Pathos
- verse 15—Notice we are to be diligent in the practice of all three areas, so much so that our students can see it evidenced in our personal growth
- verse 16 – Notice the reemphasis of verse 12 (life) and verse 13 (doctrine) and the serious admonition Paul gives to Timothy (and to us). Notice which one is mentioned first. We are being watched. Our lives to speak volumes and our lives will affect our students.

In concluding this section, consider the following questions: (1) Do you find these three components important to effective biblical communication? (2) Is one component more important than the others?

# THE LAYOUT OF A MINISTRY TEACHING PLAN

## BASE THE TEACHING PLAN ON SCRIPTURE

There are two key areas when teaching the Scriptures. First, remember *what we teach* and next, remember *why we teach*. As leaders, we must guard our teaching as based on Scripture—the *what*—and we must seek building our students into full maturity in Christ—the *why*. These two areas are based on some foundational Scriptures.

First, *based on Matthew 28:19–20, we are to make disciples.* This is done as we teach students to obey everything Christ taught the Twelve. The three basic presuppositions in this command are:

- We must teach all the *information* Christ taught in the Gospels.
- We must teach for *application* seeking our students to obey Christ.
- We must teach for *transformation* for students to habitually be conformed to the image of Christ.

Second, *based on Colossians 1:28–29, we are to teach with all wisdom with the goal of each student coming into full maturity in Christ.* Reading through Colossians, one quickly realizes the wisdom referred to is not based on the teacher's strengths, talents, or knowledge, but on the Word of God (3:15–16). We teach the Word in order to present our students to God as fully mature in their faith. This is a serious stewardship issue and should never be taken lightly (Hebrews 13, 17).

Third, *based on the Pastoral Epistles, we are to teach the Word boldly and clearly (1 Timothy 4:13–16; 2 Timothy 4:2–4).* As previously mentioned in this chapter, as pastors this is our highest calling; therefore, as youth pastors we must understand the immense responsibility to teach the Word of God through the examples we live and the lessons we give (1 Timothy 4:15).

Finally, *we are to teach "the whole counsel of God"* (Acts 20:27). Paul so thoroughly equipped the Ephesian church leaders through the Scriptures that he declared he was free of the blood of that city (v. 26). He taught them the encompassing foundation truths that would prepare those leaders to carry on ministry. Paul equipped these people for ministry because he knew he would not always be with them. Obviously Paul had a comprehensive teaching strategy. He taught these people daily for two and a half years—plenty of time to teach the whole counsel of God. I see a tremendous student ministry principle within this passage. As youth leaders, we have these students for only a few years and then they graduate. We must equip them for ministry while they are in school and prepare them for life. We must have a comprehensive strategy for teaching.

## BASE THE TEACHING PLAN ON A SCHEDULE

Do you remember our hypothetical leader at the beginning of the chapter? Everything was ready to go for the evening's youth meeting—well, everything except the lesson. I realize that as you begin to look at the following information you may begin to feel like you are trying to swim in a two-hundred-foot pool. You may not have even considered a five level teaching plan. After all, many youth leaders are simply worried about trying to figure out what to talk on in their next youth meeting. But as we have seen already, teaching God's Word is so much more sober than merely trying to pull off a fast one on the students. And if your goal is to bring students to full maturity in Christ, how does one bring them to this place?

As you begin to process through the following material, my encouragement is not to be overwhelmed. Take what you can and start where you can. And as you have read about in our essential of building a leadership team, use other adults to assist you in these measures.

# DEVELOP AN OVERALL PLAN FOR YOUR DEPARTMENT

In my first youth ministry, someone presented this idea to me. When I first heard this, I actually laughed. I thought how stale and legalistic this would be; yet as I matured in ministry, the more this concept made sense. I know of very successful student ministries who have applied this model to their ministries.

Years ago while in my church in Seattle, I grabbed some "Starbuck's Time" with my dear friend and coworker Monte to talk about the question, "What do we want our students to learn during the time we have them from the sixth to twelfth grade?" As he was the lead with middle school and I with the high school students, Monte and I wanted to develop a big picture approach to our teaching ministry. Since we had a twice-a-week meeting schedule, this meant we had 718 opportunities for a student to learn the Word of God within that time frame. (This did not include our church services, any accountability groups, discipleship appointments, etc.)

## OUR MIDDLE SCHOOL DEPARTMENT PLAN

We began to write out our basic goals. We decided the middle school teaching ministry would focus on:

1. *Biblically centered teaching on salvation.* Both of us had the conviction that too many children have just gone along with the ecclesiastical language of "Jesus in your heart," and we wanted to make sure each student could articulate a genuine, personal, born-again experience.

2. *Teaching basic doctrine.* As much as a middle school student could

grasp these treasures at this particular level, we wanted to cover the simple truths of doctrine. Not necessarily in a traditional catechistic format of oral recitation but to truly begin to engage their minds.

3. *Helping students understand the greater application to the basic stories they learned as younger children.* We did not want to ignore the stories they learned as children yet neither did we want to simply teach them again at a children's level. For example, so Jonah is a really cool kid story, slime and all, but let's now take this story into the realm of why God had prepared the fish. God wants even the ungodly to repent so we need to be ready to share.

4. *Beginning to formulate the foundation to Christian character.* By now you understand we must be about teaching for life change. Yet we desired the students not to mechanically do the right thing (legalism, behaviorism) but to begin to own their faith as they learn a sense of biblically based right and wrong.

## OUR HIGH SCHOOL DEPARTMENT PLAN

While there would be some carry over from middle school, we decided the high school ministry would utilize a four-themed matrix approach. Below is the chart designed for you to use this concept as a planner form for your own topics:

## PLANNING TOPICS FOR STUDENT MINISTRY

| DOCTRINE (how I believe) | APOLOGETICS (how I know) | NURTURE (how I grow) | MINISTRY (how I serve) |
|---|---|---|---|
| | | | |
| | | | |
| | | | |
| | | | |
| | | | |

Some of these topics were done on Sunday mornings (our teaching time). Some were addressed on Wednesday nights (our reaching time). Some were covered at different parts of the year. But I made sure all four areas had significant focus at some point during the school year. So, how are we going to get there? This will not automatically happen. You must be intentional. You must have a strategy. Here was mine:

1. *Doctrine—How I Believe.* Personally, my goal was to cover ten doctrines every two years with the "major" doctrines covered annually. Each time a certain doctrine was taught it would have its own designated series so while a doctrine would be covered more than once, it was not going to be the same series. In other words, the same doctrinal truth but taught in a different series.

2. *Apologetics—How I Know.* As one may understand, doctrine and apologetics are strongly tied together. Doctrine focuses on what is truth, while apologetics focuses on how we know a doctrine is truth. For example, in the doctrine of Scripture one can teach the inspiration and preservation of the Word of God, how we received the canon, the claims of Scripture, etc. Yet in an apologetic series on Scripture, one can teach on the internal, external, and bibliographical evidence that validate Scripture. One of the greatest reasons I believe we are seeing so many of our evangelical students drift away is the lack of solid apologetic teaching. I beg of you, engage their minds, make them think, and do not allow bumper sticker answers!

3. *Nurture—How I Grow.* When we think of growth, we typically think of the needed disciplines of spiritual maturity. This is true. Yet move your students past what they should do to how they can do! Teaching them how they can study Scripture is much more significant than the guilt trip of asking if they read their Bibles. Yet spiritual growth is even broader than a list of disciplines. We want to see students develop a personal, intimate, and obedient walk with the Master. The indicative that a student is truly maturing is how they think, act, and speak when we are not around and they are on their own.

4. *Ministry—How I Serve.* What comes to your mind under this category? It probably has to do with teaching students how to share their faith or serving in the church or community. These are quite true. Teach the spiritual gifts and how to be effective in ministry. But I also would personally focus on various forms of relationships in this category. More than just friends and family, relationships should include our church relationships and responsibilities. Introduce your students to the "one another's" that appear in the New Testament. I would say these are foundational for mature interpersonal personal relationships. And it is through healthy relationships that we learn to serve. I hope your mind is at work right now!

My eventual goal was to develop a repeating three-year middle school plan and a four-year high school plan. For example, in ninth grade we teach doctrine, in tenth we teach apologetics, and so on. The only struggle Monte and I had in building this teaching matrix was the inevitable "problem" of having new students enter into the ministry. Praise God for this type of problem! Where we settled was as laid out above—the four basic categories listed, yet the topics would remain fluid and developed into the annual teaching plan.

One more suggestion would be to develop a personal discipleship "status sheet" each student would maintain, if they so chose to do this format. I was actually moving in this direction in our ministry before I left the church to teach in the classroom. The concept was to have a comprehensive listing of subjects that a student could pursue during their high school years. With a combination of the weekly meetings, special core classes, and personal discipleship times, the student could learn a number of Bible-centered subjects and topics. This way at graduation, the student and we leaders could look back and know he or she had been taught the whole counsel of God. I would encourage you to strongly consider developing something like this within your own ministry. Some ministries do this based on grades, some on topical levels, but develop a plan.

While this may sound extreme to some of you, it at least guarantees the student ministry is focused in its teaching efforts. Sadly, from what I have seen, many youth leaders do not know what they are doing two weeks from now. Maybe having this type of plan should be considered.

## DEVELOP A ONE-YEAR PLAN

Even if you are not ready to build a total ministry picture, you can at least start at this point: a one-year plan. Traditionally many senior pastors develop a yearly teaching schedule. I believe this should be no different within student ministry. There are so many needs, issues, and doctrines that must be taught to our students and we only have (at the most) seven years to do our best to equip them for life. We can either approach our teaching with a reactive method or a proactive method. I prefer to be proactive. Looking over my student ministry career, I greatly valued using a yearly plan within my ministry. This kept me on focus throughout the year and strategic in the curriculum plan. And I still do the same today in the academic world of teaching in a university.

Keep in mind if you have two different weekly meetings, you are going to have two different teaching plans. While I had one chart, there were two columns; one column for Sunday and one column for Wednesday evening. These two different programs should have different purposes and different target audiences, so this should be noted when planning out your teaching schedule. I do want to point out that while your programs operate separately, I found great benefit in occasionally having some sense of continuity as well, especially if there was a seasonal theme.

## BUILDING THE TEACHING PLAN

At the latest, begin to build your teaching plan during the summer before the new school year. It would even be best to get a jump on this during the end of the current school year. First, build your summer teaching schedule and then focus on building the school-year schedule.

How does one build a teaching plan? Begin by planning out the basic topics and series you believe God would have the students look into as a group. My approach was to literally write out the series and topic ideas on note cards and spread them across my desk. Then I would think through which would better fit a Sunday series (more for mature believers) and which the midweek series (more for students newer to Christianity). These were typically designed as a monthly series usually three or four weeks in length. Next I would literally move the cards around the desk to see which series would go best seasonally and during what part of the school year. Finally, I had to consider any special days I wanted to build around.

I want to mention that I have found it wise to stay balanced in the topics. For example, coming right off a serious series such as suicide, eating disorders, or abuse, I recommend following this with a lighter topic, such as friendship. This kept things balanced. But to do this series transition effectively you need to start and stop the series well and communicate the transition or you may confuse your students, especially if they miss the closing lesson to "Battling Destructive Behaviors" (heavier) and they walk into a new series on "You've Got a Friend in Me" (lighter). This is why one needs a strong promotion plan.

I would also strongly encourage you to utilize input from others. Bounce your ideas off of godly students and leaders. There is much wisdom in many coming together. My teaching ministry became much stronger when I would utilize a team around me. Some churches will use a teaching team and/or a planning team.

I would encourage you to use apologetics on your outreach night. The apostles originally used apologetics to nonbelievers. I think we have become shy of this tactic in our zeal to be "seeker friendly." While I want to reach seekers, I want to reach them with truth. Currently there is a saying I say many times throughout my classes, "People do not want our answers until they own the question." Unbelievers have great questions about God so let's go into it!

## THE FOCUS OF THE TEACHING PLAN

What is the purpose (or program level) of your series? This will determine so much of what you speak on. While you may do things differently, the emphasis for my Sunday's lessons would be "deeper life," concentrating more on doctrine, exegetical teaching, or ministry training. The midweek's emphasis would be on life issues that all teenagers (both saved and lost) are dealing with. These would be the areas such as destructive behaviors, family issues, and questions about Christianity. Sunday was more instructional, whereas Wednesday more practical. This created a more specific strategy to what and when the topics were covered.

## PRACTICAL MATTERS

Okay, you have the teaching plan. What's next? Here are three practical next steps:

*First, type it out into your planner form.* Keep a record or log sheet of what you are going to teach and what you did teach. This is a great personal record for you and can be a quick resource for anyone who wants to know "What have the youth been learning?"

*Second, communicate the teaching plan in advance to your leaders, parents, and students.* You can make this into an attractive handout. Before I would go public with this, I believe it is wise to go over this with your leaders so they can see the spiritual direction for the year before others do. Make it available at parent meetings, your ministry site, i.e., a youth center, put it on the church website or on social media. And definitely share this with the church leadership.

*Third, implement the plan!* Unless God directs you otherwise, stay with it. I am often asked, "Isn't this legalistic to have a teaching plan?" I trust we have established the rationale for planning ahead at the beginning of the chapter. In addition, keep in mind that the Jews during the time of Jesus were used to the systematic reading and teaching from the "Law and the Prophets" at each Sabbath within the synagogues. Jesus Himself participated in this type of teaching.

There will be times God does want you to change direction. When this is true, obviously you must heed to the Spirit of God and not hold on too tightly to "your" series or lesson. Stay sensitive to the Spirit, and you will know what God is up to!

The one-year plan involves the individual series. The traditional Sunday school curriculum has been the standard thirteen-week period. This has been referred to as "the quarterly" (i.e., four quarters of thirteen weeks, equaling fifty-two weeks). Although many pastors and Christian educators have moved away from this format, I still think there is benefit for a strong, deeper-growth program. It allows both the teacher and student the time to cover the material at a deeper level without having to rush through. This type of series also benefits in the context of a discussion-oriented learning environment.

However, for a larger, seeker-oriented type program, I recommend the use of the three- to five-week short series. This short series has each lesson built to connect together and communicate an overall theme. This way you have time to communicate your theme with the reality that many of your students are going to have a hit-and-miss attendance rate.

Many great resources exist on how to put together a series. I would also recommend looking through many different youth curriculum books and websites for ideas. This will allow you to see how various youth workers have put together their materials into a short series. While I am a firm believer in "home cooked meals are better than pre-cooked microwave meals," I do suggest buying some curriculum even if just for the benefit of an ideas resource.

Now the moment you have been waiting for. Let's give our hypothetical youth worker some pointers on how to develop a lesson! Turn to chapter 10.

---

# NOTE

1. Haddon Robinson, *Biblical Preaching*, 3rd ed. (Grand Rapids: Baker, 2014). See also Andy Stanley and Lane Jones, *Communicating for a Change* (Colorado Springs: Multnomah, 2006).

# 10

# THE ESSENTIAL OF
# A BIBLICALLY CENTERED LESSON

hapter 9 chronicled the needs and benefits of an organized teaching plan, along with instructions on how to develop such a plan. Now the moment you have been waiting for. Do you recall the hypothetical frustrated youth leader at the beginning of that chapter? This chapter will focus on the specifics of developing the actual lesson.

## THE LAYOUT OF A SPECIFIC LESSON
### THE HOOK, LOOK, AND TOOK

This simple layout has been used in education for years and is used in both biblical and secular contexts. This layout is certainly not the "only" method of lesson development—there are a variety of proven methods—yet it is one in which I have found very effective in my own personal lesson and sermon preparation. Below is my own definition of the three steps.

*The HOOK*, or the introduction. "Why should I listen?"
*The LOOK*, or the main body. "What does God say?"
*The TOOK*, or the closing. "How do I apply this to life?"

Think about some of the recent marketing you have seen that use this approach. These three components also seem to show up in various television commercials. Go ahead, choose a recent radio or TV commercial you have heard or viewed and consider if you see these being used.

In my programming course at the university, we look into how to best promote our student ministry events. We even see these three in how one can do their ministry promotion. Think of it as follows:

*The HOOK*—you capture the attention.

*The LOOK*—you cover the subject.

*The TOOK*—you convince the observer to action.

## THE TIMING OF EACH ELEMENT

While there may not be nor should be a hard rule to the time breakdown of each element, consider the following as a positive breakdown for each element:

*The HOOK*: 10 to 15 percent

*The LOOK*: 70 to 80 percent

*The TOOK*: 10 to 15 percent

So when it comes to the time you have to present the specific lesson, be aware of the total time needed. If an entire lesson is forty-five minutes in length, then break the lesson down appropriately. Once this is done, look at your outline. Assign each element (and main point in the outline) a specific allotment of time and possibly write these into your own notes. Finally, have some form of a timer visible for you when you are speaking. If you choose to have a visible timer, I suggest not making the timer visible to the audience. There is nothing like a group of students yelling out, "Hey bro, your time is up!"

## THE TRANSPORTING OF EACH ELEMENT

You have possibly heard of or even used the analogy of public speaking in terms of the flight of an airplane. If not, then consider your talk like an airplane flight:

*The HOOK:* Departing off the ground and ascending to the desired height

*The LOOK:* Cruising altitude

*The TOOK:* Descending and the landing

During my time of ministry in the Northwest, we lived just south of Seattle. This put our home quite close to Seattle-Tacoma Airport. The chairman of our church board was a pilot with Alaska Airlines. He told me that most hazardous issues of flight typically take place either with the takeoff or with the landing. As one who does not enjoy flying, I am not sure if this made me feel any better or worse! Just like a flight, so many negative issues with our lessons or sermons are seen either at the beginning or the end. Imagine the speaker who stays on the runway in the introduction but won't get the plane off the ground. Or how about the speaker who continues to mention "and in conclusion" over and over again? It is like they were hovering the plane over the airport. You want to yell out, "You are clear to land, land the airplane now!"

## THE TRANSITIONING OF EACH ELEMENT

Transitioning is absolutely necessary! Weak transitions can make the lesson disjointed and can cause the speaker to lose the attention of the audience. Strong transitions will keep the lesson flowing and the audience engaged. The lesson should be one talk and not three talks. Make the lesson build to your final conclusion; thus, the importance of a central theme and an objective statement. Thinking like a passenger on a flight, one wants a smooth takeoff, smooth flyover, and smooth landing. No one wants a bumpy ride, especially not this guy!

## THE DESCRIPTION OF EACH ELEMENT

### The Hook

Some may not think the first step is important, yet if you do not capture an audience's attention right away, you may never get it. And once their minds are on another journey, they are probably not going to be with you. This is even more so true today with the accessibility of smart phones. When you combine the attention span of an adolescent with an electronic device, you may be done speaking before you even start. I am not suggesting those of us in student ministry become all about entertainment; I am suggesting we become more creative.

Powerful hooks raise a hunger for what is next. Jesus used hooks. Many times Christ used questions to create the conversation. His healing ministry could be seen as a hook. These miracles did create the desire for the people to listen to Him. Christ used word pictures, stories, object lessons, and many other approaches, all of which caused the audience to listen closely to what He would say next.

Some simple examples of effective introductions that hook your listeners would be: a brief drama, a video clip, recording and playing back "on the street" interviews, small group discussions, or a student testimonial.

Here are a few tips in regard to the Hook. First, whatever type of hooks you decided to use, stay fresh with them and mix them up. For example, starting off each week with an online video clip will become very predictable and ineffective. So utilize a variety of methods but whatever you choose, make sure it makes the listener desire to know more. Second, make sure the Hook does not give away too much of the Look. Think of a movie trailer versus reading a review of the movie online. The trailer creates the desire to go see the movie while the review can give away too much of the movie. Third, recognize that one can even use the Took as a closure to the Hook. For example, you can have a student sharing a testimony raising awareness of the issue, your lesson explains what the Word says about this issue, and the student can cap off the lesson how following Christ has helped them through the issue. Fourth, the Hook should raise the question and not give the answer. Save this step for the Look.

### The Look

This is the most important aspect of the lesson. This is the main course of the meal. As has already been mentioned, teach the Word of God. Make the emphasis of the lesson the Word of God. Break the lesson down into the three or five main parts. Under each main point I recommend two to three supportive points. Work through each main point by making each main point similar in weight or content to the other points. In other words, do not have a long "point one" and then quickly fly through the other points.

### The Took

Similar to the Hook, some may not think this step has value but how wrong this thinking is. When one reads through Jesus' Sermon on the Mount (Matthew 5–7), you will see the importance of His conclusion. He gave the information but taught for application, as in His story of the wise man and foolish man who each built his well-being on different foundations:

> Everyone then who hears these words of mine and does them will be like a wise man who built his house on the rock. And the rain fell, and the floods came, and the winds blew and beat on that house, but it did not fall, because it had been founded on the rock. And everyone who hears these words of mine and does not do them will be like a foolish man who built his house on the sand. And the rain fell, and the floods came, and the winds blew against that house, and it fell, and great was the fall of it. (7:24–27)

The Took should include two key segments. I refer to these as "the review and the renew." In the review segment, step back and review the basic high points of the lesson. You are not teaching the lesson again, just simply going over the important points. This way you are smoothly connecting the lesson together. Each point should have a legitimate reason for being in the outline so tie these together.

Once this is done, move into the renew segment. Romans 12:1–2 calls us to renew our minds through Scripture and this is what we desire the listener to do—to have their minds and lives conformed to the will of God. In this segment, provide specific action steps as to how one can apply the lesson to real life. When working with students, especially concrete thinking middle school students, be very aware to give bite-size action steps. Go beyond "So read your Bible" to providing a very simple strategy how they can read their Bible during the following days.

Personally, I greatly valued using our small groups (discussion/disciplship groups) right after I finished my own wrap-up to the lesson. The small group leaders had the lesson ahead of time, complete with discussion questions. I wanted each leader to review the lesson with their students and then focus on application. One caution is to be sensitive to each student. While I wanted our leaders not to settle for traditionally safe answers, I also did not want them to "call out" a student or make them feel pushed into a spiritual decision. Second Timothy 2:7 (NIV) states "Reflect on what I am saying, for the Lord will give you insight into all this."

# DEVELOPING THE LESSON

When it's time to prepare the actual lesson, be sure to ask the following questions (and then find the answers):

1. What is my topic?
2. What is my key Scripture?
3. What is my main point? (Some call this *the big idea*.)
4. What is my outline? (Write out the Hook, Look, and Took. Then focus on the key areas, typically three to five points for the Look and begin to put it together.)
5. What are my supporting areas? (The extras, such as the object lesson, video clips, etc.)
6. What is my application? (Some call this *the big question*.)

## THE STRUCTURE OF THE LESSON

As one considers developing a lesson, you have to make some basic decisions on the structure of the lesson. Will the lesson be?

- a solo lesson or part of a series?
- topical or textual?
- group discussion, lecture, or an interactive combination of both?

There is much debate in the church as to "which structure is correct." For example, some believe topical is best because it meets the needs of the people. Others believe textual (exegetical) is best because the focus is the whole Word and not just parts. Take some time and work through the ups and downs of each of these options, using the chart below.

## KINDS OF LESSON STRUCTURES

| STRUCTURE | POSITIVES | NEGATIVES |
|---|---|---|
| Solo lesson | | |
| Series | | |
| Topical | | |
| Textual | | |
| Group Discussion | | |
| Lecture | | |
| Interactive Combination | | |

## THE SENSITIVITY OF THE LESSON

Have you ever been embarrassed when you say a certain word, knowing full well the meaning of the word, to then see a room full of teenagers laughing? No, they are not laughing with you; they are absolutely laughing at you, and it is all because what you said and what they heard were two different things. Or maybe you heard a person from a different cultural background use a word that was quite offensive and insensitive to your audience, and they just sat there in shock. It was nothing profane or intended. It was just two different backgrounds yet this stopped effective ministry from taking place because the audience was thinking about the particular comment and not the sermon. How can we guard against this happening?

The answer is to recognize the role of semantics and stasis. *Semantics* refers to the idea that words may have many meanings and a variety of connotations. These meanings can be different across regions, cultures, subcultures, age groups, and over time. We can even see this when one is reading from an older translation of the Bible and today's culture has a different definition of the word. The consideration of semantics is desperately needed as student ministry communicators are engaging to an adolescent culture that is changing at such a rapid pace.

*Stasis* refers to the idea that all language-based communication deals with abstract thought. Language itself has such limitations. What language really does is seek to provide names or descriptions for things, processes, and relationships. The names are abstractions; they are not the things themselves. This is especially evident in today's postmodern culture.

The word *stasis* is used in the medical world and refers to the normal flow of a bodily fluid or semifluid. In the sense of linguistics, communication is flowing. We use the common phrase today of "being on the same page." When both people are speaking of a topic at the same level of abstraction or at a level of abstraction that is close enough for communication to work, it is said that they have achieved "stasis."

If the speaker and the listener are not on the "same page" with people, things will be misunderstood and can even become volatile. Without stasis, communication breaks down and without achieving stasis, it may turn out to be explosive. Know your surrounding and know your culture.

We can express the difference between semantics and stasis this way: Semantics focuses on the specific word; stasis focuses on the broad body of communication.

## THE STYLE OF THE LESSON

Biblical speaking can be seen in two categories: preaching and teaching. Some are more comfortable with topically oriented speaking while others are comfortable with textually oriented speaking. In addition, each one of us has a particular style when it comes to speaking. Consider four different styles from biblical communicators as demonstrated in Scripture by four different people:

- Nathan—the *Storytelling* Speaker (2 Samuel 12:1–14)
- Nehemiah—the *Motivational* Speaker (Nehemiah 2:17; 4:1–20)
- Peter—the *Confrontational* Speaker (Acts 2:14–39; 3:11–26)
- Paul—the *Classical* Speaker (Acts 17:16–34)

I must point out that I do not seek to label each of these four styles with these four communicators. We can see from studying Scripture that these men could also use other styles as well. Yet each person demonstrated a particular speaking style at a key point in his life. You may have a style that more naturally fits how God made you yet you must be wise enough to adapt other styles as necessary.

## THE SETTING OF THE LESSON

As you prepare your lesson or series, you will need to consider the setting where you give your talks. For example, what type of talk would you give while the students are sitting on the grass near the lake? Would the same lesson look different if it were delivered inside the youth room during the school year? Of course you would seek to adapt your style and even the layout to your lesson based on the setting. The setting can either be a help or a hindrance to your teaching ministry!

Think through what setting is the best to fulfill your lesson aim. Investigating how the Master Teacher approached His teaching you will realize He taught in many different settings, including (1) the synagogues (Luke 4:15), (2) people's homes (Luke 10:38–42), and (3) outdoors (Matthew 5–7).

As you consider your own teaching location and setup, think through the:

- *Structure.* Is the lesson going to be more serious or more relaxed?
- *Style.* Is the lesson more educational (master teacher), experiential (inductive), or relational (group discussion)?
- *Setting.* How long will the lesson be? In what shape are your chairs and the room set up? Is the environment going to strengthen or detract from your lesson?

## THE SCHEDULING OF THE LESSON (AND SERIES)

When putting together each lesson and your overall lesson plan, you should consider various issues. Being aware of these and taking advantage of them can greatly benefit your overall teaching ministry.

### Think Seasonal

Contemplate what topics would match up best during what part of the year. Obviously Christmas topics are an obvious choice but think through other ways you can "make the most of every (teaching) opportunity." Use the Christmas season to teach on the importance of the virgin birth, the deity of Christ, or fulfilled prophecies of the coming Messiah. In the spring, look into doing an apologetic series on the resurrection of Christ. One year we even put the resurrection "on trial" at the conclusion of this type of series by creating a courtroom setting and having a legal team represent each side if the resurrection. On a personal note, as one who is the twelfth great-grandson of Governor William Bradford, I would read from the journals of the early English settlers of Plymouth, Massachusetts, and share of their theology and reliance on the Lord during the Thanksgiving season. The Jewish tradition is one of using the seasons to teach the next generation. I think we could benefit from this style of teaching.

### Think School Year

Look at your school year and think through the busy times and the quieter times. Also think through the seasonal slumps that students go through during the school year. I say this because I watched twenty years of Christian students "falling" in the fall. They enjoyed a great summer of relationships, no homework, and ministry opportunities but when they go back to school, it was game on! While I am the first to say "Don't shy away from admonition," I realized what they needed in the fall was a ton of love, encouragement, along with the spiritual challenge.

One must also consider other variables within the school year. When are the students hit hard with midterms or finals? You may want to have lighter topics during those times. To illustrate this, here is a lesson I learned the hard way when it came to the end of the school year. I realized that the incredible series I had already written entitled "We're Outta Here" (eschatology) was scheduled in late May and early June. But the problem was my students were toast. Much of this was due to the school systems in our area committed to four to six hours of homework per evening. So when it came to the end of the school year, they were fried. I realized I needed to drop my grandiose plan and go with some simply light topics. Instead we went with more of a fun and celebrative atmosphere and short series.

### Think Special Days

What are some of the built-in special days that have local, regional, or even national significance? Over the years in student ministry there are some more prominent movements you may want to partner with, such as "See You at the Pole." Maybe there is a significant Christian collaborative ministry effort in your area that you want to join with. Is your church having a special anniversary? And do not forget graduation! These are all different opportunities that you can take advantage of within your teaching-plan map and the planning of your weekly series. You may want to build in some other special days as well.

*Think Siesta*

Sometimes you just need to take a break! For instance, when you finish a series this would be a good time to have a solo lesson, have a guest speaker, use one of your students to give a talk, or have an open question and answer time. While it is not necessarily wrong to do one of these in the middle of a series, I think is it more advantageous to not break up the flow of a series; so consider waiting to pursue one of these lessons until the series is completed.

In addition, when it comes to your midweek or Sunday evening programs, consider taking a program night off once a quarter. For example, at the end of the summer when school is about to start, do not meet during the typical midweek time. Many families are trying to fit in some last-minute school shopping or even trying to squeeze in a few days of family vacation before school starts. I personally did not have a midweek service in between Christmas and the new year. This was similarly done during the week of spring break. By doing this, you are also demonstrating to parents that you value them, having "permission" to do family outings during a natural time when families do. It took me over fifteen years to finally give myself permission that it is okay to not meet *every* Wednesday throughout the year.

# WHEN YOU ARE A GUEST SPEAKER

At times you may be called on to speak before another group. Whereas I used to be speaking before the same students each week in my own church, now I am the guest speaker for someone else. The following steps I developed were for my own personal growth as a guest speaker yet you may find them of interest as well. Even if you never guest speak, the principles are very practical in your own ministry when you are the consistent speaker to the same students.

## QUESTIONS TO ASK BEFORE WRITING THE LESSON

Get answers to these questions before you begin to prepare your talk:

1. Who am I speaking to? Know the age group, culture, spiritual background (unsaved or saved), biblical knowledge, belief, and behavior. Are your listeners primarily introversive or extroversive; are they apathetic or passionate?

2. Why am I speaking? Know the purpose of the lesson and the ministry level. Is your talk part of a series, or a single talk?

3. Where am I speaking? Consider the location, atmosphere, and room size.

4. When am I speaking? Take into account the time of year, time of day, length of lesson, etc.

5. What am I speaking on? Are you given a topic or responsible for your own topic—and is the topic part of a series?

## QUESTIONS TO ASK YOUR HOST

1. *The Audience.* What denomination is this? Are there certain doctrinal issues to be aware of? Is this a single group or part of a collaborative effort? What seems to go well and/or not well with your students? Should I have an awareness of any recent issues?

2. *The Adult Leaders.* Will there be other adult leadership present? What are their roles? Can I meet them beforehand, especially for communication and for prayer?

3. *The Appearance.* Do you want handouts, visuals (i.e., PowerPoint), student interaction, etc.?

4. *The Arrangement.* Will I follow the worship time? Will you introduce me, should I introduce myself, etc.? How do you want me to close the lesson?

5. *The Actual Lesson.* Would you like me to send you the lesson beforehand? Do you want me to write group discussion questions?

## QUESTIONS OF PERSONAL INTEGRITY

*Whenever you speak before an outside group* (or even before your own group of teens), be able to answer these three questions, ideally in the affirmative.

- Do I comprehensively know the subject matter? (Logos)
- Do I consistently live the subject matter? (Ethos)
- Has God burned this subject matter within me? (Pathos)

As you put together your teaching plan and each lesson, never forget your ultimate purpose. The apostle Paul provided a picture of his shepherd's heart for the Galatian people when he wrote this little phrase, "until Christ is formed in you" (Galatians 4:19). This is what it is all about!

STUDENT MINISTRY

# ESSENTIALS

## PART 3: REACHING

# 11

# THE ESSENTIAL OF
# COMPETENT PROGRAMMING

As you read this chapter title you may be thinking, "Events or programs are not essential to salvation, and youth events aren't even in the Bible. After all, God does not need some pizza party to see students come to Christ."

I am glad you are thinking and, don't be shocked, I would somewhat agree with you. God does not need anything we do nor even need us to bring salvation and He certainly does not need pizza, loud bands, inflatables, or amusement parks. Events or programs by themselves do not save anyone. They are simply a tool. There is nothing spiritual or "anointed" about a ministry tool. Programs or events are nothing but a tool. Yet just like a surgeon's tool can be used to save a life, so a ministry tool (an event) can be used to save a life.

Later, in chapter 13, we will consider how to build intentional outreach events, but for now, let's consider some foundational aspects that undergird the logistics to such an event. One immediate criterion is when one defines an event; the greater perspective is that an event forms only part of an overall program. And for a program to be effective, this must be part of a larger picture as well. Therefore, in this chapter we will look into: (1) investigating why one would have programs; (2) understanding a four-level strategy to ministry; and (3) ten foundational principles of programming.

# WHY HAVE PROGRAMS?

When I use the word *program*, I also think of synonymous terms *structure* and *project*. The Scripture never opposes structure. It does oppose the misuse of structure. Both Old and New Testaments reveal that God demands His people to rely on Him, not on a program (the structure). This included religious activity and national activity.

## GOD IS A GOD OF ORDER IN THE NEW TESTAMENT.

Religiously, consider the worship system of ancient Israel. A simple read of the Old Testament reveals the Jewish people began to revere the *form* of worship instead of the *One* they were called to worship. This was still taking place during the time of Christ. Jesus quoted Hosea 6:6 as He rebuked the Pharisees saying, "Go and learn what this means, 'I desire mercy, and not sacrifice.' For I came not to call the righteous, but sinners" (Matthew 9:13). God is the One who set up the worship structure so He is not against structure! He is against us forgetting the purpose of the structure.

Nationally, consider ancient Israel's military. God was not opposed to Israel having a military; rather, He implemented it and even commanded them at times to use their military. The issue was not having the military; the issue was trust. God warned His people not to trust in their military for victory but to trust in Him for victory. "Some trust in chariots and some in horses, but we trust in the name of the Lord our God" (Psalm 20:7). Notice that King David, himself a successful military leader, wrote this for use in national worship. So whether it is corporate worship or national security, having a structure, or program, in and of itself is not evil. It is when we trust in our program that we sin.

Knowing that programs are not innately evil, we can understand that structure is actually of God because it is who He is. Scriptures reveal God is an organized, creative, and structured God. From the beginning in Genesis 1–2, we learn of God's first "project" as the Master Designer as He put all things together. He called everything He made "good." To this present time, science still cannot comprehend the vastness of His great cosmos and the intricacy of His finite details.

In that passage we also read of God's finest "project" as He made a human being "in His own image" (Genesis 1:27). After God created Adam, He saw "everything that he had made, and behold it was very good." This project of creating a human being is so lofty that humankind is still trying to duplicate it with our modern attempts of cloning. Yet even if scientists do accomplish some form of genetic reproduction, they have to start with previously created matter. Yes, God's project is very good!

Moving throughout the Old Testament, we come across physical projects that God had given specific directions to build. Consider the holy project of God's dwelling place, the ark of God's covenant. In Exodus 25, we read the intricate details given by God to His specific dwelling place. This is followed by the surrounding tabernacle in Exodus 26 and the articles of worship in Exodus 27–30. God was greatly concerned with details and with excellence.

As the nation of Israel settled in their promised land and King David's reign concluded, God's holy dwelling place received a more permanent home when King Solomon built a magnificent temple dedicated to Jehovah. Second Chronicles 2–4 provide the details to this immense project. This temple was so magnificent that dignitaries from other nations were in awe at this amazing project (2 Chronicles 9:1).

There are other Old Testament examples of God being organized, creative, and structured. As previously studied in the leadership section, we can see the story of God's rebuilding of the walls of Jerusalem as Nehemiah is chosen to take on this project. Alongside this story we read of Ezra's rebuilding of the destroyed temple. One must understand God is concerned with details and with excellence.

## GOD IS A GOD OF ORDER IN FORMING A NEW PROGRAM.

Moving through the New Testament it is easy to discover that God's new "program" is not a building made of hands but the project He does within His people. All of those in Christ are new creations (2 Corinthians 5:17), and God has placed His Holy Spirit within each believer (2 Corinthians 5:5). It is truly amazing to know that the same Holy Spirit that formerly indwelled the ark of the covenant now indwells God's people. We are His temple (1 Corinthians 6:19). We are now His adopted children, and His plan is to make us into "the image of His Son, Jesus Christ" (Romans 8:28–29).

To make a people pleasing unto Himself, God has instituted His church. This church is seen in the New Testament with the metaphor of a building. From the initial mentioning of the church, Jesus Christ told Peter in Matthew 16:18, upon the great bedrock of the Lord Himself, "I will build my church." We learn from this passage that the church *belongs* to Jesus Christ and the church is *built by* Jesus Christ. The son of a tradesman-carpenter is the Master

Builder. Later in the New Testament, Peter also referred to this building concept in his first epistle when he referred to each member of Christ, "You also, like living stones, are being built into a spiritual house" (1 Peter 2:5 NIV). Each of us as followers of Christ are connected to one another in this great house, this invisible building called the church.

While you may wonder why we just had a brief overview of the Old and New Testament, I trust you are seeing my point. God is organized, creative, and structured. If He is this way, then do we think it out of character for us to be organized, creative, and structured? Honestly, I provide this defense of organization because I have been on church boards where leadership has resisted organization, thinking of it as of the flesh and not of the Spirit. I have also read this same mindset from a handful of my online students as well. All of us—parents, students, and church board members—need to see that God is organized, creative, and structured.

When one specifically looks at the church, it is evident God seeks structure. In the middle of a chaotic church where each was going their own way, the apostle Paul taught, "For God is not a God of disorder but of peace"; therefore "everything should be done in a fitting and orderly way" (1 Corinthians 14:33, 40 NIV). Paul warned the Corinthian believers that church expression (v. 26) does not mean a "free for all" service. While there was to be freedom of worship expression, there was also to be order. In addition to the specific church service, also consider the overview of the church itself. Both Acts and the Pastoral Epistles reveal specific structure laid out by God for His church. This is why God had these passages in the Word of God. In addition the creative and organized God has also provided each believer with certain spiritual gifts to do His work as they work in unison. Through this orchestrated endeavor of the church under His leadership, we see our God using a program, or structure, in His mighty plan.

## SO WHY USE PROGRAMS?

Here are two key reasons to use programs in ministry: (1) to keep us focused on our mission and (2) to help us fulfill our mission. Let's look at each.

### Programs keep us focused on our mission.

It is great to have lofty dreams about what can happen in ministry. It is equally great to have those dreams consist of well-meaning intentions. But how many times do dreams translate into reality? For example, I would trust each one of you has a commitment to fulfilling Christ's mandate of disciplemaking (Matthew 28:19–20). But how many student ministries actually develop students into mature disciples of Jesus Christ? While each leader's intention may be good, I wonder if true discipleship is happening in each student ministry.

What causes the breakdown between good intention and good implementation is usually due to a lack of a proficient course of action—a game plan, also called a program. This is where programs are beneficial. Note the following benefits that programs can have in focusing us on our mission:

- Programs can *clear* us toward fulfilling our stated purposes of youth ministry.
- Programs will *commit* us to see these purposes are met.
- Programs will *contribute* to us developing a means to accomplish these purposes.
- Programs will *communicate* to others the seriousness of our commitment.

As you know, one of your ministry purposes must be the spiritual growth of your students. And this must take place with one's commitment to the clear, correct, and life-changing teaching of God's Word. So when you begin to have a strong Bible study program in place (i.e., your Sunday school), this helps fulfill these four benefits. If you did have a disciplemaking structure in place and simply left spiritual growth to naturally happen, it probably wouldn't happen. (Again, for those who are struggling with the concept of structure, please read Acts 2:42–47. There was immediate follow-up and the church intentionally met every day for spiritual growth.) We all have been moved to start a Bible study, an accountability group, or something of that nature that never began to meet. How many times at the end of a camp week do we hear, "Dude, we need to start accountability" but it stops before it even starts. Without the structure in place, we simply forget, let it go, or move on to something else. Good intentions will fail without good structure. Our programs can keep us focused on our mission.

### Programs help us fulfill our mission.

Programs not only demonstrate our commitment to being focused on our mission, they also give us the means to carry out these purposes of our mission. Continuing with our previous case study, as we provide a strong growth-level program, we will see God begin to develop the depth of these young disciples. Note the following two benefits that programs can have in fulfilling our mission:

- Programs will help us *consistently work* toward fulfilling our stated purposes.
- Programs will help us *carry out* these stated purposes.

Here is a real ministry example of *focusing* and *fulfilling*. As a student pastor, I truly believed in developing students into becoming strong and effective leaders (my good intention). But in ministry this does not automatically happen. So to assist this purpose I provided our high school students with a summer leadership class (structure). We were using this program (structure) as a specific step in training potential student leadership for the coming school year as we were moving into campus-based home groups. Instead of assuming leadership would automatically occur, I offered this class to take specific action steps in developing potential leaders. Offering this class showed intentional *focus* on the mission of training leaders. Through this class I was able to *fulfill* a basic step in leadership development. Subsequently as the school year started off, I had a field of over twenty students who were feeling good about jumping into leadership positions within the high school ministry.

But why use programs? Why not just go organic and hope it all turns out? Programs give life to your philosophy. They are your direction based on rationale.

Programs are important, but remember they are only programs. The program is not to legalistically bind us but to free us. If all we are doing through programs is filling a "job description" or fulfilling moldy church traditions, then we are missing the point of true ministry! The wise student pastor has his programs serve him, not him to serving his programs. Programs may come and go. It is the philosophy of ministry that must remain constant. For the church whose famous roadblock phrase is "We've never done it that way before," may I lovingly say it was Jesus Christ who brought in a major "program change" (see John 4:23). Jesus Christ bombarded the Pharisees on their commitment to traditions and programs, which were more important to them than people. This concept of God changing man-made traditions and programs continues through the book of Acts. I've been involved in churches with both extremes: either a commitment to "do not touch" programs or little, if any, organization.

Please develop a balanced ministry. Use programs to build people. Please do not build programs by abusing/using people. *The philosophy remains resilient but the programs must be relevant.* How to best fulfill effectiveness in ministry must always come from having the calculated mind of "can we do this ministry more effectively?"

# UNDERSTANDING A FOUR-LEVEL STRATEGY OF MINISTRY

It was during the 1990s that many of us "veterans" in student ministry were introduced to the nationally known ministries of two churches: Willow Creek Community Church (Barrington, Illinois) and Saddleback Church (Lake Forest, California). These two churches were used by the Lord to provide for so many the template of how to be focused and intentional in ministry. As one who valued the resources they provided and appreciated how they refined me, I have to step back and communicate how much I treasured my university education in the early 1980s from Liberty University's student ministry program. Both of my professors, Drs. Doug Randlett and David Adams, taught each of us young men and women to be intentional, or purpose driven, in our student ministries before there ever was a nationally recognized book. This sense of ministry philosophy and intentionality in ministry was engrained into me at the age of twenty, and I have never let it go.

I say all of this to preface this content. As I have taught the following material I have had a small percentage wonder if I "stole" it from other ministries. I can sincerely say that what you are going to read came right from my notepad long before there were any electronic notepads. Our professors wanted us to develop our own philosophy of ministries and this is what I developed back in my early years in student ministry during the 1980s. I do not seek to sound defensive or apologetic; I simply want to have a clear conscience with each of you and be above reproach.

The following four levels—entry, evangelize, edify, and equip—are specifically designed for event planning. This can mean a weekly program, a monthly large group event, or just you and a student together. As you look at the explanation of each level, realize that everything you do in ministry should fall into one (or more) of these levels for effective ministry. Maybe it's just taking a new student out to build a relationship (entry) or your group involved with a service project (equip). Whatever you do, have a purpose and know your purpose. Within each level there will be an example from the ministry of Jesus and I will provide an example done in my ministry experience.

# THE FOUR LEVELS OF STUDENT MINISTRY

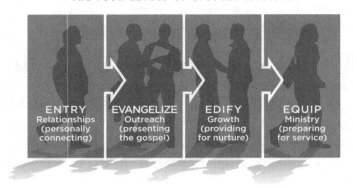

ENTRY
Relationships
(personally
connecting)

EVANGELIZE
Outreach
(presenting
the gospel)

EDIFY
Growth
(providing
for nurture)

EQUIP
Ministry
(preparing
for service)

## *ENTRY* LEVEL (MATTHEW 9:9-13)

This initial level is to provide entry-level opportunities for the unsaved to see and hear about Christ. And this comes so often through building relationships with lost students. The whole purpose of the entry level is to open the door to our student ministry. This is a visual presentation of the gospel with the goal to move to the next level.

> *Description*: A relational event, one that begins and/or develops relationships with unsaved students with the eventual goal being evangelism.

> *Goal*: For unsaved students to *come and see* Christianity.

> *Question*: "Can I trust in the followers of Christ?"

> *Examples*: Monthly events (tailgate parties, Fifth Quarters [events following high school football and basketball]), broom hockey, theme park, etc.); weekly meetings (game nights, recovery groups, investigative Bible studies, etc.); small groups and/or personal ministries (service projects, cleaning up around town, etc.); youth centers

Much of Christ's ministry was based on spending time with people. A perfect example of this is when Christ invited Matthew (Levi) to be one of His followers. The Lord then attended a dinner Matthew hosted in honor of his new friend, Jesus Christ. Also present were Matthew's "social cluster," a group of people who no Jew would identify as spiritual, holy, or noble. See the picture in Matthews's house. You have Jesus, His apostles, a new follower Matthew, and Matthew's posse. Today's culture would say "awkward."

Did this bother the Master that these people were "tax collectors and sinners" (Matthew 9:10)? I think you know the answer. And when challenged by the legalists on His associations, Jesus responded with His purpose of coming to earth and told the Pharisees to go and learn about God's mercy. These people needed a Savior (v. 13). Notice there was no Bible study, nor did Jesus give out pamphlets or even have them listen to Him preach. He just spent time with them. Jesus knew the door to evangelism was going to where the lost were and connecting with them.

An individual example of this would be for a youth leader to take out a new student for a bite to eat after school. You may also want to connect with some of your students after school and intentionally include some of their lost friends. A group example of the entry level is while in Seattle we rented out a hockey arena to play broom hockey. There was no lesson or "God talk"; it was just a place to bridge non-Christian students to our ministry. This was to build credibility, friendship, and trust. This event was strategic because we followed this up with an outreach event where the new students were invited to return. Many did return and they heard a clear presentation of the gospel; thus, the next level.

## EVANGELIZE LEVEL (MATTHEW 11:20–30)

While we use entry-level events to attract students, the entry level is worthless if we don't take students to the next level. We must verbally share the gospel of Christ.

> *Description*: An outreach event—one that clearly articulates the gospel to unsaved students and provides the opportunity to become followers of Christ.
>
> *Goal*: For unsaved students to commit to Christ.
>
> *Question*: "Can I trust Jesus Christ?"
>
> *Example*: Monthly events (food events, travel events, concerts, rallies, etc.); weekly meetings (seeker night, etc.); small groups and personal ministries (investigative Bible studies, etc.); youth centers

Christ built relationships with the lost so they would be saved (e.g., John 4:7–26). Through the power of the Holy Spirit and the language of love, Christ showed us how to lead people to Himself. As His followers, we are to carry on this work. Just like Christ with the Samaritan woman, we are to build relationships with the lost, not just for relationship sake, but for the gospel sake. To build a relationship with a lost person and never eventually share the gospel is an incomplete mission.

While in student ministry, I planned at least three to four events a school year that were designed to clearly present the gospel. These were typically held three to four weeks after an entry event. In addition to the events were the weekly midweek meetings that provided an entry point and evangelistic opportunity for students to bring their generation to Christ.

As you will read in chapter 12, I have a caution about youth outreach events. As we have moved deeper into postmodernism and post-Christianity, we need to keep in mind these unsaved students may not understand our Christian cultural phrases and gospel presentations all packaged within five minutes like previous generations. Please make sure you work hard in fulfilling Paul's prayer to present the gospel "clearly, as I should" (Colossians 4:4).

## *EDIFY* LEVEL (MATTHEW 9:35–38)

Once an individual comes to Christ he or she is a disciple. When we see a young person put their full faith in the atoning work of Christ on the cross, they have passed from death to life (John 5:24). They are a new creation (2 Corinthians 5:17) and have a new identity. They are now a follower of Jesus Christ.

Throughout the gospels and over twenty-five times in the book of Acts, the terms *disciple* was the descriptive term used for believers. This was their identity. Their allegiance and their loyalty were to Jesus Christ (Romans 10:9–10). They identified with Him in public baptism and many identified with Him in public persecution. It is interesting to note that the early believers referred to themselves as disciples while it was the secular culture who labeled them Christians (Acts 11:26). What a powerful testimony that these early believers followed Christ with such authenticity that the secular culture recognized Who they followed.

Just as in the first century, today we as youth leaders must help these newly converted youth see who they are—followers of Christ (disciples); therefore, we must assist them in doing just that, following Christ, becoming more like Christ. This is seen in Matthew 11:29 when Jesus invited lost people to take on His yoke (our salvation) and learn from Him (our growth). Our student ministries must fulfill the mandate of making disciples as we teach these young followers "to observe all that I have commanded you" (Matthew 28:20).

> *Description*: A growth event, one that calls a disciple into a deeper level of Christlikeness.

*Goal*: For saved students to come and grow in Christ.

*Question*: "Can I become like Jesus Christ?"

*Example*: Monthly events (food events, travel events, concerts, rallies, etc.); weekly meetings (Sunday services, Bible studies, etc.); small groups and personal ministries (personal discipleship, accountability, mentoring, etc.)

Even unsaved people will say that Jesus was one of the greatest teachers to have walked this earth. Even atheistic leaders have studied His teaching methods. Yet I believe He was the greatest teacher, based on some basic variables like His deity, His miracles, His resurrection; you have the idea. His word pictures were painted masterfully. His uses of real-life situations were timely and effective as they hit the heart. And His knowledge of the Scriptures was creatively woven throughout His teaching into a splendid masterpiece. Even with all of His artistry, He knew what caused us to be renewed was the Word of God (John 17:17). No matter what variety of teaching styles one will use, the Word of God must be the ultimate tool to change people's lives.

Within my student ministry, the core of the edifying were the weekly youth meetings. As I have already explained in our chapters on teaching, my personal approach was to use the midweek meeting as designed more for the unbeliever. Our students stated this was the more likely time their unsaved friends would ever come to church. Yet even while it was designed for lost students, I absolutely was committed to the Word being lifted up, taught, and explained. The topics centered on real-life issues that both saved and lost students would identify with and the Word of God provided the answers. Not only were unbelievers hearing God's answers to their issues, so were the saved. The weekly Sunday morning time was designed for deeper spiritual growth. This centered on doctrine, Bible book studies, and ministry training. Included with each lesson was a small group breakout time for the students to look at personal application and talk about the lesson.

In addition to the weekly meetings were various retreats and summer camps. As I am sure you are aware, these are great memory-filled experiences that can really enhance and establish commitments to Jesus Christ. In addition to the weekly meetings and various growth-level events, there were provided a variety of one-on-one and small group discipleship opportunities for those who truly wanted to "grow in the grace and knowledge of our Lord and Savior Jesus Christ" (2 Peter 3:18).

## EQUIP LEVEL (MATTHEW 10)

Now as your students are growing in their knowledge and relationship with Christ, we must move them along in their growth by equipping them to do ministry. As we have seen in our essentials of leadership, this is the purpose of pastors and leaders (Ephesians 4:12) and was the heart of my ministry purpose statement "developing a team of students to impact their world for Christ."

> *Description*: A ministry event—one that gives growing students an opportunity to serve and eventually take on leadership responsibility.

> *Goal*: For saved students to be equipped given the opportunities to come and serve Jesus Christ.

> *Question*: "Can I effectively serve Christ?"

> *Examples*: Monthly events (seasonal opportunities, missions trips, ministry trips, etc.), weekly meetings (leadership and serving roles in ministry, etc.), small groups and personal (ministry teams, service projects, etc.)

Do you remember the story of the feeding of the five thousand? I would love to have seen the Twelve as they frantically came running up to Jesus totally freaked because there were all these people and no one planned an after-church potluck dinner! I wonder if the Twelve were wondering if Martha was available to cater. Do you remember our Lord's response? "You give them something to eat" (Luke 9:13). He was stretching them. He was developing leadership. There are countless books on the subject of Christ's training of the twelve disciples, as well there should be. Just as Jesus taught both by life example and by involving His "students" in various roles of serving, so we need to provide our students with our examples of servanthood coupled with providing them ministry opportunities. During my ministry training in college, I read a quote that really affected me. It is a classic from Dr. Bill Bright. In explaining Jesus' training of the Twelve, Dr. Bright stated, "He (Jesus) taught them how, He showed them how, and He let them do it."[1] Our students should be players, not fans; in the game, not in the stands.

One simple event was the annual "Christmas SHINE" (Students Helping In Neighborhood Efforts). Each small group chose their own service project to get into our community and serve. This was not a fund-raiser but an act of kindness, absolutely free. There were no strings attached, and we turned down money whenever someone tried to slip us a five dollar bill. We didn't even give out gospel pamphlets. We just wanted to serve. It was fun to see the expression on the faces of those served as well as seeing our students involved in ministering in the name of Jesus Christ.

Another absolute highlight was our summer mission project. This was not a "sign up and show up" trip! These students committed to three months of solid discipleship based training (level three). I would not trade this training time for anything. I can honestly say when we arrived at the mission site, they were right with God, tight with each other, and mighty in their ministry. The success of the mission project was not necessarily what happened at the mission site; rather, what God did in these young lives as they were trained to be lifestyle ambassadors, not just event ambassadors. I would let them know that my definition of a successful missions experience was what they did with this experience when they returned to school in the fall as campus missionaries. In the next chapter, you will read about one girl who influenced her friends for Christ; her actions took place over ten years ago. Just recently she reached out to me on social media to thank me again for such training. Praise the Lord!

As ministry leaders, if we will be committed to providing a healthy production of all four levels in a balanced format, we will provide the resource for our students to become effective in their own personal growth and personal ministries of impact on their culture. To have a strong intentional outreach event, all of the above criteria is necessary. Any shortcuts taken will hurt the effectiveness of your ministry.

# WHAT GOES INTO SUCCESSFUL PROGRAMMING?

In the senior portfolio course in our youth ministries department, the seniors learn the foundations and components of a strategic, balanced, and strong student ministry. For their portfolio project, they build an entire year of student ministry, including monthly events, a week of camp, a mission trip, their annual budget, monthly calendars, and a teaching plan for 104 lessons for their weekly meetings (52 x 2 a week). Before they build the project, we cover some programming principles. The following material is an excerpt from the course notes as we cover the "Ten Foundational Programming Principles."

1. Program with the BIG PICTURE.
    • How does this program fit into the layout of the entire ministry?
    • Is this the best day, time, and location to use this program in this way?

2. Program with PURPOSE.
   - What is the specific ministry purpose of the program?
   - Does it fit with the big picture of the ministry?
   - Does it fit with where the group currently is both spiritually and socially?
   - Do we acknowledge it is expendable and not above being changed or pulled?

3. Program with a PLAN.
   - Do I have an overall written plan for this ministry?
   - Do I have the basic breakdown for each area to be covered within this ministry?
   - Do I have the specific details written down?
   - Do I have job descriptions written for each participant?

4. Program with PRAYER.
   - Was this ministry dreamed into existence through prayer?
   - Are we continuing to pray as this ministry is constructed?
   - Are we continuing to pray about this ministry as it has been implemented?
   - Do we have others praying for God to use and bless this ministry?

5. Program with PARTICIPATION.
   - Am I getting the input of others with this program?
   - Am I surrounding myself with a team of passionate and competent people?
   - Have I empowered and entrusted others in assisting me to carry out this ministry?
   - Along with my leadership team, do I have parents and students involved?
   - Have I correctly matched up the right people to the right responsibilities?

6. Program with PASSION.
   - Do I exemplify enthusiasm for this ministry?
   - Does our leadership team exemplify enthusiasm for this ministry?
   - Do our students exemplify enthusiasm for this ministry?
   - Do we give our students reason(s) to be enthused about this ministry?

7. Program with PERSISTENCE.
   - Is this ministry being done with excellence?
   - Is this ministry given opportunity to develop?
   - Is this ministry given opportunity to be reviewed and adjusted as needed?

8. Program with PURITY.
   - Is this ministry being done with all honesty and integrity?
   - Is this ministry being done in a way true to Scripture?
   - Am I and other leadership treating people with dignity and respect?

9. Program to the needs of PEOPLE.
   - What is the target audience for this ministry?
   - Is the meeting being held at the best time, place, and means to reach this target audience?
   - Are people or the structure the essential value of this program?
   - Do the participants in this ministry know that Christ loves them as seen through us?

10. Program with PROGNOSIS.
   - Are we having an immediate, small-scale evaluation?
   - Are we having a semiannual to annual, larger-scale evaluation?

When it comes to successful programming, keep this approach in mind: Use the ministry to build your students and not use the students to build your ministry. Or as someone has cautioned, "Pharaohs build pyramids, pastors should build people."

---

# NOTE

1. Bill Bright, *How to Make Your Mark* (San Bernardino, Calif.: Here's Life Publishers, 1983), 189.

# 12

# THE ESSENTIAL OF
# EQUIPPING STUDENTS FOR OUTREACH

Many years ago I was asked to take the lead responsibility of organizing the street evangelism efforts for my denomination's annual youth conference. I accepted this opportunity with open arms. I have always loved teaching youth to share their faith with other students.

And yet I immediately noticed when it came to evangelism, while all of the conference leadership agreed Jesus is the only way to God, there was a difference in methodology. I am sure you have seen this to be true as well. My simple take on why this is true is there is a wide diversity of theological perspectives on exactly what salvation is. But before I enter into that conversation, let me take you back to that hot summer afternoon.

I had a van full of students as we were driving into town ready to go confront sinners. We had just come out of a thirty-minute rally-type training time—one in which I began to feel very uncomfortable. I was responsible for the administrative duty but not the training duty. During the training we were taught to go "Romans road" on strangers and get them to pray the "sinner's prayer." There was no mention of asking the Holy Spirit to lead us, to empower us, or to bring conviction to the lost. There was no mention of explaining the deity of Christ or the resurrection of Christ. There was no mention of repentance.

There was no mention of what it means to place one's life into the leading arms of Jesus Christ. Obviously there was no mention of calling people to lose their lives to find them in Christ.

It was the judicial approach to having someone express a paragraph requesting Jesus to be the Savior to get them from hell to heaven. I think you know where I am coming from even as you just read that description.

I parked the van at a local 7-Eleven store. Out jumped the students as they spotted two female adolescents who looked to be about fourteen years of age outside the store, eating their ice cream. I listened as the students began to engage the girls in spiritual conversation and ask them if they wanted to go to heaven. The girls giggled and said sure. Our young evangelists asked them if they were sinners to which the girls replied no.

The following response is one I will never forget. "That's okay, just pray this prayer after me anyway, and you can go to heaven." The girls went along with the recitation. The teenagers jumped back in the van and off we went.

I wanted to cry after that. Seriously, I wanted to cry. I thought of these young girls and where they truly stood with a holy God. To think that they were told they were going to heaven because they "prayed the prayer." Later that day I shared this with my leader. While he understood and agreed with my concerns, I was never asked to lead this effort again.

Please do not get me wrong. I was delighted that teenagers volunteered to go talk about Jesus. I am not pushing them off any cliff. My intention with this story is to have student ministry leadership analyze how we are training our students to share Christ with lost people and to provide a simple structure how we can equip them to do this in a gospel-centered, Holy Spirit–empowered, relational means. In this chapter we will focus on three main areas:

1. The current spiritual condition of adolescents in the United States
2. The most effective in reaching unsaved adolescents
3. What student ministry leaders can do to equip student to reach their peers

# THE CURRENT SPIRITUAL CONDITION OF ADOLESCENTS
## WHAT IS THE AGE MOST PEOPLE ARE SAVED?

For the past few decades the consensus among evangelicals was that 90 percent of those who come to Jesus Christ will do so before age eighteen. Many of us may have heard this in various ministry settings and by various speakers. More recent research by the Barna Group indicates that of all Americans who "accept Jesus Christ as their Savior, " 43 percent do so before age thirteen, 64 percent of believers receive Christ before age eighteen, and 77 percent before age twenty-one.[1] Whether it is the traditional number of 90 percent receiving Christ as Savior prior to age eighteen or Barna's 64 percent (77 percent before twenty-one), we can see if people are going to enter the kingdom of God, most will do so in the early years of their lives.

## HOW MANY ADOLESCENTS ARE SAVED?

Only God truly knows the number of adolescents who are followers of His Son; none of us has ever seen God's database of genuine believers. Yet there is some research to give us a partial answer. In his book *The Coming Revolution in Youth Ministry*, Mark Senter notes that a 1960 Youth For Christ survey found only 5 percent of adolescents stated they had a "Christian conversion experience"; another 35 percent claimed to have some type of religious affiliation; and 60 percent considered themselves unchurched.[2]

This indicates that only five of every one hundred adolescents in 1960 claimed a Christian conversion experience. Before you say, "Come on, this was over fifty years ago" and brush this statistic away, stay with me. Those teenagers in 1960 are today's grandparents and great-grandparents of today's teenagers. I believe this statistic does have to be considered.

I assume you are wondering about the spiritual condition of adolescents in more recent years. In his 1997 release *The Bridger Generation*, Thom Rainer stated that his research revealed of those born after 1984 (his definition of millennials), 4 percent identify themselves as Bible-based believers.[3] A few years later George Barna completed a similar study. His study was sensitive to terminology, especially the definition of terms. When one speaks of labels like "Christian," "born again," and "evangelical," these terms have different meanings to different people. What was meant to a teenager in 1960 by identifying with the phrase of having a "Christian conversion experience" can mean something entirely different to a more secular culture today.

In the report *Third Millennial Teens*, Barna used various labels and found a variety of answers. For example 80 percent of adolescents claimed to be "Christian," yet only 26 percent of all adolescents stated they had an absolute commitment to the Christian faith. When asked if they were "born again" (defined by a personal commitment to Jesus Christ which is still important to them today), 33 percent of adolescents claimed this term as theirs. But the study took the labels to a deeper level. It proposed some deeper criteria to define the spiritual commitment of a teenager.[4]

When using this definition of *born again* as the foundation, the study also included the following criteria as one who believes they have a personal responsibility to share their religious beliefs about Christ with non-Christians; they believe that Satan exists; they believe that eternal salvation is possible only through grace, not works; they believe that Jesus Christ lived a sinless life on earth; and they describe God as the all-knowing, all-powerful, perfect deity who created the universe and still rules it today. (Within traditional evangelicalism, these areas are similar to the fundamentals of the faith, as described over a century ago by R. A. Torrey.) Using the above beliefs as criteria, the findings were 4 percent of adolescents agreed with these indicators. I do see a pattern.

## PUTTING THIS TOGETHER

If these single-digit statistics are sincerely close to reality as the research indicates, this means that for over fifty years the United States of America has had a 4 to 5 percent conversion rate among its nation's youth culture. When you hear people question why the current culture is the way it is, you are looking at the answer. Remember, the youth of the 1960s are today's grandparents. Think about the implications: for more than fifty years America has seen up to 96 percent of the generation's youth lacking a saving and personal relationship with Jesus Christ.

By putting this together, if the majority of believers come to Christ before age eighteen and the majority of adolescents are not confessing a sincere saving relationship with Jesus Christ, that means we as the church of King Jesus are losing. Jesus is still King, but the field is truly filled with wandering sheep who lack a shepherd. I fully understand there will be those who will downplay this information and would argue that I am sensationalizing, even fabricating, the situation. Some may even want to argue about this percentage contrasted to that percentage. I repeat what I said earlier, only the Lord truly knows the exact number of how many adolescents are sincerely born again. My encouragement is to not get so lost in the specifics that we lose sight of the big picture. Today's youth culture is quite separated from Jesus Christ.

## AN EXPERIMENT IN OBSERVATION

You have now read about the spiritual condition of today's youth culture, but now I challenge you to do your own analysis. Yet instead of going online or reading another book, I am challenging you to do something that I have been requiring my own students to participate in. For over ten years I have had the students in my introductory "Survey of Youth Ministries" course complete a Cultural Observation Project. This project calls them to attend a secular local teenage hangout to simply do a casual yet intentional observation of the culture. This project is based on Matthew 9:36: "When he saw the crowds, he had compassion on them, because they were harassed and helpless, like sheep without a shepherd." The student is not to have their electronic devises out investigating or stalking teenagers. That's just weird and wrong! This assignment is to have each student simply blend in and prayerfully observe teenagers.

The assignment is included in both the residential and the online course. The residential student has the average age of one to two years removed from high school while the adult learner in the online course ranges from mid-twenties through sixties. You can imagine what group of students is more shocked and moved. It is the adult learner. So many times I read the same basic response as I grade the reaction papers as so many of them say they must now get involved in student ministry.

When you do your own observation project, an easy place to observe is at the local mall. When you enter the mall, just grab a refreshing beverage and sit in the main hallway or food court and simply watch the youth that pass you by. As you see these teenagers, look into their faces and be reminded, as Paul taught on the deity of Jesus Christ, "All things have been created through him and for him" (Colossians 1:16 NIV). Each teenager you see was created by Jesus and for Jesus. This powerful verse reveals what each one is looking for—identity and purpose. Once you throw yourself in the middle of a location where teenagers go hang out, especially some place like a local high school football game, and process what you have just seen, I am convinced you will see the data for yourself. But who is going to reach them?

# THOSE MOST EFFECTIVE AT REACHING LOST ADOLESCENTS

As leaders of students we understand that students reach students. Have you seen this true in your own life and ministry? I would understand that among children who grow up in the church their parents probably are the main influencer, but I am focusing on the 96 percent of lost students in the United States.

I have never seen a study on this subject but just through personal observation as well as the observation of many student ministry friends, saved teenagers reach lost teenagers. I have a wife who can give witness to this. I have many current university students who can give witness to this. And I have many former teenagers, now adults, who can give witness to this. As you come into contact with young disciples of Jesus Christ who did not grow up in the church, I urge you to ask them "Who was the key influencer that led you to Christ?" The answer is most often "a friend," "a classmate," or "another teen."

Why would this dynamic be true? Why would it be that saved teenagers are more apt to reach their own peers for Christ than us more spiritually mature adults? Before I provide my own thoughts, I encourage you to step away and think about this yourself. Maybe journal a few ideas down and banter your thoughts with another ministry friend.

Are you ready? Here we go. The list is modest and simply based on what I have seen and what I have heard from my own university students.

## WHY SAVED STUDENTS ARE MOST EFFECTIVE IN REACHING TEENAGERS

The reasons students are most effective vary. It can be any combination of the following—and sometimes all of these factors play a role. Students are most effective because of the following:

- *Identity.* Saved students know the culture, speak the culture, understand the culture, and are the culture.
- *Empathy.* Saved students know how the unsaved student thinks, feels, believes, etc.
- *Relationships.* Saved students are naturally engaged in friendship structures with unsaved students.
- *Proximity.* Saved students are currently in the culture and already among the unsaved student.
- *Social interaction.* The saved student is among unsaved peers for 7,560 hours between sixth and twelfth grades (6 hour school days x 180 days per school year x 7 years).
- *Credibility.* Saved students are more trusted and believed by a peer more than an adult.

When you think about it, student ministry is missional ministry. Not just the typical concept of one fulfilling the mission of Jesus in seeking and saving the lost but also missional in the strategy. As someone who grew up in a godly home preparing for overseas Christian ministry, I remember hearing both of my parents speak of the journey needed to be an ambassador for Christ in a foreign land. The journey consisted of years of higher Christian education, seeking a sending mission agency, being accepted by such an agency, years of raising support, finishing up with one year of language school. This can easily be a ten-year process from one's calling to the actual launching. Even after a missionary arrives on site, it may take years for a missionary to become integrated in the native culture so as to be trusted by the local people before there is ever any evidence of spiritual fruit.

Remember who reaches students? Our Christian youth are already on the campus and in the population. They speak the native language and know the native culture. They already have credibility and proximity. But what is missing? Who will help them see they are the players to reach the generation and who will equip them to fulfill the task?

## WHAT WE CAN DO TO EQUIP OUR STUDENTS TO REACH THEIR PEERS

One of the highlights of my own student ministry career was observing and hearing about our students connecting Jesus Christ to their friends. I have frequently stated I would rather have teenagers lead their friends to Christ than me lead their friends to Christ. Not only are they the ones who are more naturally placed to do this, but also I loved seeing their own love for Jesus and faith in God's sovereign hand grow through this experience. One verse that each of our missions team participants needed to memorize during our training time was Philemon 6: "And I pray that the sharing of your faith may become effective for the full knowledge of every good thing that is in us for the sake of Christ." When students see another individual their age open up to the person of Jesus Christ, they more deeply realize the treasure they have. To think that what they have grown up with most of their life is more than Bible stories, it is power of the almighty God to save.

The following are ten areas that are essential to create a culture of outreach in your own student ministries and in the lives of your students. I call these the ten axioms of training students to reach their generation. The premise of each of these axioms is that we as student ministry leaders personally own these and implement them into the life of our ministry structure and ministry culture. Once these are in place, we encourage our students to own these and embrace them into their own lives.

### AXIOM 1: *INTENTIONAL.*
### You have to be on purpose. (Missional)

Both leaders and students need to be intentional. They need to be on purpose (i.e., be missional). Here is how they can do this:

*Leaders.* When we see someone, do we see a person Jesus died for and desperately loves? Are people something we use as a means to an end or do we use our resources to reach people? Does our own ministry value people as eternal beings created in the image of God? Do the students see this evidenced in how our ministry treats people?

*Students.* Urge your students to step into their school each morning seeing it as the mission field where God has called them. Teach them intentional living. Every relationship with a lost person needs to be focused to give that person the opportunity to come to Christ.

## AXIOM 2: *INSPIRATIONAL.*
### You have to be persuasive. (Motivate)

*Leaders.* I have often asked myself the question, "When people see me, would they want what I have?" Is the joy of the Lord truly my strength? Does my life make people attracted to Jesus Christ (Titus 2:10)? I am not suggesting that Christians always need to have a goofy smirk on their face. I am suggesting what Paul and Silas modeled for us in a Philippian jail right after they illegally had their backs beaten: joy, worship, and contentment in the middle of a rocking prison experience. Their calmness and joy got the attention of a certain jailor, and a church in Philippi was born (Acts 16:22–34).

*Students.* Our students need to understand that their lives must be filled with joy and not a complaining spirit. Paul speaks of this in Philippians 2:14–15 when he called us to stop complaining and shine like stars. A powerful witness to lost students can take place during your youth meetings when your students are positive during worship and the teaching of the Word. Also, encourage students to have positive social media postings!

## AXIOM 3: *INFLUENTIAL.*
### You have be in position. (Model)

*Leaders.* We sometimes refer to this as "a divine appointment." The Scriptures give us so many characters who were at the right place at the right time. Paul during the shipwreck is a great example of this (Acts 27–28). Another example is Esther. Her relative Mordecai, who also knew the power of position, recognized God's divine hand in her position as queen when he admonished her to speak up and defend her people by saying, "And who knows but that you have come to your royal position for such a time as this?" (Esther 4:14 NIV). We as leaders can seek positions of community influence as coaches, substitute teachers, tutors, committee members, etc. We can also have our ministries be in places of influence. Let our lights shine!

*Students.* Encourage your students to be involved in their school and community. Affirm them when they want to be involved in marching band, sports teams, and student government. Keep reminding them to be Pauls and Esthers. Be in places of influence so that where there is a need, Christian students can lead.

## AXIOM 4: *INTERCESSIONAL*.
### You have to be in prayer. (Mediate)

*Leaders.* While there is much to be said about prayer, the context within this section is on outreach; therefore we need to be praying for Christ to reach lost people. One of the greatest passages on being effective gospel communicators is Colossians 4:2–6. At the start of this "how to" approach to evangelism, Paul teaches us to devote ourselves to prayer. One of my ministry heroes, Ron Hutchcraft, uses this passage as the layout of what he refers to as the "three open prayer." Ron calls us to pray for the Lord to open three places: open a ministry door, open the lost person's heart, and open my mouth.[5] I have used this principle for years within my own ministries and my own life.

Some suggestions for creating a culture of prayer are to go on community prayer walks or have the students pray in groups for their own campus and their unsaved friends. Make sure you have group prayer time over your events. At this point, I believe I must mention I have received some push back to having any public prayer by those quoting Jesus and the "prayer closet" teaching but they are misunderstanding the interpretation. We are admonished by Christ about the motive of prayer as we should not pray to be seen of men. However, Jesus prayed in public on many occasions, including right in the middle of one of His sermons (Matthew 11:25–26). There are numerous times in Scripture we see public prayers done within groups where God was pleased and showed Himself (Acts 2, 4, 12).

Leaders, I urge you to speak much of prayer, teach on prayer, and exemplify to your students a life of prayer. When a student has an issue or a need, just stop and pray with them. Many times we will have prayer requests but also take the time to share the answers to prayer. Make prayer a vital part of the DNA of your ministry over your ministry events and the lives of the students.

*Students.* Encourage much of what was just previously mentioned for the students, to do on their own. Have your students pray in front of their peers.

While being a student pastor, I especially encouraged our young men to pray. Many times I would hear from our guys, "Dude, I don't pray." If I let this go unchecked I am only continuing to exacerbate the problem of having men who don't pray in our church and men who don't pray with their wives. Even now in premarital counseling I ask the young man to close the session in prayer. This is intentional as I want him to take the lead and have his fiancé see him taking the lead.

## AXIOM 5: *INDIVIDUAL.*
### You have to be personal. (Minister)

*Leaders.* As ministers we need to see people not as numbers or parts of larger groups but as individuals. Christ saw the woman at the well not necessarily as a Samaritan or as a woman but as a person. This is what pastoral ministry is about: caring for people as Christ cares for them. When your ministry has guests, do what you can to focus on them in an individual basis. Think through what you can do to start treating people as individuals and ministering to them in a personal way. Do your guests feel valued and significant when they are with your group?

Think of it like this: what is your favorite fast-food restaurant and why is it your favorite? I know which one is mine and both of my sons have worked for this national chain. When I go to any of these particular franchises across the country, I am consistently treated with a smile, warmth, and respect. I cannot say that for any other fast-food restaurant chain where I have been a patron. If you're not sure which fast-food restaurant I am referring, let's just say it's a "pleasure" to go there!

*Students.* Let's teach our students to be aware of the personal touch when dealing with unsaved students. Do not ever allow negative comments or a jeer to be made when the new student "Steve" is introduced from "Central High School". I actually encouraged my youth to attend another out-of-town student ministry just to see what it would be like to be treated as a new person.

## AXIOM 6: *INSTINCTUAL.*
### You have to be perceptive. (Be mature)

*Leaders.* As described in the teaching section, we need to discern the specific needs of the individual. When in the context of reaching lost students, listen to what they are saying. Don't just hear the words; sincerely listen to what they are saying.

You are going to have students visit your ministry and push back when you speak of God's truth. As Colossians 4:6 states, "Let your speech always be gracious, seasoned with salt, so that you may know how you ought to answer each person." There is typically a reason unsaved students are so quick to get reactive, angry, and/or defensive. Be patient and seek to find out where they are coming from.

*Students.* Also encourage this same grace to be given through your students to those without Christ. If you teach your students to walk in the Spirit, He will lead them into such mature perceptivity. I have observed that students seem to be more in tune with this instinctiveness mindset than sometime we adults are. They will pick up on the hurts and needs of others sometimes quicker than we do. When we see this positive action in our students, affirm them for being sensitive to the Lord and others.

## AXIOM 7: *INSTRUCTIONAL.*
### You have to be prepared. (Know the message)

*Leaders.* We as adults need to communicate the gospel in an intellectual, reasonable, and culturally understandable means. Even the apostle Paul was concerned whether his message would be clear: "Pray that I may proclaim it clearly, as I should" (Colossians 4:4 NIV). I define the gospel clearly to my university students as having two components: theologically correct and culturally connect. Share the whole plan of salvation. This includes the deity of Christ. As the perfect Son of God, He is the only one who can bring us to a holy God. Speak of repentance and surrender to Jesus Christ. Share that it is nothing anyone of us can do to achieve the forgiveness of God. It is 100 percent God's amazing grace. Salvation is not a combo meal—a little of God and a little of me. It is purely God's intervention and my faith act of surrender to Him.

Yet as we share this *"mystery"* (v. 3), we need to do it in a way that today's postmodern and post-Christian adolescents can understand. I would rather have the patience to work with a lost student helping them move toward a genuine conversion than to have us "seal the deal" (as I have heard some say) by having them repeat a prayer before they even understand the essentials of Christianity and desire to be a Christ follower.

*Student.* There are four key areas in which we can equip our students. One key area is to *equip your students with the essentials of the gospel.* Help them understand the doctrinal aspects of the gospel. The second area is to *teach them how to succinctly and sensibly share their testimony.* They can learn how to do this by writing it out and going over it with each other. The third area is to *teach them some simple tools to share the gospel*, such as the Bridge illustration from the Navigators. Yet the fourth is crucial and that is to *keep the gospel natural* and not like we are telemarketers. As already noted, our students should be looking for natural ways to connect God into the conversation.

Ultimately we need to help our students see it is the Holy Spirit who convicts lost people, yet He uses us to communicate God's truth with lost people. Help them learn to be led by the Spirit as He directs them to move the conversation forward or to step back. Do what you can to have your students learn to be patient while working with lost people. Ultimately help them see they are the key players in reaching their generation. As I used to tell my high school students, this student ministry is designed to help you fulfill your own personal evangelistic efforts.

## AXIOM 8: *INSISTENCE.*
### You have to persevere. (Be patient)

*Leaders.* This point has been referred to in the previous axiom about preparation for the moment—we are to be patient while sharing the gospel with lost students. While one's conversion is instantaneous, there is a process of one coming to faith (Hebrews 11:6). Reflect on the relationship of Jesus and Nicodemus. Jesus did not pressure Nicodemus into a "decision" during the evening of spiritual discussion (John 3), yet we see him begin to defend and identify with Jesus (John 7:49–51). Later on during the burial, while the apostles were hiding in the upper room, Nicodemus is at the grave site assisting fellow Jewish leader Joseph of Arimathea with the loving act of preparing the body of Christ for burial (John 19:39–40). While the Scriptures never directly state that Nicodemus became born again, the indication is there.

While ministering in Seattle there were two seniors who began attending our seeker Wednesday night meetings through the ministry of one of our senior girls. These two guests told me right away they considered themselves atheists. We pulled them right into our ministry and lives. It was such a reward to see them move through various stages of atheism to Christianity: being an atheist, the plausibility of a god, there is a god, this god is Jehovah God, the reality of a historical Jesus, and, well, you have the point. It was months of patience, genuine care, teaching sound doctrine, and answering questions that led to both of their conversions two weeks shy of their high school graduation. It was such fun to see God at work drawing them into their conversion. I actually laughed just a few weeks before their salvations knowing it was only a matter of time before God would do what God does! Do not see people as projects but treat them with gentleness and respect (1 Peter 3:15).

*Students.* What made the above story so rewarding was how God used one of our young ladies as His ambassador. Brittany's faithful integrity, love, and spiritual dialogue were fundamental to her friends' conversions. It was not me—it was a student reaching a student. I will never forget that Thursday morning as I walked into my office and checked my phone for messages. There was a message from Brittany, more excited than I had ever heard her. You would have thought the Seahawks just won the Super Bowl (well, that was over ten years before the Seahawks *did* win the Super Bowl). "Rich, Rich! (Name withheld) just got saved last night!" To give the backstory, after our Wednesday night meetings most of the students would go out to eat. My encouragement had been for our students to use this time for ministry. After they brought their lost friends to our group, go out and be "normal" with their lost friends but look for ways to open up spiritual conversation. Praise the Lord, the students began using times like this for ministry. It was after such a time at Red Robin and on their drive home this young lady met Christ. Just think what your students could do! Yum . . .

## AXIOM 9: *INVOLVEMENT.*
### You should work in partnership. (Act as a team)

*Leaders.* Evangelism should be seen as a team approach. When we consider evangelistic involvement with others, I think from both the individual and organizational perspectives. In chapter 15, "The Essential of Partnering with Other Ministries," we will focus on some principles regarding this subject. Allow me to focus on the individual approach. Have you ever seen how God orchestrates events in a lost person by bringing various believers into their life? It is like you having a friendly conversation about the Lord with a lost student. God then uses that to spark a spiritual interest in his or her heart. While unknown to you, God begins to use some students to take the conversation further. Ultimately He has another faithful ambassador who answers the intimate questions of faith as this lost student comes to Christ. This may even be your own story of grace.

So who led this young person to Christ? While so many would say it is the last person mentioned I say it was God who used a team (1 Corinthians 3:6–7). Maybe we should stop putting the emphasis of evangelism on the "soul winner" as we have treated evangelism like a business person making sales and begin to embrace the team approach where God receives the glory. Leader, please teach your students to work together.

On a side note, make sure the ministry structure is set up in such a way so to have your various ministries and meetings working together. This has been mentioned in chapter 10 when speaking of the teaching series and meetings in collaboration with each other. Using one weekly meeting to spend time in prayer, Bible teaching, and focused communication of the other meeting committed to outreach can prove very advantageous.

*Students.* So much of what the student should be doing in partnering with others may already be evident to you as you have read the previous section. Encourage your students to interact with each other as they graciously share Christ with their lost friend. Remind them people are not projects, and they should not have a "mob" mentality over a lost person. Rather they should reach out with grace. Continue to remind them to partner with your ministry structure as you seek to help/assist them in their evangelistic efforts.

One final thought about partnering: Our students must remember the only kingdom to be built is the one of Jesus Christ and not their own church. Their concern about their lost peers being saved is greater than having the lost teenager attending their youth ministry. They need to work together with the students from other churches as well to advance the kingdom of Jesus Christ.

> Only let your manner of life be worthy of the gospel of Christ, so that whether I come and see you or am absent, I may hear of you that you are standing firm in one spirit, with one mind striving side by side for the faith of the gospel. (Philippians 1:27)

When it comes to involvement, remember that successful youth evangelism should see student ministry leaders and the saved students working in partnership for the gospel. The three components of outreach involvement are shown in the following circle chart. Starting with the strategic structure (base of circle), the leaders should develop a ministry structure that includes equipping their saved students for personal evangelism as well as ministry events designed for clear gospel presentations. Moving to the saved students, these students should be the ones integrating Christ into the lives of their seeking friends. As the saved students are personally sharing Christ with their lost peers and the leadership provides various outreach events, the seeking student should be able to experience the gospel from both a personal peer relationship and a community of believers. Thus, a student ministry should be assisting each Christian student in his or her personal outreach efforts. We as leaders should simply be the background of outreach as the saved students are at the foreground. By incorporating this model, leaders are properly equipping the youth to do the ministry and not doing the ministry for the youth.

## THREE COMPONENTS OF OUTREACH INVOLVEMENT

AXIOM 10: *INDWELL IN THE SPIRIT.*
You have to do this in the Lord's power. (Employ *His* might)

*Leaders.* Make this front and center—only Jesus is the One who will build His church, and it is His church to build (Matthew 16:18). And how this is to be done is by the power of His Holy Spirit. In the book of Acts, the Holy Spirit is mentioned sixty-seven times and in almost each case the verse has to do with His work of building up God's church. Understand this for yourself before you teach this to others. Anything you do or any ministry you create must be accomplished through His undergirding and strength. Anything short of this is robbery of the glory of God.

*Students.* Teach your students to be filled with the Spirit. This is so imperative as it is only from Him that we can overcome fear but have power, love, and discipline (see 2 Timothy 1:7). It is only through Him we can guard what God has given us—His truth and His message (2 Timothy 1:13–14). And it is only through Him that the spiritually dead can have life (Titus 3:5–6). They need to realize that they are not responsible for "saving someone." The work of salvation was fulfilled by Christ on the cross and the work of causing someone to repent of their sin and turn to Christ is the Holy Spirit (1 Peter 1:2). We are just the ambassadors. The Holy Spirit is the One to do the convicting and the calling.

Currently each fall the Liberty University youth ministry department hosts a large outreach event. This event lasts nine evenings and attracts over 25,000 people annually. For years I have had the responsibility of training and organizing the gospel presentation. It is such a reward to come alongside the students who I love, serve, and mentor in the classroom as together we present Christ. I coach, but they are the players. I equip, but they are the speakers. They are the ones who share Christ. As we conclude our prayer time each evening before the event begins, I see the nervousness on their faces. I want to share with you what I share with them each night after our prayer time, "Share God's truth, be filled with God's Spirit, love these people, and let Jesus be the Lord of the harvest. The pressure is off!" The relieved looks on their faces is priceless.

## PUTTING THIS ALL TOGETHER

Of course much more is available about presenting the very good news known as the gospel. I encourage you to find resources that will enable you to further equip your students. There are many fine ones available.

According to the US Census Bureau, there were 41,844,000 youth in between the ages of ten and nineteen in 2012. This is 14 percent of the total United States population.[6] When one factors in the 96 percent statistic in Rainer's *The Bridger Generation*, this means we are looking at 40,170,000 adolescents who are in darkness and need Christ. This leaves us with 1,674,000 students who need to become serious about reaching their generation. They are already called to be His ambassadors. We must equip them to effectively reach this generation for Jesus Christ.

---

## NOTES

1. George Barna, "Evangelism Is Most Effective Among Kids," Barna Update; http://www.barna.org/flexpage.aspx?page=barnaupdate&barnaupdateid=72 (Wheaton, Ill.: Victor Books, 1992), 129–30.

2. Mark H. Senter III, *The Coming Revolution in Youth Ministry* (Wheaton, Ill.: Victor Books, 1992), 129–30.

3. Thom S. Rainer, *The Bridger Generation* (Nashville: Broadman & Holman, 1997), 169.

4. George Barna, *Third Millennium Teens* (Ventura, Calif.: Barna Research Group, 1999), xx.

5. Ron Hutchcraft, *Called to Greatness* (Chicago: Moody, 2001), 61–65.

6. "Age and Sex Composition in the United States: 2012," Table 1: Population by Age and Sex: 2002"; http://www.census.gov/population/age/data/2012comp.html.

# 13

# THE ESSENTIAL OF
# INTENTIONAL OUTREACH EVENTS

S tep back for a moment. Once you have understood the essential of competent programming (chapter 11) and the essential of properly equipping your students as the players to reach this generation (chapter 12), it is time to look into the mechanics of designing an effective outreach event.

This chapter will focus on ten major administrative and ministry areas that should be considered when putting together your evangelistic event. Clearly these ten areas are not the only issues or needs that you will have in developing an event. They are simply to get you started and guide you along the way.

Two things to keep in mind as you look at these ten areas. First, these areas are actually "steps," as they move chronologically from purpose and planning to the nuts and bolts of pulling off the event. Second, these ten steps directly focus on the level two event—the *evangelizing* event; however, many of these same principles can apply to events within the other three levels of ministry—events of *entry* that *edify* and *equip*.

## STEP 1: YOUR PURPOSE

As in the case of every student ministry event, you must have purpose. Choose and define what will be your purpose. Since this event is going to focus on the target audience of spiritually lost adolescents, you can either use the entry-level approach (level one) where there is the visual presentation of Christ or the evangelistic approach (level two). Will your outreach event be to open doors for future ministry as you have a "fun" and low-key time of relational building (entry) or will it be to directly share the plan of salvation (evangelistic)? You need to establish your purpose.

Once you have *strategically chosen* the purpose of the event, you have to *successfully communicate* this purpose to others. Success at this will lead to triumph; failure will lead to tragedy. Effective ministry depends on this point. You can have the greatest outreach event planned since Pentecost but if the right people aren't behind it and ready for it, it may not be as successful as you had desired.

### To Who Do I Communicate the Purpose?

Here are the five audiences to whom you must communicate effectively in order to have a successful event:

1. *The adult leadership team.* I suggest this is the first place to start. After all, they are the ones who typically carry out much of the work.

2. *The students.* As the players, they are the ones who are going to bring in the lost students.

3. *The church leadership.* Consider the benefits of the backing you can get if you get your pastors and adult leaders excited about your upcoming event. If they can be enthusiastic about the upcoming event, they will have significant influence with the next two groups.

4. *The parents.* If you can get the parents excited about the outreach event, this should help their own child to attend and have their child attend with a lost friend. This is another way your ministry can partner with parents.

5. *The church body.* If the members and regular attenders of your church become excited about this student ministry outreach, just contemplate the many benefits this brings to who you are as a student ministry and your place in the church.

### How Do I Communicate the Purpose?

1. *The adult leadership team.* This starts back at the beginning of your planning stage for your ministry year. The leadership team should have known about this for months and should have already bought into this back then, especially if they were part of the planning. By

this time in your training, your leaders will already understand the four levels of ministry and will know what to expect with this event.

2. *The students.* Obviously you must publicly explain this purpose when you announce the event. Do this creatively and passionately. But to be more effective than just the group announcements, you need to identify who are your influential students and go after them. If they can get excited about the event and own the vision of this purpose, they are the ones who influence their peers and hopefully will invigorate others in your group. As I continue to read through the Gospels, I see this principle in the ministry of our Lord. The people were amazed at His teaching, were in awe of His miracles, and kept bringing more people to come to see and hear Jesus.

3. *The church leadership.* Secure a meeting with your senior leadership (the senior pastor would be ideal) and explain what you are doing and why you are doing it. Ask them to help "our" student ministry by getting behind this event and using their influence to help the adult ministries to become excited about this event as well. Then set up a specific strategy how they can do this.

4. *The parents.* So much of youth events' attendance goes back to properly communicating to parents throughout the year using as many means as are available. Just like your strategy with students, use the public forum to explain the purpose and also use the personal touch. You should be doing this with parents anyway but also use your leaders in this process. As you do this, hopefully their child is excited and the senior leadership is doing their part. This means the parents are hearing about upcoming events from three sources.

5. *The church body.* Ideally, you have the senior pastor and senior leadership communicating this event. With them on board, request their permission to allow you to present a quality promotional piece, whether a video presentation, public announcement, or creative bulletin insert, during one or more of the morning services. During this time, explain why you are doing this event and ask the church to get involved in any way they can to see God use "our" youth ministry as these students are on the cutting edge as cultural missionaries to their generation. Next, have this event tactfully promoted throughout the church building. Make this event visible! Finally, maybe you can have your students visit adult groups to share their vision for this event and ask for prayer as they are inviting their friends.

# STEP 2: YOUR PLAN

Once you establish your purpose, begin to plan out your organizational structure. Over the years I developed my own organizational system consisting of some simple planning tools: an event planner form, an action item timeline form, a budget form, and an organizational flow chart. While this may sound like a lot of paperwork, by using these tools, we were able to organize the events, budget accordingly, and have each team member carry out specific tasks. The time spent on planning ahead was an investment and not a waste of time.

I encourage you to search online for such resources or ask other student ministry professionals what they use. A number of student ministry books include such forms. For you who are creative, work on developing your own forms. My forms were very basic yet functional. Many readers could develop a much better system than I did. If you are not the creative type, reach out to others who are to help.

# STEP 3: YOUR PROMOTION

You can have a great purpose and a great plan but you must get the word out to lost students if you want them to come to the event. Within my planner form I had two charts to assist me in planning out the needed promotion. One had the promotional ideas all listed in two categories of external (community) promotion and internal (church) promotion. The second chart focused on the timeline of promotion based on the ideas.

## THE SEVEN W'S, PLUS THE HOOK, LOOK, AND TOOK

The rapidly developing electronic age of social media can be a valuable resource in spreading the word about your events, so don't overlook Facebook and the like for promotion. No matter what type of promotional method you choose to use, I teach our students to follow seven crucial areas of promotional communication (the seven W's):

- *Who.* Communicate the specific *age group* who you are inviting.
- *What.* Communicate the *name* or *theme* of the event.
- *When.* Communicate the *date* and *time* of the even, including the ending time.
- *Where.* Communicate the *location* of the event. If you are traveling to the location, also put where you are initially meeting and returning.

- *Why*. Communicate the *reason* the student would want to come.
- *Worth*. Communicate how much the event will *cost to attend*.
- *With*. Communicate the *church* or *organization* to who you are *connected*. Make sure you put your church's contact information. This is crucial, especially if this is an outreach event! Unsaved parents may have no idea who "Ignite" is but if they see a line that explains this student ministry is from First Community Church, complete with the church's contact information; they will have better assurance of its identity and credibility.

As mentioned in chapter 10, much of promotion is similar to the same method used when developing and presenting a lesson. Keep in mind the benefit of:

The *HOOK* (to capture their attention).

The *LOOK* (to cover the information).

The *TOOK* (to convince them to attend).

## THE BEST COMMUNICATION: PERSON TO PERSON

Finally, I honestly believe the most effective means of promotion is person to person. It is what worked in the Gospels and the book of Acts. This is the benefit of your students having the vision of outreach and being equipped to naturally connect with their peers. As your students are excited about the Lord Jesus and their student ministry, they will want to bring their generation to these events. Use the promotional means of getting the word out but energize your students to be the ones to bring in lost teenagers. *People typically will not attend a function unless they know someone who will be there.* This is true for not just for students, but people of all ages.

If this event is not correctly promoted to lost students and you only have your church group show up for the outreach event, something broke down. You will not have a genuine outreach event without any unsaved people there! To help encapsulate this concept, study the descriptive lines below:

*Public Promotion*: Information / Fact-based / Supportive

*Personal Promotion*: Invitation / Friend-based / Students

Therefore, be excellent and creative at your public promotion. It is within this promotional aspect where you provide the necessary information about the event for both the potential visiting students and their parents. This information is usually fact-based (the time of the event, the location, any cost involved, the sponsoring church or organization, etc.). Yet while this information is needed, it typically plays a more supportive role and not a primary role in the decision of the lost student to attend.

As already noted above, very seldom will a teenager attend an evangelical event simply by observation of an event's promotion. As adults we must keep in mind teenagers are social beings. They do life in groups; therefore, encourage and equip your students to take the lead in inviting their unsaved friends to the event in a very personable way. They are the key influencers because students reach students. While using the students as the primary means of bringing in the lost, provide excellent promotional materials and resources that your students can utilize as a tool to communicate the event to their friends.

# STEP 4: YOUR PAYMENT PLAN

## THE FIVE CHOICES

The next step is to determine how to pay for the event. Typically there are five varied methods to budget for ministry. Below is a list for you to consider. Many times ministry events can be done in a collaborative way.

- *Self-Providing.* Provided from within the student ministries by the individuals themselves.
- *Support/Fund-raisers.* Provided from within the student ministries but receive monies from outside sources.
- *Sponsors/Scholarships.* Provided for by church people and/or outside sources (businesses, organizations, etc.).
- *Special Offerings.* Provided by the church or smaller groups within the church.
- *Submitted Church Budget.* Provided by the church as part of its entire church budget.

## WHEN TO CHARGE FOR EVENTS

Each event may be approached differently. You may have many events that are entirely paid for by an admission charge (self-providing). Most of my events were done by this means. However, for many of the larger events it is beneficial to use a combination approach. A simple house rule is *use your submitted church budget for your ministry programming and use the self-providing method (students) to pay for the events.*

I believe it is very appropriate to charge for events. These are typically social events for your students. Think about it, they pay to go to other events in their lives like their high school games and the movies. These are all places where they go to have a good time "above and beyond" their normal routine. While I would never charge for anything held during our weekly meetings, I did not have a problem charging for the events that are additional to the overall weekly program. Charging for your special events is different than charging students to "come to church."

## WHAT TO CHARGE FOR EVENTS

With all this as context, the event has to pay for itself. How one does this may be done creatively but each expense item needs to be accounted for. So how much do you charge? Carefully note the following questions:

- What is your means of paying for the event?
- What are the total expenses of the event?
- What is the legitimate estimate of how many students are attending?

It then becomes a matter of simple math. In using the *self-providing* method, you would take your total expenses and divide the number by how many students are expected. That is your ticket price. For a combination approach, it is a little more complex. This is where utilizing planner forms and budget forms are beneficial. One suggestion is to use your *submitted budget* for larger expenses (i.e., transportation), donations from *sponsors* for smaller areas (i.e., refreshments), and use the *self-providing* method as the students pay for the rest. When attending events that are more entertainment based, like going to a theme park or a concert, I find it wise to have the student pay for their own ticket and the other methods provide for additional costs.

# STEP 5: YOUR PLAYERS

Once again notice the value of building a hardworking and competent team. By utilizing an organizational chart, you can divide each event into various divisions, areas, and teams. Use both your adults and students within these various areas of the event. I preferred having an adult who is an advisor over each specific team and then bringing in a student who shared in the oversight of that area. While I am never suggesting we as adults abdicate leadership, *student involvement is crucial to an effective event.* Student involvement normally depends on the age of the youth. I preferred juniors and seniors in key leadership positions. Of course one should also use more students to be involved in the various teams. Giving responsibility to students may be a little taxing, but be creative on how you can involve people with the skills and abilities God gave them. On a different note, be careful in putting any student in responsibilities during the event that would detract from them being with their visiting friends. After all, this is their top priority.

# STEP 6: YOUR PASSION

This is one of the foundational programming principles. It has to start with the leader in order to be caught by the adults and leadership students. There should be a sense of excitement and anticipation mounting before the event. We have all sensed this feeling before the big game or before the concert. And we all can understand this mounting sense of excitement when as children we counted down the days to Christmas. Are you feeling it now? Are you getting pumped up? The steps used in promotion can be tremendous contributors in developing a sense of passion for the event. And you as leader have the chance to be communicating with your students that in "x" amount of days you will all have the chance to present Christ and to see lives come to Him. That should get people passionate!

# STEP 7: YOUR PROGRAM

## SCHEDULE

Type out a basic schedule (also referred to by others as a cue sheet, or timeline). This should include everything from when you first arrive and conclude when you finish with cleanup and turn out the lights. Each transition should be identified in the schedule.

## GAMES

Do you have any games you are planning on incorporating into your schedule? While you may decide to integrate a variety of such games, I found two different categories of games to be helpful during the actual event: *crowd breakers* and *crowd mixers*.

In *crowd breakers* students come on stage to do some type of feat or challenge, similar to a game show. In the crowd breaker, there are a few participants while the majority of students watch; thus the word *breaker*, as this is helping break the ice. One word of caution is to make sure you guard one of the foundational principles of respecting people. These breakers should never be used to mock or belittle a student but only to build up students.

With *crowd mixers* you engage most if not all of the students in some type of game or challenge. Significantly, you want each one involved and no one on the sidelines observing. This type of game may vary in length as it may be brief or be the majority of the event.

## DECORATIONS/ATMOSPHERE

When I use the word *decoration* please do not think of streamers and balloons. I am referring to the decor of the event. If it is a "fifth quarter" event, then make the football theme bigger than life. Be creative and have the environment take on the look and feel of your theme.

## REFRESHMENTS/FOOD

While food is optional, I seriously recommend it at your outreach events. You also need to keep in mind the time of day and the length of the event. If your event is during a typical mealtime, then you better provide a meal. If it is at other times, provide more of a lighter spread, typically snack food. Personally, I valued using the refreshment time to be a great opportunity for interaction and was built into the schedule accordingly. As one takes a look into the ministry of Jesus Christ, food was often present (Matthew 9:9–13; Mark 6:34–44). And if it wasn't, He could make it happen. It's your call if you want to use refreshments or not, but it sure is a good option to consider!

## MUSIC/WORSHIP

There are different thoughts on using worship for an outreach event; i.e., can an unbeliever truly worship God, etc.? You may choose to use music or not use music. I have my own thoughts based on John 4, but I will say this—while I personally am not convinced a lost person can truly worship God from the heart until the Spirit is in them (John 4:21–24), an unsaved person can see the majesty of God (Psalm 19:1). Thus times of worship can be used to reveal our great God to the lost. We see this principle in a Philippian jail (Acts 16:25–30). Besides, students love music!

My personal take on this is to keep a balance on the time. While music can be used to pull students together and quiet their hearts for the Word, I also told our leadership I did not want a "full worship experience" when our target audience was lost students. This type of intimate worship is what we do for our times together. This may be an odd way to put it, but do you remember the time you were with a friend who took you into another group of friends and all of their conversation was about things that you had absolutely no idea about? You felt really awkward and totally out of the conversation.

## THE GOSPEL PRESENTATION

If your purpose is an evangelistic outreach event, then you will need to culturally communicate the gospel of Jesus Christ. As already mentioned in the chapter on equipping students, we must make sure the gospel is clearly communicated. This can take place in a variety of ways. What I found so exciting was having students be the ones who gave the gospel presentation of Jesus Christ, shared their testimony, or did the counseling. However while we do want student involvement, we also want those representing the gospel to be authentic in their lifestyle and qualified to accomplish the ministry. Finally, prepare for harvest! Make sure you have prepared the correct people to be available to speak with students afterward. In addition, have available various materials for those who are investigating Christianity and follow-up material for any who receive Christ.

# STEP 8: YOUR PERSONAL TOUCH

As seen throughout much of this book, the ministry is not the program. Ministry is all about people. Keep everything you do at a personal level and with a personal touch. One way to assist this is implementing a greeting or hospitality team. Please note that this team should be pleasant and not overbearing. We have all entered the store or the used car lot and had the school of piranhas come after us. Yet even with a hospitality team in place, the most important person of personal touch is the student who brought the new student. Encourage and even teach your students how to connect their friends socially to others in the group in a way that is pleasant and not overbearing. Something our team began doing was making up guest bags for each of the first-time visitors. The bag consisted of things students like: candy, movie tickets, more candy, and a ministry information card thanking them for coming. People will ultimately return if they feel loved, accepted, and safe.

# STEP 9: YOUR PERSPECTIVE

The day for the event is finally here! You have done the hard work. All of the planning and preparation are completed. Now the event is actually upon you. Just like a sports player going into the first game of the season, you will have this adrenaline rush mixed in with anticipation, excitement, and this nervous sense of "did I forget something?" As you now begin the event there are five things to keep in mind. As the leader:

1. *Keep your EYES open!* You are the "producer" and "director" of this event. This event was probably birthed in your heart. Of all people, you know how it should look and be implemented. Be noticing the students who are there, especially the new ones. Be noticing the parents as they drop off their kids. Be looking for any areas that are struggling. And be noticing what God is doing at the event. After all, isn't this Who you are doing this for?

2. *Make sure the event is EFFECTIVE.* This is similar to the first point. If your game is not doing well, then drop it! If the band leader gets mad and leaves before the worship set, move on. If you have this great outreach retreat planned, complete with all of your talks written, and it is only your churched youth who have registered, then change the talks. (These are all real-life situations I have had to work through.) Do what is needed to be effective and be flexible as needed. Don't ever forget the student ministry code: Semper Gumby—Always Flexible.

3. *ENJOY the event!* Don't get so caught up in the details you forget to enjoy watching the event unfold. Take time to notice the great job your leaders and students have done in putting all of these dreams into becoming a reality. Enjoy your leaders. Enjoy your students. Laugh with them! And don't ever be too high and mighty not to get down and dirty with the events.

4. *ENCOURAGE those around you!* As you are going through your event, remember to be an encourager. I am convinced a *great leader* is a *great motivator* and a *great motivator* is a *great encourager*. We are so good at noticing people doing something wrong; how about noticing people doing something that is right? We are so good at telling people where they are failing; what about telling people where they are succeeding? Without positive feedback being given, how are your students and leaders going to know what they did was done correctly? Encourage your players as you go throughout the event. And when it is all done, *thank each one* of your leaders and workers for the specific role they played in making the event a success.

5. *Exude ENTHUSIASM during the event!* Romans 12:11 (NIV) states, "Never be lacking in zeal, but keep your spiritual fervor, serving the Lord." While we serve our Lord Jesus Christ, we are commanded to keep up tenacity and enthusiasm. According to

Strong's Concordance, the Greek word for *fervor* is *ze,* which refers to boiling with heat or to be hot, as one would boil hot water in a kettle. We are to be "boiling" about what is going on! We must be the ones to set the temperature. So even when things aren't going as planned, put your game face on and keep going. Everyone can still have a good time if people have enthusiasm.

## STEP 10: YOUR PRAYERS

Just because we are looking at this last does *not* signify prayer is something we must add on to make the entire event look spiritual. Prayer is the most vital of the ten steps. *Nothing of eternal significance ever happens apart from prayer!* Throughout each of these steps, I believe you should be praying. Prayer has been a vital part in the chapter on equipping students to reach others for Christ. Prayer is one of the ten foundational programming principles (chapter 11).

Involve your church in tangible ways to pray for this event. Involve your students in tangible ways to pray for this event and for the Lord to open the blind eyes of their generation. And obviously each of your adult leaders needs to be lifting these areas up to the Lord. Let's spend time talking to God about lost people and not just us talking to lost people about God.

As we close this chapter, please remember what was mentioned at the beginning of chapter 11: *Events or programs by themselves do not save anyone. They are simply a tool. There is nothing spiritual or "anointed" about a ministry tool.* Yet just like a surgeon's tool can be used to save a life, so a ministry tool (an event) can be used to save a life.

## GAMES, PIZZA, AND NEW LIFE

It was a Friday night middle school event. After the local football game there would be pizza, some crazy games, and a gospel presentation at Grace Church. Nothing that any other youth ministry has probably not done; just your basic fifth quarter gathering. As our team planned out the event, promoted this in the schools and with the students, set up the fellowship hall, secured the pizzas, and had prayer, we anticipated God to show up.

When I first met her that night over twenty years ago, Holly was in the eighth grade. Her friend Emily had recently been saved and wanted Holly also to come to Christ. After the games and pizza, the students all sat on the floor for my talk. I will never forget her face being so expressive and taking it all in as I shared the message of Jesus. God had prepared this precious young lady's heart. It was that night she reached out to the Lord and He saved her. Later, she wrote about that night and beyond:

> Growing up in the Catholic Church, I had been to many church events, but never one event where the gospel was clearly shared. When I came to the event with my friend Emily, I simply expected a pizza party. I am so grateful that I came away with a relationship with Christ. I am thankful for youth staff who clearly shared the gospel that night. Since the gospel was shared in my youth ministry regularly, I knew where I could bring friends to hear the truth. Today I have the opportunity to regularly plan ministry events for children, both in and outside of the church. I know firsthand how vital it is to share Christ's message of salvation at these events. You never know who God might send your way with a heart prepared in advance to receive His truth.

Many years have passed and Holly has been faithfully serving Jesus in France with a Christian evangelistic organization for over ten years. So while God does not need a pizza party to see students come to Christ, He sure can use it. I like mine with cheese and extra pepperoni.

# 14

# THE ESSENTIAL OF

# CAMPUS MINISTRY

Education is a subject that everyone would consider important. Governments on all levels—local, state, and federal—spend billions. Most modern cultures have established educational systems that have compulsory attendance expectations. Public education is typically considered the default option, when it comes to education.

With that in mind, your students and their parents have varied educational options, including home education, religious schools, private schools, and prep schools. Some may have opportunities for charter and magnet schools, online education, and private Christian schools. There's no doubt that the educational decision (for our kids) is an important one for parents and is never made lightly.

Our family made the educational decision early . . . private Christian education. We quickly learned that that decision involved considerable financial sacrifices (no break, even when you're on church staff . . . what's with that?!). But we were happy to make that sacrifice (which typically meant driving old vehicles, questionable home repairs by me, McEating out, and staycations or visiting relatives). At one point we attempted home education for two of our kids, the main reason being that our kids needed and wanted to try this option.

Then there was a time when our two older kids came to us (in their final middle school years) and requested that we allow them to attend public high school. We were a little disconcerted but our kids reassured us that they "were good." In other words, Christian education had given them a solid foundation and they were ready for public school.[1] So we have experienced three different genres of education.

Each school day millions of kids make their way to public schools, whether they want to or not. Our culture has conveniently assembled students in designated locations (usually determined by a family's residence, although I am a proponent of school choice, regardless of where you live) throughout our communities. While some might perceive these schools as citadels of educational safe zones (and in some cases, somewhat exclusive, with no visitors allowed), we in student ministry should see public schools as opportunities of ministry and service. Some corporately paint public schools as the enemy, while I would propose that they are simply victims of the enemy (our ultimate spiritual enemy). We cannot expect (spiritual) regenerated behavior and thought from (spiritual) unregenerated people. For those of us whose lives are faith based, we were, at one time, spiritually dark and void. I would characterize many public schools as a place that is spiritually null at worst and spiritually inquisitive at best. For the youth leader, this is where opportunity presents itself. There needs to be some initiative where public schools and people of faith interface.

## THE SIMPLE STRATEGY: BUILD RELATIONAL BRIDGES

The simple strategy of campus ministry is the building of relational bridges between public educators and people of faith (those who have a Christian worldview). More important will be the opportunity of dialogue between the two entities, which historically has been polarized due to strongly embraced ideologies. Having a dialogue will hopefully open up both sides, with a new understanding and perspective from each other's point of view. When this is accomplished, a new modus operandi of sensitivity and cooperation is possible. Another aspect of simple campus ministry strategy is our theology—a theology of mankind that says everyone, including students in public schools, was created in the image of God, and what He says about His creation of mankind is "that's good." Our inner theology of mankind should determine what our outward attitude and approach to those who might be different in their educational upbringings.

# VALUES, ETHICS, AND PUBLIC SCHOOLS

Considerable discussion and research continues on the topics of values and character education. Clearly values inculcated within the development of students have supporting contexts, including family, but it would be naïve to think values and character are solely taught within the family context. It is important to recognize the prominent role the family plays in the development of one's values. Yet within our current culture, educational systems have become a strong, and in some cases, a surrogate role, for the inculcation of values.

While this could be perceived as an opportunity, others may perceive this as a dilemma. According to Gretchen Wilhelm and Michael Firmin,[2] implementing some facsimile of values or character education within schools leaves the door open to a variety of subjective and situational ideas, thus polarizing further opinions on what values should be embraced. This type of ambiguous thought has led to a suspicion of public education that, at its minimum, has not been collegial, and at its maximum, has been contentious and reactive.

There has been a propensity for adversarial and combative attitudes toward public education from people of faith, causing an attitude of frustration and distrust from public educators. Consider this example from Sheldon Berman, "Consideration of ethics is an area that becomes contentious for schools, with some individuals wishing to promote particular religious principles within the curriculum and others advocating for value neutrality."[3] While I would be the first to admit that there is a lot wrong with public education, there are significant areas of agreement that should be identified. While this author's motivation is more related to ministry opportunity, from a more pragmatic standpoint, this motivation could be more in the realm of understanding instead of misunderstanding public educators. We need to attempt to identify those areas of commonality, specifically on the subject of values, within the context of public education. Character education is the vehicle that public educators use (or should use), and once a closer look is taken at the values embedded within character education, people of faith may be surprised at the number of values with which they are in agreement.

## VALUES RECONSIDERED

There is a middle path schools can follow to help students reflect on the values we hold collectively as a society. The great contribution that the Character Education Partnership and the character education movement has made to this debate is to help adults see that we can come to agreement on such collectively held values as trustworthiness, respect, responsibility, justice, fairness, caring, and citizenship. The middle path of affirming these values while engaging students in dialogue about moral issues provides an opportunity for schools to nurture moral and pro-social behavior.[4]

I have had a specific interest in those values and ethics that coincide with a Christian worldview; in other words, identifying those values and virtues that educators would agree with, in the context of public education. In her master's thesis, Michelle Jaye said,

> Perhaps this ambivalence springs from a desire to be profoundly respectful, to accept all beliefs, all perspectives, all ways of existing in our pluralistic and highly complex society. However, it is increasingly evident that an education system lacking a nucleus of core ethical principles leaves students unprepared and ill-equipped to make wise and judicious decisions, not only in school, but in all facets of their lives.[5]

There is an apparent sense that core values exist in education. For some, these core values would be comprised of beliefs in inclusion, the sanctity of the classroom, embracing and celebrating diversity, educating for democracy, and support of collegial growth. Others have identified liberty, social justice, loyalty, and competence. Still others have observed the core values of participation, diversity of opinion, learning from conflict, reflection, critique, and acceptance of mistakes.[6]

Values have been defined in terms of positive characteristics such as honesty, loyalty, cooperation, democracy, and freedom. Patricia and Jacob Cohen break down values into individual traits, in terms of process, social, and abstract ends, strengths, and life goals.[7] Some other examples of values would include politics, religion, work, family, friends, money, leisure time, school, love and sex, material possessions, personal tastes, aging and death, health, multicultural issues, and culture.[8]

## ETHICS AND VIRTUES

According to the Catholic Education Resource Center, ideals that cross over culturally are called *cardinal virtues. Cardinal* is from a Latin word that means "hinge," that on which something turns or depends because most virtues are somehow related (see www.catholiceducation.org). These cardinal virtues would include wisdom, justice, self-mastery, and courage.

*Wisdom* is the virtue that enables us to exercise sound judgment, engage in careful consideration, and maintain intellectual honesty. It also enables us to plan and take the right course of action in our pursuit of the good. *Justice* is an outward or social virtue, concerned with our personal, professional, and legal obligations and commitments to others. A sense of justice enables us to be fair and to give each person what he or she rightly deserves. *Self-mastery*, by contrast, is an inner or individual virtue. It gives people intelligent control over their impulses and fosters moral autonomy. A ten-year-old who throws frequent temper tantrums or a teenager who spends six hours a day in front of a television and cannot complete his homework are examples of individuals who lack self-mastery. Lastly, *courage* is not simply bravery but also the stead-fastness to commit ourselves to what is good and right and actively pursue it, even when it is not convenient or popular.[9]

The Josephson Institute of Ethics, a leading proponent of character education, focuses on virtues. This institute is a popular source of information on character education and ethical decision-making. The mission of the Institute is as follows, "To improve the ethical quality of society by changing personal and organizational decision making and behavior." This organization has been working in the business and education world for twenty years doing research and seminars about the importance of ethical decision making. The institute has come up with six pillars of character, and they believe they are universal values that can help to unite a fractured society: trustworthiness, respect, responsibility, fairness, caring, and citizenship.[10] With a culture that believes in moral relativity, these values are designed to be a filter through which ethical decisions can be made more effectively.

The list of the six pillars of character is by no means an exhaustive list of moral virtues. Most of these pillars are in other character education curricula, likewise not issued by the Josephson Institute. They are meant to be a starting point to help guide people in making better decisions. These six pillars of character have close biblical parallels behind which Christians can rally. The names and terminology may be different, but the idea behind these universal ideals comes from the Bible and sometimes they are characteristics ascribed to God Himself. A close examination of these pillars and their biblical parallels should help to clear up any doubts a Christian may have about supporting this form of character education.

There can be much debate over what constitutes a culture of integrity and the type of character education a culture is disseminating. From the Christian perspective, there has to be some distinctive. In *Issues Facing Christians Today*, John Stott lists several essential "marks" of a Christian mind.[11] In essence, they are values embraced by Christians, with some varying degrees of explanation and incarnation. They include: (1) a supernatural orientation, (2) an awareness of evil, (3) a conception of truth, (4) an acceptance of authority, and (5) a concern for the individual.

Robert Kunzman[12] holds that students need to learn to relate to other students and be respectful of each other's personal beliefs. He suggests schools should no longer hold to a doctrine of neutrality and silence, but rather schools should aid students in their discussions of religious plurality. Kunzman is not concerned with what schools are teaching, but rather he is concerned with what schools are not teaching. There is a lack of education regarding the pluralistic religious beliefs of America. While a Christian worldview might consider the exposure of other religious beliefs as detrimental in a student's progress toward spirituality, it could be perceived as an opportunity to present and explain the Christian worldview.

In his provocatively titled book *The Death of Character*, Professor James Hunter makes an interesting comment on character. Hunter says that character does not require religious faith but does require the conviction of truth to be made sacred while having those convictions reinforced by habits formed within their moral community.[13] In other words, a person of character would be steadfast in wisdom and would be a person of his word. For a person to go outside the boundaries of his moral community in biblical time, meant facing the consequences with the stigma of being an apostate, heretic, or a sinner, with the penalty of these acts being severely punished. The Scripture clearly gives examples of transgression and sin, with the antithesis of faith and obedience. These are examples for all mankind.

While Mr. Hunter says that character doesn't require faith, it should be mentioned that people of faith not only hold to sacred convictions, but also hold to sacred truth and are able to glean from its spirituality. God made His expectation clear that people are to be holy, not just on the outside but also on the inside (which seemed to be a much higher priority based on the passage of Scripture, "The Lord does not look at the things people look at. People look at the outward appearance, but the Lord looks at the heart" [1 Samuel 16: 7 NIV]).

# A CONSENSUS LIST OF VALUES

For decades, Christians (and more specifically Christian educators) have been at odds with public education. Commonality between the two groups is something that has been avoided or unidentified. As a Christian educator teaching practical ministry at the university level to youth ministry students, I am looking for ministry opportunity, not unnecessary polarization. With that said, here's my list of values that we agree with public schools:

1. Self-esteem
2. Personal integrity (honesty, etc.)
3. Racial acceptance
4. Drug-free/against substance abuse/teen smoking
5. Patriotism
6. Mentoring
7. Stewardship of nature
8. Self-worth
9. Courtesy/etiquette
10. Character development
11. Dealing with conflict
12. Health (habits)
13. Knowledge (education)
14. Sexual responsibility
15. Spirituality
16. Sanctity of life
17. Improved lifestyle
18. Compassion for the less fortunate
19. Need for positive role models
20. Leadership

Among these twenty may be some values that cause you to scratch your head. I'll pick two: sexual responsibility and sanctity of life. At first glance, you could say, "No way!" If I could challenge your thinking . . . we collectively embrace these values but we may define them differently. For example, people of faith will default to the Scriptures for its teaching on sexual responsibility, and I would suggest that the Scriptures are pretty clear. Public education defines this in the context of mechanics and as long as you get the mechanics right, you'll be okay. Sexual responsibility in the context of a loving husband and wife is almost considered abnormal and unattainable. The value of sanctity of life is one that I believe the public school and the Christian community collectively embrace, but we are at polar opposites when it comes to defining it. As people of faith, we define this as the unborn within the body of a mother, with no age restrictions. Public education tends to define this as protection for baby seals, whales, and vegan extremism. My point is this . . . we actually do agree with public schools, when it comes to values on many topics. These could be starting points of conversation rather than points of contention. I am suggesting that until we identify those values we agree on, we will have a difficult time having any opportunity of ministry within our public schools when we start at where we disagree.

Schools are already, in many cases, in a lockdown mode, for obvious safety reasons. Our agenda needs to become the agenda of the school . . . which is a reflection of the values they embrace. Are there values that we'll disagree on? Of course (e.g., faith in Christ, creation, absolute truth as defined in Scriptures, against immoral lifestyles, the role of the church, the propensity for human nature to sin, etc.). But if we have no audience, then we are simply talking to ourselves and amongst ourselves.

# AN INCARNATIONAL WITNESS

We have been discussing campus ministry on a macro level. Remember, God "gave us the ministry of reconciliation" (2 Corinthians 5:18). The definition of *reconcile* is to close the distance between two parties that have been estranged from one another. Typically we see the terms *reconcile* and *estranged* in the context of divorce. One term is good and the latter is bad. In campus ministry, we have the opportunity to close the distance between students and God, with the goal of reconciling them to God. In other words, reconciling is closing the distance. So if we are closing the distance, then there so much that can be included in this ministry of reconciliation . . . pretty much anything we do with students in mind. This can be a freeing proposition that removes the idea of an agenda, program, or schedule into a relationship that is all about just being. The added beauty of this relationship is that if a student declines anything remotely spiritual, we don't abandon them. We simply continue the relationship, with the assurance that we are still closing that distance between them and God.

On a micro level, we can see elements of the way campus ministry should be done, with Christ's example of an incarnational witness in John 1:1–5, 14. God took the first step. This kind of initiative in campus ministry takes on the appearance of being open-minded to what public schools have to say. This is not an endorsement of all things in public education, but it is being quick to listen and slower to speak. The contrary tends to be the expectation.

## GOING WHERE THE STUDENTS ARE

Reaching students where they are is another initiative. For the most part, we expect students to come to us. Campus ministry turns that upside down. To actually be in the students' world of public schools and activities raises the bar for those in student ministry. I know students appreciate it when they see their youth leaders in their universe. Initiative also looks like being nonjudgmental. We simply overlook any outward appearances and stereotypes. Our mission is to get below the surface and to get to know the student within. We view students as more than just a soul. I'm convinced that if students get any hint that all we care about is their soul, we may lose opportunity and credibility. Students are more than souls and when Christ changes lives, He changes their eternal destinies as well as other parts of their lives, including relationships, lifestyles, emotions, and in some cases, their very lives. In other words, the entire person is important and valued . . . for life now and in the hereafter. Students are interested in living, not dying. Our theology of salvation should not be limited to life after death. It should include life while we live, and that message resonates with students. So the term *soul winning* may be misunderstood at best and archaic at worst. We will need to use clarity in our attempt to explain what our agenda is, as well as how we plan to go about it.

## BEING A PERMEATING SOURCE OF LIGHT

Christ's example of an incarnational witness can also *be characterized as permeation.* Just as light permeates a dark room, His light is everywhere the body of Christ is. Campus ministry can be that light in public schools. There's some good news and some bad news. The good news is that you don't need many Christian people to be that light. The minimum requirement would be one. After that, the ministry can exponentially grow as numbers are added to the leadership team. The bad news is that you may not be welcomed. I don't want to paint an overly optimistic picture when it comes to the possibilities of campus ministry, but there will be those who would rather you not be involved with their school. The reasons are many but it could come down to misperceptions of religious people, a negative view of outsiders, a previous bad experience, or even personal conviction. Regardless, the not-so-easy task is to dispel any misperceptions and build a positive reputation of who we are and Who we represent.

We need to have a well-thought-out strategy that incorporates the agenda of the school. So if our attitude is to serve the school and embrace their agenda, then there is a strong possibility that we will have opportunity for ministry. Serving can take the form of coaching, teacher's aide, recognizing office staff, score keeping, substitute teaching, chaplain, being a part of anti-bullying campaigns, attending school board meetings, participating it parent/teacher organizations or booster clubs, hall monitor, guest lecturer, helping with pregame meals, etc. You don't have to look very far to see what could be done to serve a school.

A third characterization of Christ's incarnational witness is *His identification with people*. He met people and identified with their greatest needs. Our role in campus ministry is to take time to understand students. Finding that common ground may take some time but we need to go no further than our own adolescence. Hopefully we haven't deleted all those memory files from our adolescent years. My guess is that some memories are so vivid that we can't forget them. Fast-forward to students today. Sure their vocabulary has changed and their platforms for communication continue to test technological boundaries, all for the purpose of dodging parental and adult eyes. But some of the same needs are still there, including being accepted, someone believing in them, being valued, being understood, and being loved. Let me add one more . . . someone who knows their names. As we move among a predominantly unbelieving student audience, we can be assured that we are empowered by Christ to do so. For some, it will mean crossing barriers of culture, race, and age. We need to make sure that we are comfortable moving among them, and they are comfortable with us being there. That can be a delicate balancing act but one that needs to be achieved nonetheless. We love and accept students for who they are, as we shine that "little light of mine."

## HANGING WITH A PURPOSE

Finally, in campus ministry, we are hanging out with purpose. For some, hanging out looks like wasting time. It is not. Hanging out is costly and time consuming, but it is necessary. So our hanging-out time needs to be planned and productive. There are three key elements when it comes to exposure to students: being seen, being known, and being understood. Hanging out with purpose can accomplish the first two elements. For those who are in vocational student ministry, time is the one thing they don't have. Yet to be effective in campus ministry, youth pastors and leaders need to have flexibility of time.

As a former YFC director, I practiced what I called "comp" time with my staff (and with me). "Comp" or compensated best describes this. If there was an event or activity that we wanted to do that was related to campus ministry, that staff person did not have to come in the next morning. Their time was compensated. We did this because I didn't want my staff to hesitate when it came to doing something that would be an opportunity of being seen, known, or understood, but would also take some time out of their traditional schedule (there's nothing traditional about student ministry schedules). Human nature would flinch if it came down to participating in an extraordinary activity or event, if it took away personal or family time. But if that time is compensated, youth workers would be much more enthusiastic about attending those events or activities. This is sensitive kingdom thinking.

So campus ministry is time consuming but it is also costly. Campus ministry can nickel and dime you to the poverty level. It takes money to get into games, plays, and other events. Often youth workers will find themselves needing to attend more than one event in an evening. I know that ministries have to live within their means, but I would encourage ministries as a whole to look after these expenses. I would not want my youth leaders to hesitate to do ministry simply because they couldn't afford a few dollars. I think it's a great investment for funds to be set aside for those minor charges and expenses that youth workers experience when trying to do campus ministry.

## A WAITING MISSION FIELD

Campus ministry is essential in student ministry. There has been much said about missional churches with a "new" way of thinking, when it comes to thinking more like a missionary except the context is within our own country. This way of thinking (ministry) will determine how ministry is done. A simple definition of a missionary is a person who takes the gospel to other cultures beyond the reach of the church.

I would suggest that our public schools have become that mission field and student pastors and leaders have an incredible opportunity to take the gospel to this culture within a culture. The apostle Paul put it this way, "When I am with those whose consciences bother them easily, I don't act as though I know it all and don't say they're foolish; the result is that they are willing to let me help them. Yes, whatever a person is like, I try to find common ground with him so that he will let me tell him about Christ and let Christ save him" (1 Corinthians 9:22 TLB). Their language is different. They wear different clothes. Their food is different. Their gods are different. Sounds like a mission field to me.

# NOTES

1. Their rationale for attending public school was a mix of an access to friends, educational opportunities, and of course, athletic opportunities and competition. Our talk about attending a public school went something like this: "The difference between you and other students in school is that you can recognize a cow pie when you see it. Other students do not always recognize those cow pies, and in many occasions, they stand in them, without even knowing it." They understood my farm analogy.

2. Gretchen M. Wilhelm and Michael W. Firmin, "Character Education: Christian Education Perspectives," *Journal of Research on Christian Education*, 17, no. 2 (2008): 182–98.

3. Sheldon Berman, "The Bridges to Civility: Empathy, Ethics, and Service," *The School Administrator*, 55, no. 5, 27.

4. Ibid.

5. Michele P. Jaye, "A Compass in Every Pocket: Nurturing Ethical Behavior in Schools," master's thesis, Royal Roads University, Colwood, British Columbia, April 2006. Cited in G. Jorgensen, "Duet or Duel?" *Journal of Moral Education*, 35 (2): 179–96.

6. Pat Williams-Boyd, *Educational Leadership* (Santa Barbara, Calif.: ABC-CLIO, 2002).

7. Patricia Cohen and Jacob Cohen, *Life Values and Adolescent Mental Health* (Mahwah, NJ: Lawrence Erlbaum Associates, 1996).

8. Sidney B. Simon, Leland W. Howe, and Howard Kirschenbaum, *Values Clarification* (New York: Time Warner, 1995).

9. Kevin Ryan and Karen E. Bohlin, *Building Character in Schools* (San Francisco: Jossey-Bass, 1999).

10. The six pillars of character, from *the Six Pillars of Character Series Annnotated Teacher's Edition* (Los Angeles: The Josephson Insitute 2012). See also http://www.josephsoninstitute.org/sixpillars.html.

11. John Stott, *Issues Facing Christians Today* (Grand Rapids: Zondervan, 2006).

12. Robert Kunzman, *Grappling with the Good: Talking about Religion and Morality in Public Schools* (Albany, N.Y.: State University of New York Press, 2006).

13. James Davison Hunter, *The Death of Character: Moral Education in an Age without Good or Evil* (New York: Basic Books, 2000).

# 15

## THE ESSENTIAL OF

# PARTNERING WITH OTHER MINISTRIES

After being in local church youth ministry in locales like Southern California (they definitely march to the beat of a different drummer), Knoxville (where it's all about orange Volunteers at the University of Tennessee), and then Alberta, Canada (hockey, hockey, and hockey), I had hit an impasse in my ministry.

I loved ministering to the students I was endeared to and loved the context of the church I was in. But I was restless and wanting to reach out to students in a way that I couldn't in the role I was in. Then an opportunity came across my desk to minister to students on a larger scale and in a different context. The vetting process was thorough and my learning curve was substantial. The hardest part of my decision to cross this ecclesiastical fence was the expectation of raising my own salary. But my wife and I were all in, and I transitioned into a very interesting and fulfilling journey, from a local church youth pastor, to the executive director of Youth for Christ in Edmonton.

There are freedoms and responsibilities in the local church context, as well as the Christian organization context, often called the parachurch. Frankly, I've never been a fan of the term *parachurch*. It carries a negative connotation as other prefixed words, like *parapsychology*, *paranormal*, etc. In other words, parachurch

STUDENT MINISTRY ESSENTIALS

organizations are outside the norm and may appear a bit odd and out of the ordinary, even to the extreme of something to be feared and avoided. For the most part, Christian youth organizations are not of the mainstream but are not abnormal. Of course, there are some who feel the opposite is true. There simply are a myriad of parachurch or Christian youth organizations that are contributing to God's kingdom work, as well as making attempts to minister to students. While some organizations have been birthed out of local churches, many have been birthed from church and Christian leaders who have had a vision and burden to do something outside the walls of the church, and frankly, beyond the church's capabilities.

We have to come to the harsh reality that the church can "send out" but it cannot always "go out." Acts 13:1–3 is a good example of this. When Paul and Barnabas were sent out, a Christian organization was created that had an interesting relationship to the church at Antioch. Paul and Barnabas reported back to this church, yet neither the new churches started on this trip nor the mission organization itself appear to become part of the organization of the church at Antioch. This is not an indictment on the church at Antioch. It's simply a matter of function. Yet the relationship with the people of the church in Antioch remained intact, with a keen interest and involvement in this missionary endeavor.

# VIEWS OF THE PARACHURCH

In *The Church and the Parachurch: An Uneasy Marriage*, Jerry White describes six theological perspectives regarding the legitimacy of the "parachurch."

1. *Local church only.* The view judges any structure outside the local congregation as illegitimate. All mission sending or other efforts must be under the direct authority of a local congregation.

2. *Temporary legitimacy.* This view believes that the local church is God's primary agency for ministry in the world. However, para-local church structures have been raised up for a temporary corrective influence on the local church. When the church begins meeting the need as it should, para-local church structures should disappear.

3. *Two structures.* The local church and the mobile church are two distinct biblical structures in God's plan. The local congregation meets the growth needs of a body of believers. The mobile function is the mission outreach of evangelizing and discipling in the world.

4. *Church planting.* This position gives legitimacy to para-local church societies as long as their goal is church planting. It is insufficient to

simply perform a part of the function of a church, such as evangelism, if a direct result is not integration into an existing congregation or planting a new one.

5. *Dual legitimacy.* Dual legitimacy indicates that both the local congregation and para-local church are legitimate expressions of God working in the body of Christ. It permits varied kinds of structures both in missions and local expressions. Since all are part of the broader body of Christ, individual believers, though part of a local congregation, express their ministry to the world in a variety of semiautonomous structures. This differs from the two-structure view in that it does not require the two-structure analysis and would allow for nonmobile para-local church agencies (a rescue mission, a local businessmen's outreach, a seminary) and non-missionary specialists.

6. *Anti-institutional.* This view looks upon the church in its institutions, organizations, and buildings as ineffective and unnecessary. It seeks nearly total freedom in individual expression with resistance to authority from either a local or para-local church. The defining characteristic of a Christian youth organization is that it stands outside of the organizational structure of well-established religious bodies. The autonomy of the Christian youth organization from established religious bodies allows a much greater degree of flexibility for innovation than is possible within an established organizational hierarchy. Christian youth organizations are often the creation of an entrepreneur or a small group of motivated people who seek to achieve specific ministry goals.[1]

This author embraces the fifth theological view of the parachurch, dual legitimacy. There is much debate over legitimacy in the first place but I would argue that Christian youth organizations are simply a mobile extension of any church ministry. One opinion on parachurch groups is somewhat supportive. "Parachurch groups can fulfill a variety of legitimate functions in the Christian world but one of the key issues is that of discerning when and where the parachurch starts to usurp the functions of the church. This raises important questions of accountability and transparency as they connect to influence and power...as long as parachurch groups have clear and very limited purposes, they can be very helpful as a means of encouraging discussion and action on various issues."[2]

# THE ROLE OF CHRISTIAN YOUTH ORGANIZATIONS

Christian youth organizations have been around since the nineteenth century. Now, well into the twenty-first century, Christian organizations (from church planting organizations to music producers to publishers, Christian colleges and private schools, cross cultural ministries, foster care homes, just to name a few) continue to flourish. In the context of student ministry, there are campus-focused ministries, short-term mission organizations, residential and service-oriented camps, conferences, music festivals, and others. To ignore and not take advantage of these Christian youth organizations would be a mistake. You could characterize these ministries as niche ministries that have a franchising edge. Many have a history and have continued making ministry modifications for effectiveness and relevancy among teenagers. Some have even modified their names but have maintained their mission and message.

Being in student ministry as long as I have, one gets quite familiar with fast-food restaurants. So in my many student ministry related travels, I look for certain franchises where I can expect a quality treatment as a customer, value, and product, no matter where I visit their locations. (If I'm in the West, it's In-N-Out Burger; in the South, Chick-fil-A and Cook Out; central US, it's Culver's. Now there's always that other McPlace when I can't find anything else . . .). So when it comes to Christian youth organizations, you get a sense of what they do well, and you have an expectation that hopefully they will meet. Why? Because this is their mission and expertise. While I could consider replicating something they do, why not consider a level of outsourcing and alignment of my student ministry with Christian youth organizations that are determined by a number of things: my mission purpose, timing, financial considerations, partnership and identification, students' motivation, marketability, and an overall kingdom mentality (this is bigger than my ministry and will contribute something not only to my students but also to the bigger picture of the kingdom of God).

## AUTONOMY VERSUS INTERDEPENDENCE

Although Christian organizations are organizationally autonomous, they typically function with a considerable degree of interdependence with established religious organizations. In one article researcher Ed Stetzer described a healthy ministry that he consults with: "I was struck by their health and sense of family. Even as they disagreed, the focus was family and graciousness in their disagreement. People were allowed to ask questions, leadership was transparent, and trust was present."[3] Mark 10:45 and Luke 19:10 also make it clear as to the ultimate mission of any organization is the same as Christ's mission: to seek and save the lost." I would suggest that the ultimate ministry goal is summarized in Matthew 28:18-20. Obviously there are axillary ministry activities that are associated with the primary goal of presenting a message of hope that can only be found in Christ but you cannot ignore Matthew 10:42 or Mark 9:41 as an act of good works that gives human relief to human suffering.

Many Christian youth organizations publicly promote that one of their goals is to "come alongside" the local church to assist in fulfilling its mission as well. However noble this may sound, some perceive this as actually invading the territory of the local church in order to form an artificial organization foreign to the New Testament's mission plan:

> Essentially, they can do what the name suggests: they can work alongside the church to support the church. Seminaries can train pastors, as long as there are clear lines of ecclesiastical accountability (as with my own seminary's requirement of ordination and presbytery call for professors). They can provide excellent conferences for pastors and people which allow for fellowship and encouragement. They can enable pastors working in small churches where they see little week-by-week encouragement to gather together to meet with others in similar situations. They can promote clearly-defined single issues, such as complementarianism or principled confessionalism, and provide material for churches who address such matters in their regular ministry. They can even produce occasional statements on key issues of contemporary interest, such as ethics or inerrancy. We might say that they can fulfill handmaiden functions that help the church but they should never seek to lead or control the church.[4]

There are others who continue to stir this debate of legitimacy toward Christian youth organizations.

> You step out in faith to explore compassionate gospel ministry to the homeless or international students or battered women or veterans. You even discover other Christians who are doing the same ministry. In fact, they've formed an organization to coordinate their work more effectively. So you join up. And then you tell your pastor the good news that at long last you're putting his words into practice.
>
> To your shock, he doesn't celebrate this new venture of faith. He begins to lecture you! He talks about the dangers of parachurch organizations and the centrality of the local church.

Are there dangers and theological challenges for parachurch work? Yes, most significantly, there's the danger of replacing the bride of Christ with another organization that Jesus didn't establish. The parachurch can easily become a pseudo-church.[5]

One writer makes this comparison between churches and Christian youth organizations:

Becoming a Christian means being adopted into God's family. And joining a local church is like showing up at the family dinner table. Don't tell me you belong to God's "universal church" if you don't prove it on earth by binding yourself to a local church. That's like saying you belong to the family but never showing up at family events.

Working for a parachurch ministry, on the other hand, is like playing for a soccer team. You know how soccer teams work. Team members are selected, and then they gather to play soccer. They don't gather to receive math tutoring, to brush their teeth, to give and receive family love, or to care for the elderly. They gather for one purpose and for a limited season of involvement: to play soccer.[6]

## BEING DEPENDENT AND ACCOUNTABLE

Those who say that Christian youth organizations are outside the perimeters of the local church have not experienced the dependency on the local church that Christian youth organizations have. This dependency does not validate organizations' existence, but it certainly confirms the community aspect of a local congregation and Christian youth organizations. Numerous times when I worked with Youth for Christ we relied on our local congregation of people to assist us, whether it was personally or for the sake of our ministry. We were involved in a loving community of people who were genuinely concerned about the well-being of our ministry as well as our personal well-being.[7] The community aspect of our relationship with this church was paramount. Our local congregation provided a loving and involved relationship that made my Christian youth organization involvement and my local congregation involvement an engaged one.

Accountability was another aspect of the relationship we had with our Christian youth organization and our local congregation. People who knew us would inquire as to how we were doing as well as how the ministry was functioning. It is refreshing to be able to answer honestly to people who have your best interest at heart. Being within a local congregation does not necessarily mean being under the authority of a local congregation when it comes to the operations of an organization, but it does place those workers or employees of those organizations personally under that authority, and they will have an impact on that organization.

Recall Jesus' statement that if a Christian who sins against you does not listen to your concern after you tell him, "take one or two others along with you, that every word may be confirmed by the evidence of two or three witnesses. If he refuses to listen to them, tell it to the church; and if he refuses to listen even to the church, let him be to you as a Gentile and a tax collector" (Matthew 18:15–17).

This implies, as one large church concludes, "Christians are to be members of churches where they are held accountable to walk in a way that pleases the Lord. If there were no relationship of accountability, it would be meaningless to 'tell it to the church,' because the offending person would simply say, 'That church has no jurisdiction over me.'" From the Matthew 18 passage as well as 1 Corinthians 5:2–5, that large Midwest church concludes "The teaching of the New Testament on church discipline implies that church membership (involving mutual accountability among the members) is the will of God for all Christians."[8]

Most Christian youth organizations have bylaws and articles of operation. While organizations might not use the biblical verbage of "church discipline," my experience is that strong organizations evaluate performance on a regular basis, both at the board level, as well as the direct ministry staff level. So "discipline" takes place in the form of making changes, whether that be personal or corporate. Leadership is always under scrutiny. While it is important that Christian youth organizations have strong doctrinal statements, organizations should also have a good understanding of local church leadership.

There is no question that some Christian youth organizations have slid into a self-preservation mode and should take serious ministerial inventory as to the validity of their prolonged existence.[9] Because Christian organizations are under the mandate to be Christian, not only to have members who are Christians, the organization itself can and must experience the impact of the Word of God and the Holy Spirit. Because Christian organizations also experience Christian community in their organizational life and function, they must exhibit the ethical mandate of demonstrating love in relationships as well as in mission. Because Christian organizations are under the mandate of theological reflection, an understanding of biblical teachings and principles is essential to each component of the organization's life and practice.[10]

## RECONCILIATION GRANTED TO CHURCH AND CHRISTIAN YOUTH ORGANIZATIONS

The Christian youth organization carries the gospel beyond the gathered church in all its form and community. It is doing something that perhaps a gathered group would not have the wherewithal or the know-how to do. Second Corinthians 5:18 (NKJV) says, "All things are of God, who has reconciled us to Himself through Jesus Christ, and has given us the ministry of reconciliation." Here is the ministry that God has given to all of us. It is the ministry of reconciliation, a coming together after a separation. This coming together is a closing of the distance between the two estranged parties. So in the biblical sense, this ministry of reconciliation is given to all of us so we may close the distance between God and man. It is this ministry that motivates the vast majority of Christian youth organizations, because they are ever conscious of the fact that so much of what they do is closing the distance between lost young people and a loving God.

We acknowledge that the local church is presented in Scripture as the sending organization (Acts 13), but we believe God has raised up Christian youth organizations—denominational institutions, mission agencies, etc.—to be servant facilitators and partners in the global task. This is going to require a new respect by Christian youth organization agencies for the primacy of the local church in God's global plan. We do not believe local churches are going to have a proper partnership with Christian youth organizations unless Christian youth organizations adopt a partner paradigm and see themselves as servant facilitators of local churches, servants who are dedicated to empowering local churches to reach the world more effectively than ever.[11] In other words, Christian youth organizations are just as much a part of the local church as the members within the local congregation. Each entity can learn from the other, and each can complement and encourage each other in carrying out the specific elements of the Great Commission.

## WHO BRINGS WHAT TO THE TABLE?

So what does the local church bring to the table? A stable environment; human resources in the shape of manpower; godly counsel; consistent biblical teaching and preaching; a community presence; financial resources; ministry opportunities; and a family atmosphere.

The Christian youth organization brings an entrepreneurial spirit, specifically trained staff and volunteers, community relationships with both Christians and non-Christians, specific ministry strategies that focus on teenagers, and a tendency to be interdenominational, with an unbiased denominational approach to student ministry.

What are the benefits? A renewed loyalty to each other; new relationships; strengthened ministry partnerships as well as more effective ministry; creating the means for church members to interact and minister to a young audience; exposing both parties to worlds they may not have been aware; partnering the enthusiasm of a student ministry with the experience and stability of a local church; combining vision and mission with mobilization. There has to be some flexibility on both sides. It may not have been done like that before. Patience will be needed simply because the pace will be hindered by the number of decision makers involved. But with open communication and clear expectations, it can work.

Are there challenges? Of course. Probably the biggest challenge is really an attitudinal challenge. Control can be a significant challenge. We are all wired for control, but biblically we are persuaded to have self-control, not control of others. So ministry entities will need to deal with this issue of control. This could be best handled by delegating to people's strengths and then letting those people control what they're supposed to control. Typically there are some right ways and wrong ways of doing things, but often the points of disagreement are in areas where it's simply done in a different way. Hopefully egos will not get in the way and there will be some yielding for the sake of the kingdom.

I have had the opportunity to work with many local churches (while being with Youth for Christ) in joint ministry initiatives, as well as the promotion of our individual ministry. I currently work with hundreds of churches with an outreach event that involves thousands of teenagers. I need an understanding of the local church culture and dynamics in order to have these joint ministry events. That includes a sensitivity to schedule demands (requiring significant planning), and being aware of financial concerns, so that the activity is worth their investment of money. So value is important, as well as the potential for ministry. Of course, communication is critical, and I must make myself available with timely responses. When a Christian youth organization displays these best practices in joint ministry endeavors, those relationships will be ones of trust, expectation, and commitment.

## EXPECT CHANGE

The only thing that is consistent in student ministry is change. This has been the modus operandi of student ministry consistently over the years, simply due to the nature of students. Student ministry demands a creative flexibility when it comes to what their ministry will look like. Student workers and leaders tend to be relatively pliable, which is pretty much a requirement for both workers and leaders. The leaders also know their limitations.

This is where a partnership with Christian youth organizations comes into play. Working with and alongside these organizational ministries is a sort of ecclesiastical outsourcing. When there is a common ministry goal, as well as a common age group to be ministered to, a partnership can truly be beneficial for the sake of the kingdom.

# NOTES

1. Jerry White, *The Church and the Parachurch: An Uneasy Marriage* (Portland, Oreg.: Multnomah, 1983), 67–68.

2. Carl R. Trueman, "Parachurch Groups and the Issues of Influence and Accountability," *Foundations*, 66 (Spring 2014): 25 ff.), an online journal at http://www.affinity.org.uk/resources. Trueman is professor of church history at Westminster Theological Seminary, Philadelphia.

3. Ed Stetzer, "Considering and Surviving Unhealthy Christian Organizations," *Christianity Today*, The Exchange Blog, June 26, 2012; at http://www.christianitytoday.com/ edstetzer/2012/june/considering-and-surviving-unhealthy-christian.html.

4. Trueman, "Parachurch Groups and the Issues of Influence and Accountability," *Foundations*.

5. Jeramie Rinne, "For the Church: How Can You Support Parachurch Ministries? *9 Marks Journal* March 1, 2011, an online journal at http://9marks.org/article/church-how-can-you-support-parachurch-ministries/.

6. Byron Straughn, "For the Parachurch: Know the Difference Between Families and Soccer Teams," *9 Marks Journal*, March 1, 2011, an online journal at http://9marks.org/article/parachurch-know-difference-between-families-soccer-teams/.

7. You can find this church in Edmonton, Alberta, Canada. Its name is Calvary Community Church, and we were active members for nineteen years.

8. "The Meaning of Membership and Church Accountability," Bethlehem Baptist Church, Minneapolis, February 1, 2001, http://www.desiringgod.org/articles/the-meaning-of-membership-and-church-accountability.

9. I personally witnessed the closure of a Christian youth organization. The board members had the courage and fortitude to conclude that their mandate had been fulfilled and there was no other choice but to dissolve and distribute their assets to other Christian organizations who are still in the process of fulfilling their mandate.

10. Ray S. Anderson, *Minding God's Business* (Grand Rapids: Eerdmans, 1986), 39.

11. Larry Reesor, "What Kind of Church Will It Take?" http://www.missionfrontiers.org/2000/05/reesor.htm (accessed September 2001).

# WHAT I DIDN'T EXPECT

Whether you are just beginning your student ministry, right in the middle of it, or are at a point that you can look back, there will always be some unexpected circumstances and experiences. My first youth ministry was in Southern California. Now I know what you're thinking . . . sand, surf, a perpetual tan. Well, the town was Holtville, California, the carrot capital of the world. (Now I have your attention.)

Holtville is located in the Imperial Valley, a couple of hours east of San Diego and a few miles from the border of Mexico. It's all sand there. No water. Just the sandy "shore." Holtville was about 3,500 people strong when I arrived (now it's about 6,000 strong). This was my first real experience with farmers. Farmers do not use watches. They use sundials. So I had to adjust quickly.

I loved it there. We had a great bunch of students. You know you're doing a pretty good job of student ministry when the local school calls you to see what your schedule is.

## THE NEW SKATEBOARD "PARK"

One of the things that is still evident among students there is their interest in skateboarding. At least that is what my guys were into. But to find a skate park anywhere nearby was difficult. So the kids and I improvised. Outside of Holtville was an abandoned airstrip. It had plenty of concrete and culverts. So I ventured out with the church van and a vanload of wide-eyed middle school guys. The van had been provided by a father of one of our students. He asked me if there was anything I needed. When anyone asks you that . . . shoot high. So I shot high and said I needed a van to haul these kids around. And he was good to his word and purchased a brand new van, with dual air-conditioning, the youth group name on the sides, and a bumper sticker that said, "If this van is being driven recklessly, please call 555-church number." So with this brand new van, I took off into the desert.

After a good day of skateboarding and relatively few injuries, I was making my way back to town, when my guys started youth group peer pressure. They all wanted to go "fun truckin." "Fun truckin" is when you take your vehicle onto the sand, deflate the tires a bit, for better traction, and then put the pedal to the metal.

So here I am, with a brand new church van, a vanload of middle school teenagers, zipping around the desert. The kids are having a great time as I zipped up and down sand dunes. Then one of kids yelled, "Spin some donuts! . . . Okay!" So in all the wisdom and discernment I could muster, I responded, "Okay!"

# THE SANDY RIDE

So I'm spinning donuts like you would in a boat. I even get creative and try to get my kids dizzy (and potentially motion sick) by spinning tight circles, wide circles, and so on. Then one of my guys makes a reasonable request, "Pastor Steve, can we open up the sliding door? . . . Okay?" Well, it made sense, being in the desert, get some air flowing through the van, add to the excitement. So again, with all the wisdom and discernment I could muster, I said, "Okay!" So the guys opened up the van's sliding door. Well, I'm still doing circles when I look off into the horizon (where I had been), and I saw one of my guys. He was waving with one arm, while running toward us. His other arm was kind of dangling limp. Anyway, I stopped and he came right up to my door. When he stopped, his dangling arm kind of swayed back and forth until it came to rest.

He looked up at me, with the posture of a middle school guy and exclaimed, "You Ran Over Me!"

"No I didn't," I answered,

"Uh huh . . . you ran over me!"

"Freddie, no I didn't!"

"Uh huh!" Then he lifted up his shirt sleeve. There was a tread mark right across his shoulder blade!

I looked back at my tracks in the sand . . . There was an impression of a middle school boy in the sand! I had run over him!

When I succumbed to youth group pressure and opened up the sliding door, Freddie had fallen out of the van when I was doing donuts. Now what really astounds me is that nobody missed him (he was a quiet kid). Maybe that's the makeup of middle school guys . . . don't "rat" on anyone . . . even when they fall out of a van at a high rate of speed.

I have to be honest. When this went down, my ministry life flashed before me. It's over. I might as well begin another ministry career or maybe pick carrots. Now in Southern California, everybody has a hotline to their lawyer. So I was mentally processing all kinds of scenarios. Fortunately for me, Freddie's mother (a single mom) loved what we had done for her two boys (Freddie was an identical twin. I guess his mom thought that if I killed one of her boys, she still had another facsimile of one to live with.) Yes, I had separated Freddie's shoulder. But it didn't go any further (and I kept my job).

So when youth group pressure begins to build, remember . . . keep the van doors shut, no matter what!

## EXPERIENCES YOU ARE NOT PREPARED FOR

While some experiences might be somewhat laughable, there are other experiences that you simply didn't get prepared for, or a course wasn't offered. Many of those experiences are very sobering. The first funeral I did was for a young man who was killed in a single vehicle accident. The parents of this young man were on the tarmac of the San Diego airport, getting ready to embark on their dream trip to Israel. The plane was instructed to taxi back to the gate, in order for officials to inform them of what happened.

No one had prepared me for this very emotional experience. When I was in Alberta, Canada, I had the very difficult responsibility of doing a memorial service for one of my teenagers. This teenager had gone through his adolescence in our youth group, and I had performed his wedding just a year earlier. Gerry had been hiking in the Canadian Rockies, when his dog went into a moving body of water and was swept away, just above a formidable waterfall (Siffleur Falls). Without hesitation, Gerry went in after his dog. It was an act of unselfishness but it was a fatal act. Gerry (and his dog) were swept away. I was there when the Search and Rescue team declared to the family that this was no longer a rescue but a recovery. Reality set in like a punch to the stomach. I did Gerry's memorial service because his body was not found immediately. His body was found eight months later (after the winter), and again I was called upon to do Gerry's funeral.

I was not prepared to visit the parents of students who were dying of some terminal disease. I was not prepared for bewildered and confused parents who called me, looking for someone to help them find their teenager who had run away . . . and then locate them, knock on the door, and try to talk them back home. I was not prepared for the mother who called me to come over and break up a fight between the dad and his son. I was not prepared for the mother who asked if I would go and see her son who was talking suicide. I did . . . cautiously (I knew he hunted).

I received a phone call from a student who informed me that this was his only phone call. He had been arrested on soliciting a minor online. He confessed the whole story to me, explaining that he was chatting with what he thought was an under-aged girl online. The conversation turned sexual and they planned a meeting. He went but was met with law enforcement, who arrested him immediately. It was a sting. There also have been those times when young unmarried couples have found themselves seeking advice for an unplanned pregnancy (abortion has never been an option), and how to tell their parents.

Just when you think you've heard it all, graduates will contact, when they are dealing with circumstances that they didn't expect (nor did you). I've been on the phone with graduates seeking prayer and advice when the phone call suddenly ended and I was not sure why or what was next. I've prayed with a high school graduate who was dealing with a student who set himself on fire in the driveway of a girl who had dissed him. There was the time when a volunteer van driver leaving the youth group accidently ran over and killed a pedestrian. The volunteer wisely kept the teenagers in the van away from the scene. Tragically, when the students of the youth group went to school the next day, classmates were visibly upset about a student alum who was killed the night before . . . only to find out it was the same victim these teenagers were kept away from, the previous night.

Then there was one of our university alumni who had one of his high school girls die in his arms, after being hit by a truck. Nothing prepares you for this. It is during these times of absolute confusion, despair, anger, and uncertainty that the student minister and worker place their dependence on God and not on a learned skill set. It is a holy dependence on the work and wisdom of the God's Spirit that enables and equips us for any worst case scenario that our students may face. It is during these circumstances that students are looking for hope and often they are looking to someone who can offer that hope . . . someone they know personally.

Then there are those experiences that you never anticipated, when it comes to student ministry within the church. I did not expect politics within the church context, but it's there. Sometimes it's beneficial but often it's detrimental. Words are said. Relationships are aligned and maligned. Usually misunderstandings are fostered because personal agendas are trumping kingdom agendas. Determining which is which can be difficult, but the short answer here is found in Proverbs: "For lack of guidance a nation falls, but victory is sure through many advisers" (Proverbs 11:14 NIV); "The way of a fool is right in his own eyes, but a wise man listens to advice. . . . Listen to advice and accept instruction, that you may gain wisdom in the future" (Proverbs 12:15; 19:20).

A plurality of leadership can minimize political maneuvering. I never expected to be asked to resign (fired). I remember the reason I was given and it went something like this, "You came here from California and brought your California ways, but in Rome, you need to do as the Romans do . . ." So I moved on . . . disappointed but still trusting Romans 8:28 that declares, "for those who love God, all things work together for good."

# THE CHALLENGE

## A LIMITED TIME. . . A SHAKY PAST

No one has made the claim that student ministry is easy. The challenges include the culture we are dealing with. Staying current is trickier than ever but while our methods may change, our message remains the same. The time frame we have to work with is limited. Typically we have a six- to seven-year window (when you take into consideration both middle and high school years) and possibly extra years, when you include the college years. This is probably a best-case scenario because students tend to move in and out. So somehow we have to shape our ministries to accommodate the gyrations of student tenure. Beyond the time frame is the time and money it takes, to facilitate student ministry.

Often student pastors and leaders follow in the footsteps of a predecessor. This can be a challenge. If the predecessor was a rock star, it will be difficult to achieve that level of expectation. The key here is to get students to follow your leadership, which is easier said than done. The short answer is the development of relationships with students and adults as soon as possible. If the predecessor was the exact opposite of a rock star, it will take some time to develop a good reputation, as well as trust among leadership and students. The challenge of church culture can be daunting. Learning to minister and work within structure and bureaucracy can be frustrating but wise student workers need to work within the structure and those within those structures . . . when the opportunity presents itself . . . offer suggestions for improvements. Daniel 1:8 gives us an incredible example of how to approach this, "But Daniel resolved that he would not defile himself with the king's food, or with the wine that he drank. Therefore he asked the chief of the eunuchs to allow him not to defile himself." Resolve. Ask. Seek permission. Offer a thoughtful alternative (in verse 12). That is the template we should follow. I have been guilty of asking for forgiveness rather than permission in the past. There may be rare times that we practice this but generally speaking, this modus operandi could cause a lot of unnecessary trouble and misunderstanding.

## WHAT THE RESEARCH IS TELLING US

Christian Smith and Melinda Denton did one of the more comprehensive studies, combining both qualitative and quantitative methodology, on the religious condition of American teenagers. They surveyed 3,290 teenagers, followed by extended interviews of 267 teenagers. Their findings were published in their landmark book, *Soul Searching: The Religious and Spiritual Life of American Teenagers*. There were some recurring themes that caught my attention:

1. Religion is a significant presence in the lives of many teenagers.
2. Contrary to many popular assumptions and stereotypes, the character of teenager religiosity in the United States is extraordinarily conventional.
3. The single most important social influence on the religious and spiritual lives of adolescents is their parents.
4. It appears that the greater the supply of religiously grounded relationships, activities, programs, opportunities, and challenges available to teenagers, other things being equal, the more likely teenagers will be religiously engaged.
5. Adolescent religious and spiritual understanding and concern seem to be generally weak. Most US teens have a difficult to impossible

time explaining what they believe, what it means, and what the implications of their beliefs are for their lives.

6. Religious congregations that prioritize ministry to youth and support for their parents, invest in trained and skilled youth group leaders, and make serious efforts to engage and teach adolescents seem much more likely to draw youth into their religious lives and foster religious and spiritual maturity in their young members.[1]

These themes reinforce the validity of student ministry on all kinds of levels. For those of us in student ministry, this comes as no surprise. We've been convinced from the beginning. For those on the outside of student ministry, looking in . . . take notice. The more we put into this thing we call student ministry, the more we will get out of it. Will there be financial considerations here? Sure. Will there be limitations? Of course. But regardless of the extent of any ministry, there must be a conscious effort to be involved in student ministry at some level. For some, it will be rudimentary and heartfelt. For others, it will be extensive and strategic. Hopefully after this read, you will become an advocate for student ministry. Your role might become the mediator and interpreter between one young generation to a more seasoned generation. I hope and pray that this book will help you decide about vocational student ministry, volunteering, leadership, or providing the resources needed to facilitate student ministry. It's essential.

# NOTE

1. Christian Smith and Melinda Lundquist Denton, *Soul Searching: The Religious and Spiritual Lives of American Teenagers* (Oxford: Oxford University Press, 2005).